CW00543367

contents

the whys and wherefores

it's my sixtieth birthday...

I'LL START AT THE VERY BEGINNING, SORT OF...
BACK IN TIME TO 2010 IT'S MY SIXTIETH BIRTHDAY. JANICE AND
I ARE IN THE LAKES TO CELEBRATE, AND AFTER OPENING CARDS AND A FEW
PRESENTS I DEVELOP ITCHY FEET AND FEEL THE NEED TO MARK THE DAY BY
DOING SOMETHING A LITTLE OUT OF THE ORDINARY. SO I DECIDE TO
RUN UP BLENCATHRA. OFF I GO, NOTING THE START AND FINISH
TIMES ON A SLIP OF PAPER AT THE CAR BEFORE HEADING BACK
TO THE COTTAGE FOR AN EXTRA-THICK SLICE OF BIRTHDAY CAKE...

(OCTOBER 15 2010)

pastures new...

OVER THE LONG WINTER MONTHS I DECIDE TO
CHALLENGE MYSELF TO RUN OVER ALL THE WAINWRIGHT SUMMITS.
ALTHOUGH I'VE WALKED A FAIR FEW, MANY REMAIN A MYSTERY TO ME
AS I'VE ALWAYS PREFERRED TO WALK OLD FAVOURITES AGAIN AND AGAIN
RATHER THAN TRAVEL FURTHER AFIELD TO WALK OVER A GRASSY LUMP OF A FELL.
BY COMMITTING TO THIS CHALLENGE I GET TO VISIT PASTURES NEW.

it's addictive!

DURING THE SUMMER OF 2011 IT'S BACK
TO THE LAKES TO TICK OFF
THE SUMMITS SLOWLY
BUT SURELY.
(JULY 10 2011)
I'M JUST TAKING
AT THIS STAGE
NOTES OF THE
ROUTE (14 MY FIRST SUMMIT) WEATHER, A SHORT
DESCRIPTION AND
THE TIME TAKEN. I HAVE NO PLAN OF ATTACK   AND JUST CHOOSE THE
FELLS I KNOW AND ARE CLOSE AT HAND TO OUR CARAVAN BASED AT BECKSES
NEAR PENRUDDOCK - HANDY FOR THE NORTHERN, EASTERN AND FAR EASTERN FELLS.
I PURCHASE ONE OF THOSE AERIAL MAPS SHOWING ALL THE
WAINWRIGHT SUMMITS AND START COLOURING THEM IN. IT'S ADDICTIVE!!!
AUTUMN TURNS TO WINTER AND IT'S ONLY NOW I DECIDE TO PUT MY
ROUGH NOTES DOWN IN A SKETCH BOOK TO MAKE THEM MORE PRESENTABLE AND
TO SHOW MY MATES AND FAMILY WHAT I'M UP TO.

rubbish...

IT'S NOW 2012 AND I'M RECORDING MORE
INFORMATION AND DETAILS READY FOR MY WINTER WRITE-UPS.
INTEREST FROM FAMILY AND FRIENDS ACCUMULATES AS I BEGIN
TO SHARE MY NOTES AND MAPS WITH THEM. THEY ARE ALL VERY
IMPRESSED - BUT I'M NOT.
(APRIL 5 2012)
WHAT DO I MEAN? WELL, MY DIARY ISN'T THAT NEAT TO
BE HONEST - IT WAS BASICALLY   MEANT FOR MY EYES ONLY, NOT FOR
GENERAL VIEWING.   ENCOURAGED BY THEIR
REMARKS I REALISE THAT   WITH A LITTLE MORE CARE AND
ATTENTION I CAN IMPROVE   THE DRAUGHTSMANSHIP (IF NOT
THE SPELLING). SO IT'S   LITERALLY BACK TO THE DRAWING
BOARD TO RE-DO THE FIRST   THIRTY OR SO PAGES!
WITHOUT REALISING   IT I HAD NOW GIVEN MYSELF AN
EVEN BIGGER CHALLENGE - THAT   OF PRODUCING A BOOK INTERESTING
ENOUGH TO ONE DAY   BE PUBLISHED.

(BIN)

A QUICK WORD ON THE MAPS

THE MAPS ARE ARTISTIC IMPRESSIONS, WITH
FULL ARTISTIC LICENCE TAKEN WHEN IT COMES
TO ACCURACY REGARDING STONE WALLS, FENCES ETC.
REGARDING CONTOUR LINES: THEY'RE THE
BEST I COULD DO GIVEN THE POOR CLARITY
OF SOME OF THE O.S. MAPS I USED FOR
REFERENCE. IT WASN'T UNTIL I
DISCOVERED A SET OF OLD MAPS FROM
THE 1970s WITH MUCH CLEARER DETAIL
THAT MY CONTOUR LINES BECAME A LITTLE
MORE ACCURATE - BUT AS THIS ISN'T A
GUIDEBOOK LESS THAN 100% ACCURATE IS
ACCEPTABLE - I HOPE!
WHAT IS ACCURATE ARE THE
ROUTES AND TIMES FROM POINT TO
POINT AND START TO FINISH. THE ASCENT
AND DISTANCES ARE AS ACCURATE AS
POSSIBLE USING BASIC MEASURING
TECHNIQUES - NO GPS OR SPORTS
GIZMOS FOR ME!

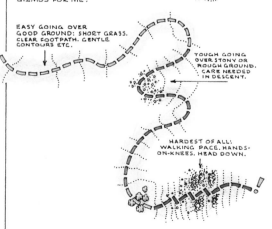

EASY GOING OVER
GOOD GROUND: SHORT GRASS.
CLEAR FOOTPATH. GENTLE
CONTOURS ETC.

TOUGH GOING
OVER STONY OR
ROUGH GROUND.
CARE NEEDED
IN DESCENT.

HARDEST OF ALL:
WALKING PACE. HANDS-
ON-KNEES. HEAD DOWN.

FOR CLARITY I'VE OMITTED ALL FOOTPATHS
OTHER THAN THE ONES USED ON MY RUNS.
I'VE USED DIFFERENT COLOURS FOR THE INFILLS
ON THE PATHS. IN GENERAL THE LIGHTER THE COLOUR
THE EASIER IT IS; THE DARKER THE COLOUR THE HARDER
IT IS. EVERYTHING ELSE ON THE MAPS SHOULD BE
SELF EXPLANATORY.
HOPE YOU LIKE...

A PICTORIAL GUIDE
TO THE
LAKELAND FELLS
being an illustrated account
of a study and exploration
of the mountains in the
English Lake District
by
awainwright

BOOK TWO
THE
FAR EASTERN FELLS

7 GUIDES

THE EASTERN FELLS	THE FAR EASTERN FELLS	THE CENTRAL FELLS	THE SOUTHERN FELLS	THE NORTHERN FELLS	THE NORTH WESTERN FELLS	THE WESTERN FELLS
35	**36**	**27**	**30**	**24**	**29**	**33**
SUMMITS	SUMMITS	SUMMITS	SUMMITS	SUMMITS	SUMMITS	SUMMITS
BOOK ONE	BOOK TWO	BOOK THREE	BOOK FOUR	BOOK FIVE	BOOK SIX	BOOK SEVEN

214 SUMMITS

...let's tick them off!

the running order...

1 THE NORTHERN FELLS **BLENCATHRA** 2 THE NORTHERN FELLS **SOUTHER FELL** 3 THE NORTH WESTERN FELLS **GRISEDALE PIKE** 4 THE NORTH WESTERN FELLS **BARROW** 5 THE NORTHERN FELLS **BANNERDALE CRAGS** 6 THE FAR EASTERN FELLS **SOUR HOWES - SALLOWS** 7 THE EASTERN FELLS **GLENRIDDING DODD - SHEFFIELD PIKE** 8 THE NORTHERN FELLS **BOWSCALE FELL** 9 THE EASTERN FELLS **GOWBARROW** 10 THE EASTERN FELLS **HART SIDE - STYBARROW DODD - WATSON'S DODD - GREAT DODD - CLOUGH HEAD** 11 THE NORTHERN FELLS **MUNGRISDALE COMMON - LONSCALE FELL - SKIDDAW - LITTLE MAN - LATRIGG** 12 THE CENTRAL FELLS **LOUGHRIGG FELL** 13 THE EASTERN FELLS **SEAT SANDAL - DOLLYWAGGON PIKE - NETHERMOST PIKE - HELVELLYN - WHITESIDE PIKE - RAISE** 14 THE NORTHERN FELLS **HIGH PIKE - CARROCK FELL** 15 THE EASTERN FELLS **GREAT MELL FELL** 16 THE NORTH WESTERN FELLS **CAUSEY PIKE - OUTERSIDE** 17 THE NORTH WESTERN FELLS **SALE FELL - LING FELL - GRAYSTONES - BROOM FELL - LORD'S SEAT - BARF** 18 THE CENTRAL FELLS **HIGH RIGG** 19 THE EASTERN FELLS **LITTLE MELL FELL** 20 THE EASTERN FELLS **CATSTYCAM - BIRKHOUSE MOOR** 21 THE FAR EASTERN FELLS **BONSCALE PIKE - ARTHUR'S PIKE - LOADPOT HILL - WETHER HILL - STEEL KNOTTS - HALLIN FELL** 22 THE EASTERN FELLS **ST. SUNDAY CRAG - BIRKS - ARNISON CRAG** 23 THE CENTRAL FELLS **HELM CRAG - GIBSON KNOTT - CALF CRAG - STEEL FELL** 24 THE NORTH WESTERN FELLS **ROBINSON - HINDSCARTH - DALE HEAD - HIGH SPY - MAIDEN MOOR - CAT BELLS** 25 THE NORTHERN FELLS **BAKESTALL** 26 THE NORTHERN FELLS **GREAT CALVA** 27 THE EASTERN FELLS **NAB SCAR - HERON PIKE - GREAT RIGG - FAIRFIELD - HART CRAG - DOVE CRAG - HIGH PIKE - LOW PIKE** 28 THE NORTH WESTERN FELLS **WHINLATTER** 29 THE FAR EASTERN FELLS **THE KNOTT - RAMPSGILL HEAD - HIGH RAISE - KIDSTY PIKE - HIGH STREET - THORNTHWAITE CRAG - GRAY CRAG** 30 THE NORTHERN FELLS **ULLOCK PIKE - LONG SIDE - CARL SIDE - DODD** 31 THE NORTH WESTERN FELLS **HOPEGILL HEAD - WHITESIDE - GRASMOOR - WANDOPE - EEL CRAG - SAIL - SCAR CRAGS** 32 THE FAR EASTERN FELLS **BEDA HEAD - PLACE FELL** 33 THE EASTERN FELLS **HARTSOP ABOVE HOW - LITTLE HART CRAG - HIGH HARTSOP DODD** 34 THE CENTRAL FELLS **RAVEN CRAG** 35 THE FAR EASTERN FELLS **HARTSOP DODD - CAUDALE MOOR** 36 THE CENTRAL FELLS **TARN CRAG - SERGEANT MAN - HIGH RAISE - THUNACAR KNOTT - PIKE O' STICKLE - LOFT CRAG - HARRISON STICKLE - PAVEY ARC - BLEA RIGG** 37 THE EASTERN FELLS **STONE ARTHUR** 38 THE EASTERN FELLS **RED SCREES - MIDDLE DODD** 39 THE NORTHERN FELLS **GREAT COCKUP - MEAL FELL - GREAT SCA FELL - KNOTT - BREA FELL - LONGLANDS FELL** 40 THE WESTERN FELLS **MELLBREAK** 41 THE NORTH WESTERN FELLS **KNOTT RIGG - ARD CRAGS** 42 THE SOUTHERN FELLS **DOW CRAG - BRIM FELL - THE OLD MAN OF CONISTON** 43 THE FAR EASTERN FELLS **REST DOBB - THE NAB - BROCK CRAGS - ANGLETARN PIKES**

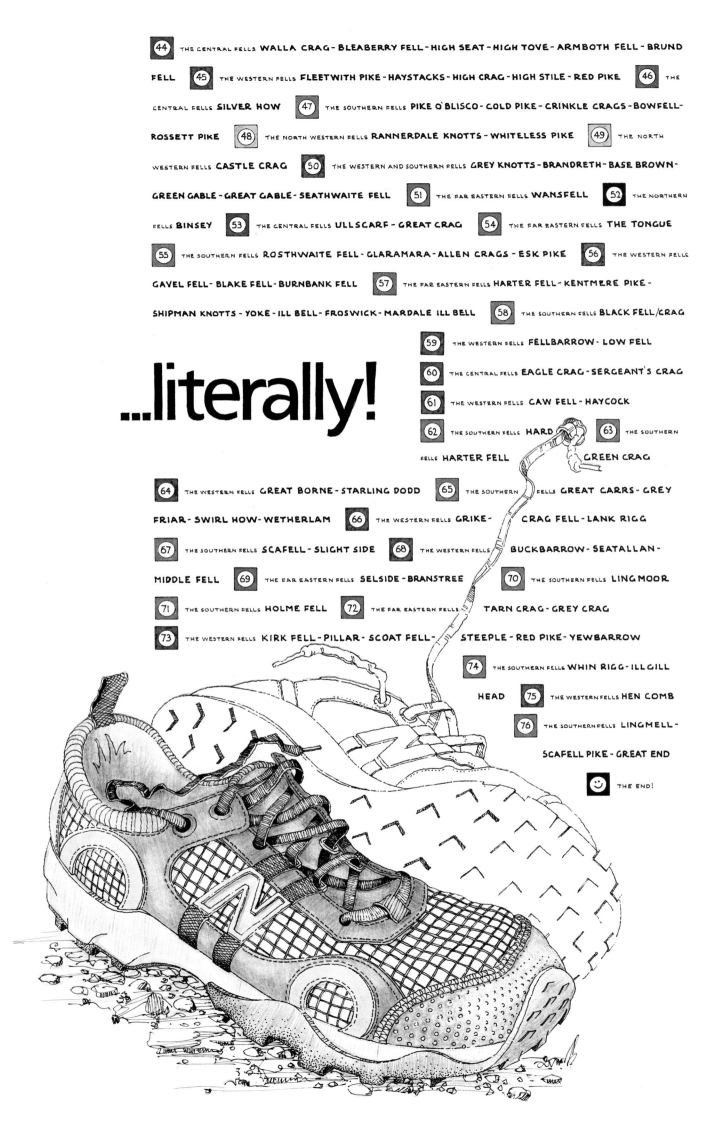

44 THE CENTRAL FELLS **WALLA CRAG - BLEABERRY FELL - HIGH SEAT - HIGH TOVE - ARMBOTH FELL - BRUND FELL** 45 THE WESTERN FELLS **FLEETWITH PIKE - HAYSTACKS - HIGH CRAG - HIGH STILE - RED PIKE** 46 THE CENTRAL FELLS **SILVER HOW** 47 THE SOUTHERN FELLS **PIKE O'BLISCO - COLD PIKE - CRINKLE CRAGS - BOWFELL - ROSSETT PIKE** 48 THE NORTH WESTERN FELLS **RANNERDALE KNOTTS - WHITELESS PIKE** 49 THE NORTH WESTERN FELLS **CASTLE CRAG** 50 THE WESTERN AND SOUTHERN FELLS **GREY KNOTTS - BRANDRETH - BASE BROWN - GREEN GABLE - GREAT GABLE - SEATHWAITE FELL** 51 THE FAR EASTERN FELLS **WANSFELL** 52 THE NORTHERN FELLS **BINSEY** 53 THE CENTRAL FELLS **ULLSCARF - GREAT CRAG** 54 THE FAR EASTERN FELLS **THE TONGUE** 55 THE SOUTHERN FELLS **ROSTHWAITE FELL - GLARAMARA - ALLEN CRAGS - ESK PIKE** 56 THE WESTERN FELLS **GAVEL FELL - BLAKE FELL - BURNBANK FELL** 57 THE FAR EASTERN FELLS **HARTER FELL - KENTMERE PIKE - SHIPMAN KNOTTS - YOKE - ILL BELL - FROSWICK - MARDALE ILL BELL** 58 THE SOUTHERN FELLS **BLACK FELL/CRAG** 59 THE WESTERN FELLS **FELLBARROW - LOW FELL** 60 THE CENTRAL FELLS **EAGLE CRAG - SERGEANT'S CRAG** 61 THE WESTERN FELLS **CAW FELL - HAYCOCK** 62 THE SOUTHERN FELLS **HARD** 63 THE SOUTHERN FELLS **HARTER FELL** **GREEN CRAG**

...literally!

64 THE WESTERN FELLS **GREAT BORNE - STARLING DODD** 65 THE SOUTHERN FELLS **GREAT CARRS - GREY FRIAR - SWIRL HOW - WETHERLAM** 66 THE WESTERN FELLS **GRIKE - CRAG FELL - LANK RIGG** 67 THE SOUTHERN FELLS **SCAFELL - SLIGHT SIDE** 68 THE WESTERN FELLS **BUCKBARROW - SEATALLAN - MIDDLE FELL** 69 THE FAR EASTERN FELLS **SELSIDE - BRANSTREE** 70 THE SOUTHERN FELLS **LINGMOOR** 71 THE SOUTHERN FELLS **HOLME FELL** 72 THE FAR EASTERN FELLS **TARN CRAG - GREY CRAG** 73 THE WESTERN FELLS **KIRK FELL - PILLAR - SCOAT FELL - STEEPLE - RED PIKE - YEWBARROW** 74 THE SOUTHERN FELLS **WHIN RIGG - ILL GILL HEAD** 75 THE WESTERN FELLS **HEN COMB** 76 THE SOUTHERN FELLS **LINGMELL - SCAFELL PIKE - GREAT END**

☺ THE END!

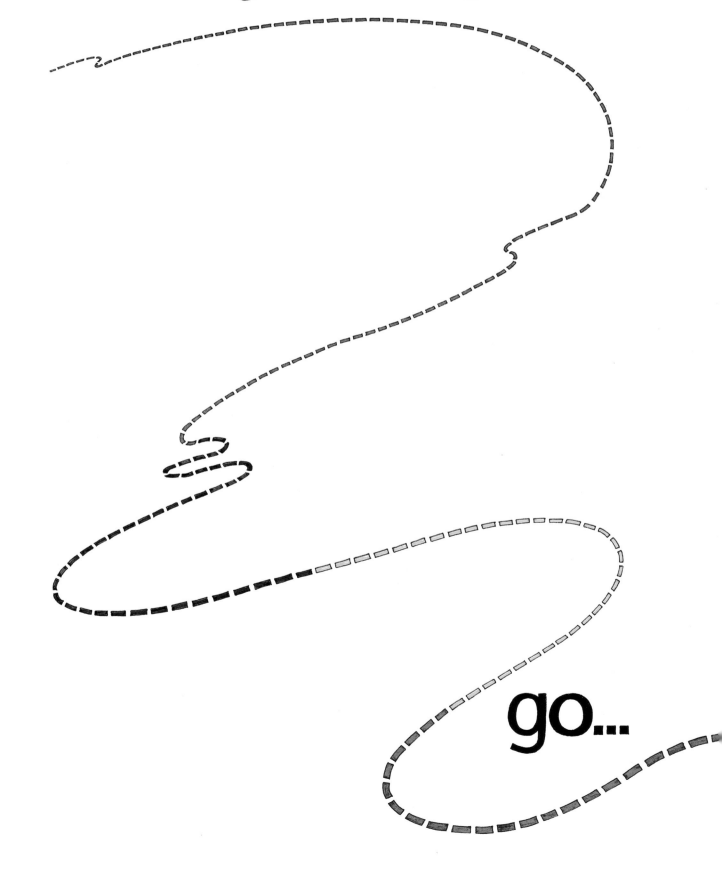

ready, steady,

go...

the NORTHERN fells

A time trial up
BLENCATHRA via Scales Tarn
& Foule Crag

IT'S MY SIXTIETH BIRTHDAY TODAY, AND AS A
SURPRISE JANICE HAS BOOKED US INTO A COTTAGE
FOR THE WEEK. I'M UP EARLY TO OPEN MY PRESENTS, AFTER
WHICH I DECIDE TO GO FOR A RUN. NOT ON THE ROAD AS
NORMAL - OH NO! - BUT UP A FELL.

I'VE NO FELL RUNNING SHOES SO I PULL ON MY ROAD SHOES AND SET
OFF TO THRELKELD. ALL THE TOPS ARE COVERED BY THICK CLOUD AS I HEAD OFF
TOWARDS MOUSTHWAITE COMB FULL OF ENTHUSIASM FOR THE JOB IN HAND.
ONTO THE OPEN FELL ON A GOOD PATH TO SCALES BECK THEN ONTO A TWISTING
NARROW TRACK TO GLENDERAMACKIN COL. UPHILL AND HARD GOING ALL THE
WAY TO ATKINSON PIKE. I STILL CAN'T SEE A THING BUT KNOW WHERE I NEED TO
HEAD FOR, AND I'M SOON AT THE SUMMIT. BEING A COMPLETE NOVICE I DON'T RECORD
MY TIME.

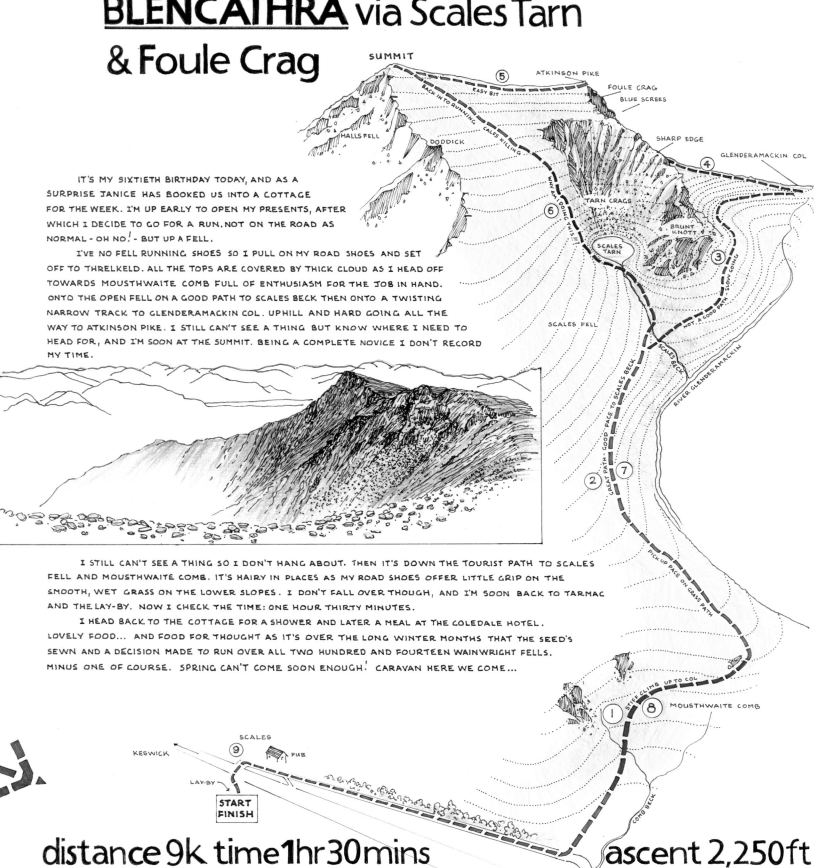

I STILL CAN'T SEE A THING SO I DON'T HANG ABOUT. THEN IT'S DOWN THE TOURIST PATH TO SCALES
FELL AND MOUSTHWAITE COMB. IT'S HAIRY IN PLACES AS MY ROAD SHOES OFFER LITTLE GRIP ON THE
SMOOTH, WET GRASS ON THE LOWER SLOPES. I DON'T FALL OVER THOUGH, AND I'M SOON BACK TO TARMAC
AND THE LAY-BY. NOW I CHECK THE TIME: ONE HOUR THIRTY MINUTES.

I HEAD BACK TO THE COTTAGE FOR A SHOWER AND LATER A MEAL AT THE COLEDALE HOTEL.
LOVELY FOOD... AND FOOD FOR THOUGHT AS IT'S OVER THE LONG WINTER MONTHS THAT THE SEED'S
SEWN AND A DECISION MADE TO RUN OVER ALL TWO HUNDRED AND FOURTEEN WAINWRIGHT FELLS.
MINUS ONE OF COURSE. SPRING CAN'T COME SOON ENOUGH! CARAVAN HERE WE COME...

distance 9k time 1hr 30mins   ascent 2,250ft

the **NORTHERN** fells

The long way round and over...

SOUTHER FELL

SET OFF FROM PENRUDDOCK WITH PLANS TO RUN UP BLENCATHRA AGAIN. BY THE TIME I ARRIVE AT MUNGRISDALE THE CLOUDS HAVE CLOSED IN AND COVERED THE SUMMIT, SO I RUN TO THE BASE OF FOULE CRAG AND TAKE A SHARP LEFT IN THE DIRECTION OF **SOUTHER FELL**. GOOD PATH MOST OF THE WAY TO THE GRASSY SUMMIT.
STEEP DESCENT ON AN INDISTINCT TRACK TAKES ME THE WRONG WAY, SO I HEAD BACK UP AND FIND THE CORRECT TRACK DOWN TO THE RIVER.
GOOD RUN – AND DIDN'T GET MY FEET WET!

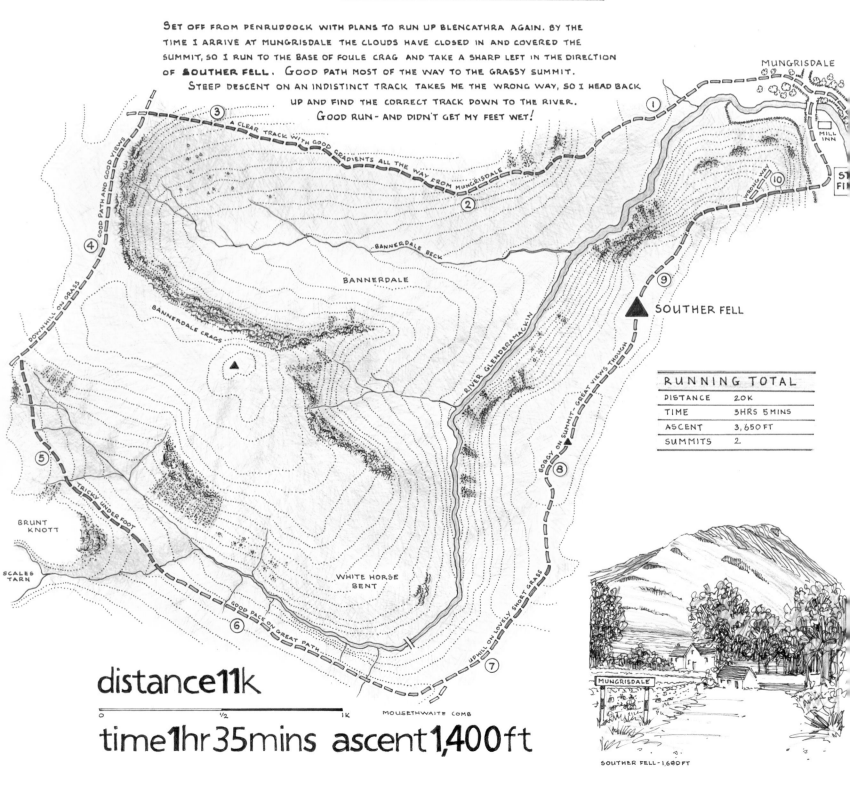

MUNGRISDALE

MILL INN

A CLEAR TRACK WITH GOOD GRADIENTS ALL THE WAY FROM MUNGRISDALE

GOOD PATH AND GOOD VIEWS

DOWNHILL ON GRASS

BANNERDALE BECK

BANNERDALE

BANNERDALE CRAGS

RIVER GLENDERAMACKIN

WRONG WAY

SOUTHER FELL

TRICKY UNDER FOOT

BRUNT KNOTT

SCALES TARN

BOGGY ON SUMMIT. GREAT VIEWS THOUGH

WHITE HORSE BENT

GOOD PACE ON GREAT PATH

UPHILL ON LOVELY SHORT GRASS

RUNNING TOTAL	
DISTANCE	20K
TIME	3HRS 5MINS
ASCENT	3,650 FT
SUMMITS	2

MUNGRISDALE

SOUTHER FELL – 1,680 FT

distance **11k**

0   ½   1K

MOUSETHWAITE COMB

time **1hr 35mins**   ascent **1,400ft**

the NORTH WESTERN fells

An old favourite-
GRISEDALE PIKE

Spent a week at scotgate site in braithwaite waiting for the 70 m.p.h. winds to drop so we could venture onto the tops... Grisedale pike just waiting for me as I looked out the caravan window. By the middle of the week the wind had calmed down and it was safe to venture out.

0   ½   1k

WHINLATTER FOREST

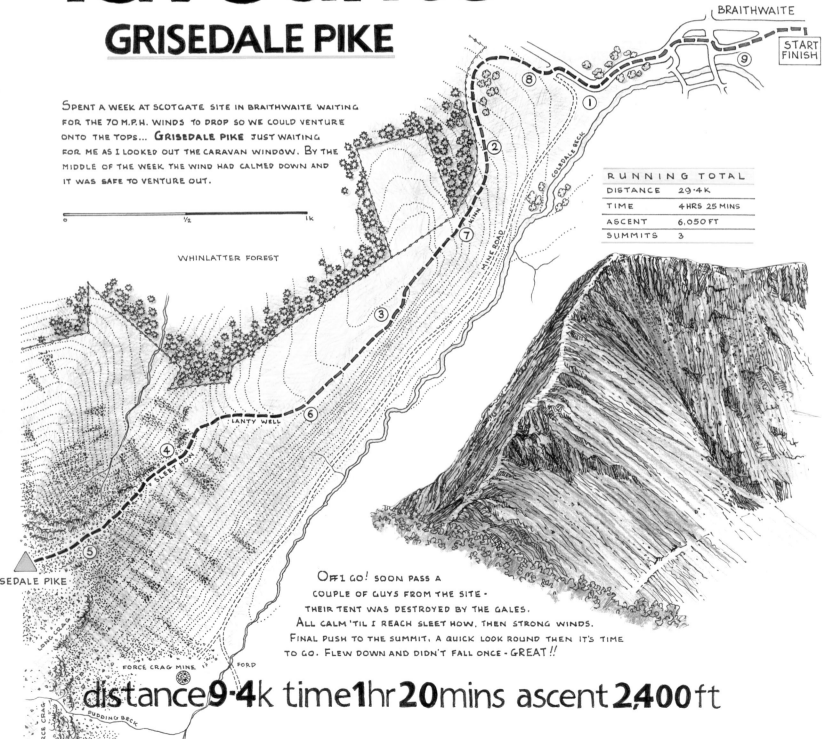

BRAITHWAITE

START FINISH

COLEDALE BECK

MINE ROAD

KINN

RUNNING TOTAL	
DISTANCE	29·4K
TIME	4 HRS 25 MINS
ASCENT	6,050 FT
SUMMITS	3

LANTY WELL

SLEET HOW

⑤

ISEDALE PIKE

LONG CRAG

FORCE CRAG MINE   FORD

FORCE CRAG

PUDDING BECK

Off I go! soon pass a couple of guys from the site - their tent was destroyed by the gales. All calm 'til I reach sleet how, then strong winds. Final push to the summit, a quick look round then it's time to go. Flew down and didn't fall once - GREAT !!

distance **9·4**k time**1**hr**20**mins ascent**2,400**ft

the NORTH WESTERN fells

Short but very sweet

straight out the door and up BARROW

BARROW GILL - LOOKING UPTO CAUSEY PIKE

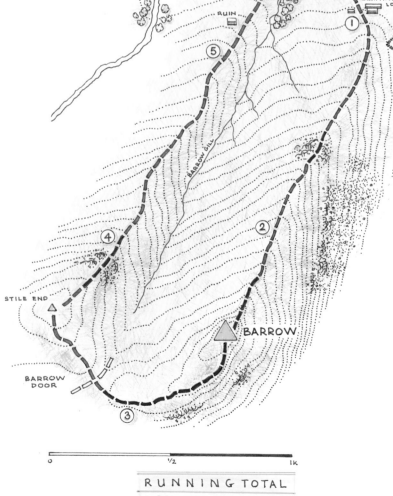

distance **6·25**k
time **38** mins
ascent **1,400** ft

STIFF LEGS AFTER GRISEDALE PIKE RUN SO
NICE EASY ONE TO GIVE THE LEGS A CHANCE TO
RECOVER. A GOOD LITTLE RUN THIS, THAT I'VE DONE
A FEW TIMES. ONE DAY I'LL GET TO THE TOP WITHOUT
STOPPING.!

IT'S ALWAYS SLIPPERY TOWARDS THE END, WITH SHORT WET
GRASS, AND THIS TIME I'M UNLUCKY AND SLIDE ABOUT 30 FEET
ON MY BUM! A NICE JOG BACK THROUGH THE VILLAGE TO
THE CARAVAN AND A HOT SHOWER.

RUNNING TOTAL	
DISTANCE	35·65 K
TIME	5 HRS 3 MINS
ASCENT	7,450 FT
SUMMITS	4

BARROW SUMM
1,494 FT —
CAUSEY PIKE
BACKGROUND

the **NORTHERN** fells

A cold and frosty start

over **BLENCATHRA** and **BANNERDALE CRAGS**

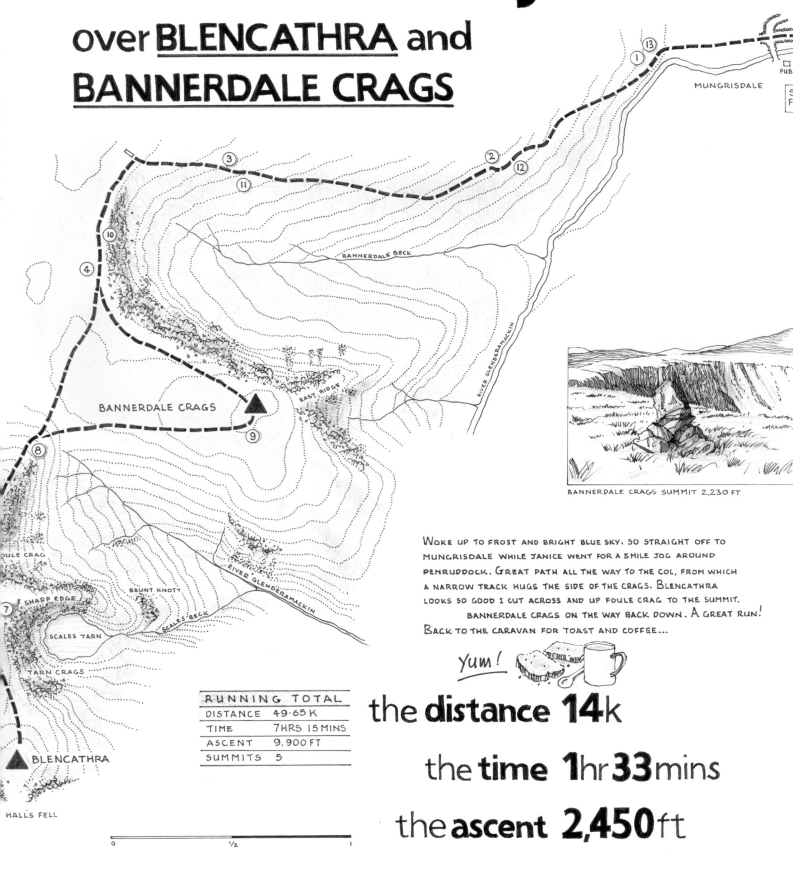

MUNGRISDALE

PUB

START FINISH

BANNERDALE BECK

RIVER GLENDERAMACKIN

EAST RIDGE

BANNERDALE CRAGS

BANNERDALE CRAGS SUMMIT 2,230 FT

ULE CRAG

SHARP EDGE

BRUNT KNOTT

RIVER GLENDERAMACKIN

SCALES BECK

SCALES TARN

TARN CRAGS

BLENCATHRA

HALL'S FELL

WOKE UP TO FROST AND BRIGHT BLUE SKY, SO STRAIGHT OFF TO
MUNGRISDALE WHILE JANICE WENT FOR A 5MILE JOG AROUND
PENRUDDOCK. GREAT PATH ALL THE WAY TO THE COL, FROM WHICH
A NARROW TRACK HUGS THE SIDE OF THE CRAGS. BLENCATHRA
LOOKS SO GOOD I CUT ACROSS AND UP FOULE CRAG TO THE SUMMIT.
   BANNERDALE CRAGS ON THE WAY BACK DOWN. A GREAT RUN!
BACK TO THE CARAVAN FOR TOAST AND COFFEE...

yum!

RUNNING TOTAL	
DISTANCE	49·65 K
TIME	7HRS 15MINS
ASCENT	9,900 FT
SUMMITS	5

the **distance 14**k

the **time 1**hr**33**mins

the **ascent 2,450**ft

0   ½   1

THE FAR EASTERN FELLS

Just in the nick of time...

SOUR HOWES & SALLOWS

Up to the lakes with Janice for a Himalaya reunion with Ian and the two Micks. Booked in at the Kendal travelodge for Friday and Saturday, with a pub meal at the Strickland Arms arranged for 7·30 p.m. Checked in at 3 o'clock so there's time for a run before dark. Changed and on the road for the short drive to Ings and the turn off to Dubbs. Park the car and set off at 3·40 p.m. There's plenty of snow on the tops, with low cloud looking to blow in from the west.

Off along a bridlepath with an easy gradient, past a frozen reservoir with no swimming signs - no chance!! Path still good. Notice Sour Howes summit on right covered in snow. Over a stile and onto thick grass and snow - very steep, have to walk. Lots of mini summits and not sure which one's the true one so visit them all. It's now 4·07 p.m... only 27 mins to reach the top - not bad. Sallows looks further away than I imagined and already the light is beginning to fade.

Set off for Sallows down a snow-covered slope. Follow a good wall to a stile and push on to the summit. It's 4·13 p.m... No time to admire the view.

Head down to Garburn Pass as Yoke disappears into the clouds. There's a good path to start with, but it soon deteriorates into a river of rocks.

It's not long before I take a tumble. Bang arm and shoulder (don't tell Janice). Eventually the path's back to a good surface and I'm retracing footsteps to the finish.

It's getting darker by the minute, but not far to go now so I'm surprised when round the bend heading towards me is another fell runner... with 2 dogs! Hope he's not going far.

Back to the car at 4·57 p.m. with the daylight all but gone.

ROUTE STATISTICS

SOUR HOWES & SALLOWS		RUNNING TOTAL
DISTANCE	9·5 K	58·75 K
ASCENT	1,068 FT	10,968 FT
TIME	1 HR 17 M	8 HRS 32 M
SUMMITS	2	7

0   ½   1
ONE KILOMETRE

SALLOWS
YOKE
TROUTBECK · KENTMERE
SOUR HOWES
WINDERMERE

Back for a hot bath, then to the pub for pork loin, black pudding and fried egg followed by Eton mess.

START FINISH

the EASTERN fells

Janice's first (and last?) fell run...
over GLENRIDDING DODD and SHEFFIELD PIKE

Up to beckses for the first time since november and the caravan was fine. First night was so cold water froze in the butt so had to fetch water from the toilet block to make coffee. Janice decided to come running with me today. Set off on a wide track leading to seldom seen (row of cottages). Steep gradient soon slows us both down as we resort to walking. Back on the saddle and we run all the way to the summit of glenridding dodd. Stiff walk up to heron crag pike followed by a run over frozen peat bogs to sheffield pike summit. Descent should be fast and easy – but it isn't! Large swathes of ice over the path make for a cautious descent all the way back to seldom seen. Find our running legs again and we're soon back to the car and a warm caravan.

SHEFFIELD PIKE SUMMIT 2,232 FT.

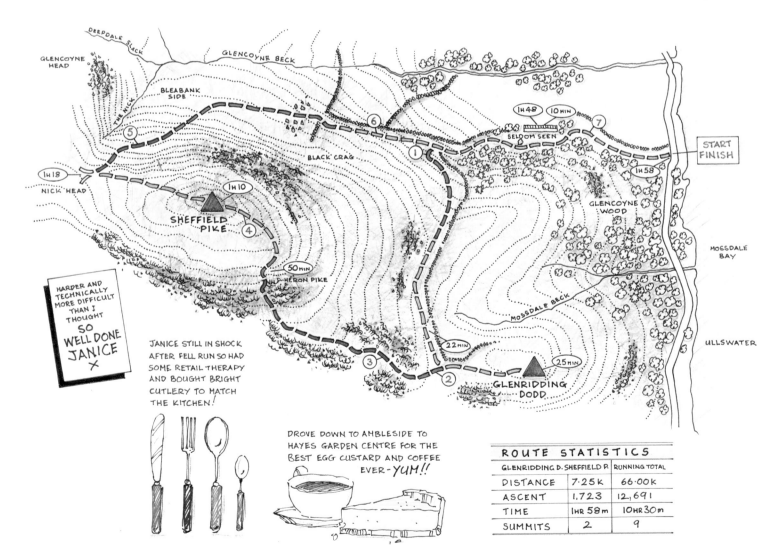

HARDER AND TECHNICALLY MORE DIFFICULT THAN I THOUGHT SO WELL DONE JANICE X

JANICE STILL IN SHOCK AFTER FELL RUN SO HAD SOME RETAIL THERAPY AND BOUGHT BRIGHT CUTLERY TO MATCH THE KITCHEN!

DROVE DOWN TO AMBLESIDE TO HAYES GARDEN CENTRE FOR THE BEST EGG CUSTARD AND COFFEE EVER – YUM!!

ROUTE STATISTICS		
	GLENRIDDING D. SHEFFIELD P.	RUNNING TOTAL
DISTANCE	7·25k	66·00k
ASCENT	1,723	12,691
TIME	1HR 58m	10HR 30m
SUMMITS	2	9

the NORTHERN fells

Another mucky morning...
...as I tackle BOWSCALE FELL

I'D PLANNED TO RUN A MULTI-SUMMIT ROUTE TODAY, BUT THE WEATHER WAS TOO BAD. OFF INSTEAD TO MUNGRISDALE FOR A RUN OVER BOWSCALE FELL. A GOOD PATH LEADS ALL THE WAY TO THE COL AT BANNERDALE CRAGS. SEE A RAINBOW OVER BLENCATHRA AS THE CLOUDS BREAK FOR A FEW SECONDS BEFORE THICK HILL FOG RETURNS. HEAD NORTH OVER SQUELCHY GROUND TO THE SUMMIT, NOTE DOWN THE TIME AND MOVE STRAIGHT ON AS THERE ARE NO VIEWS TO ADMIRE TODAY. OFF IN A NORTHWEST DIRECTION TO AVOID RUNNING OVER TARN CRAGS, PICK UP A SHEEP TROD EASTWARDS TO THE EDGE OF TARN CRAGS AND NEARLY RUN INTO TWO WALKERS WHO SUDDENLY APPEAR OUT OF THE FOG. I SHOW THEM THE WAY UP, THEY SHOW ME THE WAY DOWN. THE TARN IS AN IMPRESSIVE SIGHT - WILD AND RUGGED. CHECK TIME, THEN IT'S FULL SPEED ON A GOOD PATH ALL THE WAY DOWN TO THE MAIN ROAD AT BOWSCALE. THE LAST MILE ON THE ROAD IS PLAIN SAILING, IF NOT A LITTLE FURTHER THAN I THOUGHT.

A GOOD RUN IN TRICKY CONDITIONS.

RIVER CALDEW

MOSEDALE BRIDGE

BOWSCALE

1HR 10

⑥

⑦

⑧

TARN SIKE

⑤

55MIN

BOWSCALE TARN

TARN CRAGS

④

40MIN

BOWSCALE FELL

BULLFELL BECK

WHICH WAY NOW?
LET'S ASK THIS
FELL RUNNER...

THE TONGUE

MUNGRISDALE

①

RIVER GLENDERAMACKIN

START FINISH

BOWSCALE
SUMMIT 2,306FT
LOOKING WEST
TO SKIDDAW

②

0	½	1k

ROUTE STATISTICS

BOWSCALE FELL		RUNNING TOTAL
DISTANCE	9·65K	75·65K
ASCENT	1,450FT	14,141FT
TIME	1HR 17MIN	11HR 47MIN
SUMMITS	1	10

the **EASTERN** fells

Janice
runs again...
this time over **GOWBARROW**

AFTER THE WETTEST APRIL ON RECORD IT WAS GOOD TO HAVE SOME DRY WEATHER ON OUR RETURN TO THE LAKES. A TEATIME RUN WITH JANICE PROVED A BIG SUCCESS. SET OFF FROM WATERMILLOCK CHURCH ACROSS A WATERLOGGED FIELD - WET FEET ALREADY! A GOOD TRACK TAKES US THROUGH WOODS TO THE RUINED SHOOTING LODGE. THE PATH IS A LEVEL TERRACE BUT VERY SLIPPERY UNDERFOOT, WITH MUD AND PINE NEEDLES EVERYWHERE. CONTINUE TO THE SEAT AT YEW CRAG FOR BRILLIANT VIEWS OF ULLSWATER AND DISTANT FELLS. NO TIME TO SIT DOWN THOUGH. WE RETRACE OUR FOOTSTEPS ON AN UNDULATING PATH BACK TO THE RUIN. JANICE WAITS WHILE I POP UP TO THE SUMMIT ON A BLACK PEAT PATH (ONLY SLIP ONCE). QUICK LOOK AROUND THEN DOWN TO JANICE AND BACK ON THE SLIPPERY PATH TO WATERMILLOCK.

BLUE STILTON TOP

JANICE IN GOOD MOOD, SO HAD A GOOD TEA - SPECIAL PORK PIE SALAD - YUM!

START FINISH

14 37M

11MIN

SWINBURN'S PARK

KIRKSTY BROW

SHOOTING LODGE RUIN

25MIN

1H4MIN

GOWBARROW

AIRY CRAG

50 MIN

COLLIER HAGG

GREEN HILL

HIND CRAG

RA FORGE

COLLIER HAGG BECK

DOBBIN WOOD

SEAT

38MIN

YEW CRAG

0   ½   1K

THE SUMMIT 1,579 FT- LOOKING TO GREAT MELL FELL

RUNNING TOTAL	
DISTANCE	85·9K
TIME	13 HRS 24 MINS
ASCENT	14,920FT
SUMMITS	11

distance 10·3k **time** 1hr 37m **ascent** 779ft

the EASTERN fells

The green green grass...

of HART SIDE, STYBARROW DODD, WATSON'S DODD, GREAT DODD and CLOUGH HEAD

the **distance**
17·75k

the **time**
2hrs **35**mins

the **ascent**
2,750ft

RUNNING TOTAL	
DISTANCE	103·7 K
TIME	15 HRS 59 MINS
ASCENT	17,670 FT
SUMMITS	16

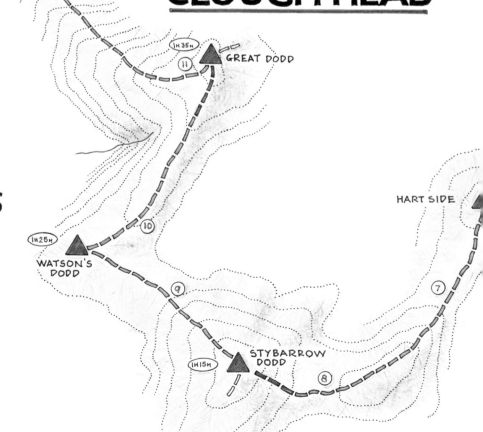

HIGH CLOUD LEVEL AND NO CHANCE OF RAIN MEANS I CAN GO FOR A MULTI-SUMMIT RUN WITH CONFIDENCE. JANICE DROPPED ME OFF AT DOCKRAY AND I ARRANGED TO RING HER FROM THE TOP OF CLOUGH HEAD SO SHE COULD PICK ME UP WITHOUT ME HAVING TO HANG AROUND GETTING COLD.

A LONG RUN IN TO MY FIRST SUMMIT HART SIDE. THE ROUTE TAKES ME ALONG THE GLENCOYNE VALLEY ON A GOOD TRACK WITH GOOD VIEWS. IT'S EASY GOING 'TIL I REACH THE WALL LEADING CLOSE TO THE SUMMIT, WHERE ROUGH GRASS AND STEEP GRADIENT MAKE FOR SLOW GOING. EVETUALLY REACH HART SIDE SUMMIT AFTER FIFTY FIVE MINUTES - AND STILL FOUR MORE TOPS TO GO!

BETTER GET A MOVE ON
STYBARROW DODD IS IN FULL VIEW ACROSS DEEPDALE VALLEY. SOON ARRIVE AT ITS SUMMIT IN LESS TIME THAN I THOUGHT. A FEW WALKERS ON RAISE ARE ON THEIR WAY TO HELVELLYN. MY EYES AND FEET TURN NORTHWEST AND ONTO WATSON'S DODD, THEN STRAIGHT ON TOWARDS GREAT DODD.

NO ANSWER
LEGS FEELING GOOD AND TICKING THE TOPS OFF AT A GOOD PACE. CLOUGH HEAD LOOKS A LONG WAY OFF (IT IS!), SO DOWN TO CALFHOW PIKE FOR A QUICK LOOK DOWN ST. JOHN'S IN THE VALE, THEN IT'S OFF TO CLOUGH HEAD. TRY TO RING JANICE BUT NO ANSWER!!! GOOD JOB REALLY - THE WIND'S TOO STRONG AND THE WIND SHELTER TOO SMALL.

STYBARROW DODD
FROM BROWN CRAG

CLOUGH HEAD SUMMIT
PLENTY OF WIND - NOT MUCH SHELTER

PICK UP THE PHONE!
HEAD NORTH. BLENCATHRA LOOKING GOOD. DOWN A TRAIL ON SHORT GRASS. SPOT A GROUP OF 4×4s ON THE COACH ROAD IN THE DISTANCE. GLAD TO REACH THE COACH ROAD MYSELF. RING JANICE. THIS TIME SHE ANSWERS... SHE'LL PICK ME UP IN TWENTY MINUTES... I BETTER GET A MOVE ON! 'ROAD' SURFACE TOO ROCKY FOR ME TO RUN ON SO HEAD ONTO THE GRASS VERGE. SAY HELLO TO A GROUP OF TEENAGERS. ONE IN A WHEELCHAIR. CATCH UP WITH AND PASS THE 4×4s AND FINISH AT THE FARMSTEAD OF WANTHWAITE. JANICE WAITING JUST UP THE ROAD. FEEL PLEASED WITH MYSELF - LONGEST AND BEST RUN YET.

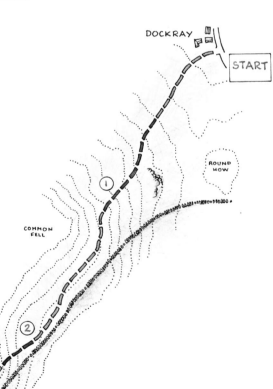

DOCKRAY

START

ROUND HOW

COMMON FELL

SWINESIDE KNOTT

BROWN HILLS

SCOT CRAG

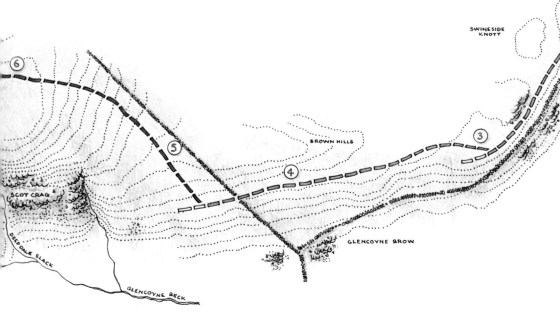

DEEP DALE SLACK

GLENCOYNE BECK

GLENCOYNE BROW

The Queen's Diamond Jubilee

11 June 4th 2012

the **NORTHERN** fells

Stunning views from start to finish...

as I stride out over
MUNGRISDALE COMMON, **LONSCALE FELL**, **SKIDDAW**, **LITTLE MAN** and **LATRIGG**

the **distance 21**k
the **time 3**hrs**28**mins
the **ascent 4,033**ft

RUNNING TOTAL	
DISTANCE	124·70 K
TIME	19 HRS 27 MINS
ASCENT	21,705 FT
SUMMITS	21

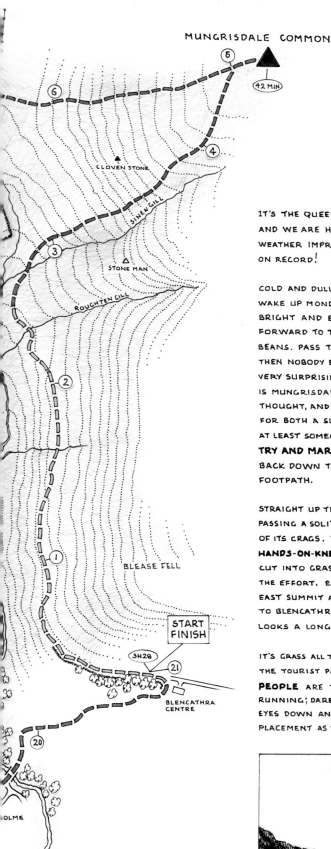

MUNGRISDALE COMMON

⑤
42 MIN

⑥

④

CLOVEN STONE

SINEN GILL

③

STONE MAN

ROUGHTEN GILL

②

①

BLEASE FELL

START
FINISH

3H28

㉑

BLENCATHRA
CENTRE

⑳

HOLME

RIVER GRETA

LONSCALE FELL

IT'S THE QUEEN'S DIAMOND JUBILEE WEEKEND AND WE ARE HERE FOR A FULL WEEK. HOPE THE WEATHER IMPROVES AFTER THE WETTEST MAY ON RECORD!

COLD AND DULL ON SATURDAY AND SUNDAY BUT WAKE UP MONDAY TO A CLEAR BLUE SKY. OFF BRIGHT AND EARLY TO THRELKELD. LOOKING FORWARD TO THIS ONE, SO OFF I GO, FULL OF BEANS. PASS TWO LADIES DOG WALKING AND THEN NOBODY ELSE FOR THE NEXT HOUR - NOT VERY SURPRISING AS MY FIRST SUMMIT (HA HA) IS MUNGRISDALE COMMON. IT'S FURTHER THAN I THOUGHT, AND CONDITIONS UNDERFOOT MAKE FOR BOTH A SLOW ASCENT AND DESCENT. AT LEAST SOMEONE HAS MADE A SMALL CAIRN TO **TRY AND MARK THE HIGHEST POINT!** HEAD BACK DOWN TO THE MAIN SKIDDAW HOUSE FOOTPATH.

STRAIGHT UP THE FLANK OF LONSCALE FELL, PASSING A SOLITARY WALKER, WITH GOOD VIEWS OF ITS CRAGS. THE GRADIENT STEEPENS TO **HANDS-ON-KNEES PACE** USING GOOD FOOTSTEPS CUT INTO GRASS. IT'S HARD GRAFT BUT WORTH THE EFFORT. EASY RUN ACROSS GRASS TO THE EAST SUMMIT AND GOOD VIEWS ACROSS THE VALLEY TO BLENCATHRA. SKIDDAW TO THE NORTHWEST LOOKS A LONG WAY OFF, BUT VERY INVITING.

IT'S GRASS ALL THE WAY NOW TO **JENKINS HILL** AND THE TOURIST PATH FROM KESWICK. **LOADS OF PEOPLE** ARE TRUDGING ALONG, SO HAVE TO KEEP RUNNING; DAREN'T STOP, TOO MANY EYES WATCHING. EYES DOWN AND CONCENTRATE ON FOOT PLACEMENT AS THE WIDE PATH IS VERY STONY.

AFTER A COUPLE OF LITTLE UPHILLS I ARRIVE AT THE SUMMIT CAIRN AND SHELTERS WITH **BEAUTIFUL VIEWS** IN EVERY DIRECTION. I SPEND FIVE MINUTES SOAKING IT ALL IN AND REFUEL WITH ONE OF JANICE'S **CEREAL BARS - YUMMY!** I'VE BEEN ON THE GO FOR TWO HOURS NOW SO IT'S A WELCOME BREAK.

AFTER TEN MINUTES I DRAG MYSELF AWAY, AND WITH **A SPRING IN MY STRIDE** HEAD OFF TO LITTLE MAN FOR AN EVEN BETTER VIEW. IT'S DOWNHILL NOW, NON-STOP FOR THE NEXT HALF HOUR. **HOARDS OF WALKERS** ARE STILL ASCENDING SKIDDAW, THE WIDE FOOTPATH STILL VERY STONY, BUT I SPOT A GOOD GRASS TRACK A COUPLE OF METRES AWAY AND STICK TO IT ALL THE WAY DOWN BEFORE JOINING THE MAIN PATH FOR THE LAST TWO HUNDRED METRES TO GALE ROAD.

KNEES STARTING TO COMPLAIN NOW, SO IT'S A RELIEF AS I START THE SHORT ASCENT ACROSS LUSH TURF TO THE TOP OF LATRIGG. A SHARP LEFT TURN AT THE SUMMIT POINTS ME BACK TOWARDS THE START-FINISH AS I REALISE THERE'S **QUITE A BIT OF RUNNING STILL TO DO -** AND NOW MY WHOLE LEGS ARE STARTING TO TIRE. DOWNHILL I GO, AT A MORE GENTLE ANGLE, BEFORE CROSSING GLENDERATERRA BECK THEN ASCENDING TO THE BLENCATHRA CENTRE AND CAR. **PHEW...!** THAT LAST SECTION TOOK SOME DOING. A GREAT RUN THOUGH.

EAT ANOTHER CEREAL BAR, FINISH OFF MY DRINK, WIPE THE SWEAT FROM MY EYES AND THEN IT'S BACK TO PENRUDDOCK FOR A SHOWER.

INTO KESWICK THAT NIGHT TO WITNESS THE LIGHTING OF **A BEACON ON CATBELLS** - NOT VERY IMPRESSIVE - A BIGGER AND BETTER BEACON APPEARED ON TOP OF **LATRIGG** AS WE MADE OUR WAY BACK THROUGH KESWICK TO THE CAR. GOOD EFFORT.

LOOKING FORWARD TO THE REST OF THE WEEK AND HOPE THE WEATHER HOLDS UP. WE SHALL SEE.

the CENTRAL fells

More trail than fell
as Janice runs again

LAST DAY OF OUR WEEK IN THE LAKES, LEAVING THIS AFTERNOON AFTER MORE RAIN FORECAST FOR TODAY AND FRIDAY. NOT DONE TOO BAD WITH THE WEATHER, THOUGH, AND MANAGED TO FIT A COUPLE OF LOW-LEVEL AND HIGH WALKS BETWEEN THE SHOWERS. TODAY'S RUN STARTS ON THE ROAD TO TOWN END THEN JOINS THE COFFIN ROAD TO RYDAL – EASY RUNNING – BEFORE CROSSING THE BUSY A591 FOR LOUGHRIGG TERRACE.

RUNNING TOTAL	
DISTANCE	134·8 K
TIME	20HR 56MIN
ASCENT	22,705 FT
SUMMITS	22

JANICE CONTINUES TO RED BANK ROAD LEADING HER BACK TO GRASMERE, WHILE MY EYES TURN TO THE SUMMIT. A SHORT BUT STIFF CLIMB LEADS ME TO THE SUMMIT CAIRN. THE RAIN'S HOLDING OFF, SO IT'S QUICKLY DOWN TO RED BANK. ONCE BACK ON TARMAC MY PACE PICKS UP AND I'M FLYING ALONG – ALL THE WAY BACK TO GRASMERE. I RUN PAST THE GARDEN CENTRE (NO TIME FOR A SCONE TODAY) AND THROUGH THE VILLAGE TO ARRIVE BACK AT THE CAR, A 'GLOWING' JANICE AND THE LAST CEREAL BAR – YUMMY!

FOR MORE DETAILS OF SCONES, CAKES AND CEREAL BARS – SEE FOLLOWING PAGE.

the distance 10·1k
the time 1hr 29mins
the ascent 1,000ft

Eat cake-
lose weight!

best pre-run cake
FRUIT SCONES
...ARE TO BE FOUND AT
GRASMERE GARDEN CENTRE.

best for
on the go
**JANICE'S CEREAL
BAR**

...TO BE FOUND IN LARGE AMOUNTS HIDDEN
(FROM ME) IN THE GARAGE FREEZER, I THINK.

best post-run cake
EGG CUSTARD or LEMON MERINGUE
...TO BE FOUND AT
HAYES GARDEN CENTRE, AMBLESIDE.

...or could it be the fell running?

the **EASTERN** fells

Loneliness of the long distance fell runner

SEAT SANDAL, DOLLYWAGGON and NETHERMOST PIKES, HELVELLYN, WHITE SIDE and RAISE...

...and hardly saw a soul!

IT'S THE PENULTIMATE DAY OF OUR HOLIDAY AND IT'S BEEN A MIXED BAG OF WEATHER.
WITH A GOOD FORECAST FOR TODAY I WAS UP BRIGHT AND EARLY RARING TO GO...
...BUT IT WAS RAINING!
STILL, MY MIND WAS SET. SO I DROVE TO GRASMERE, PARKED THE CAR ON THE A591 AND
SET OFF BACK UP THE ROAD TO MILL BRIDGE AND THE FOOTPATH TO GRISEDALE HAUSE.
LET THE FUN BEGIN...

THE WELL-GRADED PATH, SANDWICHED BETWEEN TALL BRACKEN, CROSSES
STREAMS AND TWISTS AND TURNS FOR OVER TWO KILOMETRES.
I QUICKLY FIND RUNNING WHILE VIDEOING TAKES A BIT OF
CARE - ONE EYE ON THE VIEWFINDER, OTHER ON THE PATH.
STEADY NOW..!

BLUE SKIES AHEAD...

THE RUNNING COMES TO AN ABRUPT HALT AS THE NATURAL PATH GIVES WAY
TO MAN-MADE STONE STEPS. I PUSH ON PAST A WATERFALL AND ARRIVE WET
AND SWEATY AT HOUSE MOSS, FAIRFIELD JUST VISIBLE NOW THROUGH
THIN CLOUDS AS THE RAIN STOPS. AT HAUSE GAP I BEAR LEFT UP A VERY
SLATEY PATH FOLLOWING A COLLAPSED WALL TO THE SUMMIT CAIRN
OF SEAT SANDAL. FIFTY SEVEN MINUTES TO REACH MY FIRST PEAK
AND FIVE TO GO, NOT COUNTING LOWER MAN... BUT ONCE ON TOP OF
DOLLYWAGON PIKE THINGS SHOULD IMPROVE.

BRILLIANT VIEWS...

I TAKE A PANORAMIC SHOT AS THE CLOUDS DISPERSE, THEN MAKE A VERY STEEP
DESCENT ON GRASS TO THE GRISEDALE TARN PATH FOLLOWED BY A CALF-CRUNCHING
CLIMB UP THE STEEP GRASSY SLOPE OF DOLLYWAGON PIKE. THERE ARE
BRILLIANT VIEWS OF FAIRFIELD AND ST SUNDAY CRAG FROM THE SUMMIT,
SO OUT WITH THE CAMERA, VIDEO ON, AND OFF WE GO ON A CLEAR PATH
TO NETHERMOST PIKE. TOUCH THE CAIRN IN ONLY EIGHTEEN MINUTES
THEN SUMMIT HELVELLYN IN ANOTHER TEN.

FIRST ONE OF THE DAY...

RETRACE MY FOOTSTEPS TO THE
WIND SHELTER AND MEET MY FIRST
WALKER OF THE DAY, A LADY FROM
CARLISLE. SIT AND EAT MY CEREAL
BAR, TAKE A QUICK DRINK, THEN
HEAD BACK OVER THE SUMMIT AND
DOWN TO LOWER MAN... STILL NOT
A SOUL IN SIGHT.

EASY PEASY...

THE DESCENT IS EASY - A GREAT PATH
FOR RUNNING, EVEN WHILE
HOLDING A CAMERA. I PUSH ON
TOWARDS WHITE SIDE AND ARRIVE
IN ONLY TWENTY EIGHT MINUTES
FROM HELVELLYN (WOULD HAVE
BEEN FASTER IF NOT FOR THE CAMERA).
LEGS STILL FEELING GOOD AT THE ROCKY TOP OF
RAISE BEFORE DESCENDING TO STICKS PASS. NOT A
GREAT PATH NOW AND I END UP WITH WET FEET.

A BIT OF BOTH...

HEAD WEST AT STICKS PASS TOWARDS MY FINISH AT STANAH. NOT FAR
FROM THE FINISH I COME ACROSS A SMALL PARTY OF YOUNG PEOPLE
COLLAPSED IN A HEAP AT THE SIDE OF THE PATH HOLDING ONTO, LEANING
AGAINST OR DISAPPEARING INTO HUGE RUCKSACKS. THEY SAY I MUST BE
MAD OR SUPER FIT. 'A TINY BIT OF BOTH', I REPLY. I SET OFF FOR THE
FINAL DESCENT THEN INSTANTLY FALL OVER. FEELING A COMPLETE IDIOT
I RECOVER, HAVE A LAUGH AND LEAVE THEM BEHIND.
SOON AT THE FINISH - GREAT RUN!
FIND MY BUS PASS AND WALK A HUNDRED YARDS TO THE BUS STOP. CHECK
TIME. OVER THIRTY MINUTES TO WAIT - OUCH! SO OUT COMES THE THUMB
AND WITHIN FOUR MINUTES A YOUNG GUY PICKS ME UP AND DELIVERS ME
SAFELY TO GRASMERE. THANKS YOUNG MAN...

NETHERMOST PIKE FROM GRISEDALE

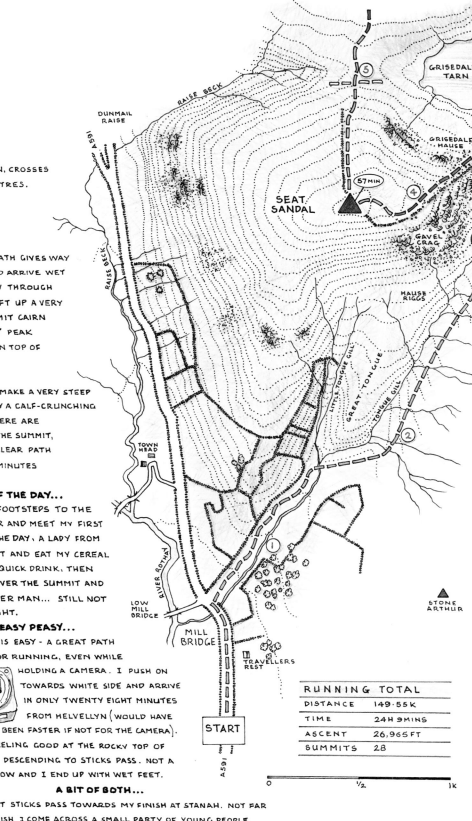

RUNNING TOTAL	
DISTANCE	149·55k
TIME	24H 9MINS
ASCENT	26,965FT
SUMMITS	28

THE END

distance 14·75k   time 3hrs 13mins   ascent 4,260ft

the **NORTHERN** fells

Bad weather brings
a change of plan
-a short run over
HIGH PIKE and CARROCK FELL

INSPIRED BY BRADLEY WIGGINS WINNING THE TOUR DE FRANCE AND THE SUCCESS OF THE BRITISH ATHLETES AT THE LONDON OLYMPICS I HAD PLANNED TO RUN A MULTI-SUMMIT EXTRA-LONG ROUTE OVER THE FAR EASTERN FELLS. BUT GUESS WHAT?.. YES! BAD WEATHER. LOW CLOUD AND DRIZZLE FORCES A CHANGE OF PLAN...

HIGH PIKE FROM CARROCK FELL

NIP UP TO MOSEDALE JUST TEN SHORT MINUTES AWAY TO TACKLE HIGH PIKE AND CARROCK FELL. UNABLE TO SEE EITHER SUMMIT FROM THE ROAD, SUCH IS THE VISIBILITY.
SET OFF AT A GOOD PACE ON A WELL-DEFINED MINE ROAD AND SOON ARRIVE AT DRIGGITH MINE. PUSH ON AND CROSS THE FELL ON TOUGH GRASS, GAINING HEIGHT ALL THE TIME UNTIL I HIT THE SUMMIT - BULLSEYE!
TOO DAMP AND MISERABLE TO SIT ON THE STONE SEAT AND ADMIRE THE VIEWS.
HEAD DOWN ON A CLEAR PATH FEELING RATHER PLEASED WITH MYSELF FOR HITTING THE SUMMIT OF HIGH PIKE WHEN I REALISE I'VE GONE TOO FAR AND MISSED THE TURNING FOR CARROCK FELL!
HEAD EAST AND CONTOUR ROUND MILTON HILL TO PICK UP THE CORRECT TRAIL. THE WAY SOON BECOMES LOST IN A PEAT BOG AND MY WARM, DRY FEET ARE TREATED TO FIFTEEN MINUTES OF COLD BLACK PEAT OOZING BETWEEN MY TOES AS I TRY TO PICK MY WAY OVER TO THE ROCKY SUMMIT SOMEWHERE IN THE DISTANCE.

THE SUMMIT, 2,157 FT, LOOKING TOWARDS BLENCATHRA

CARROCK FELL · 2,174 FT

ARRIVE AT SUMMIT CAIRN AS THE CLOUD AND MIST
DECIDE THEY'VE HAD ENOUGH AND FADE AWAY. I DROP
DOWN STEEPLY TO THE NORTH OF THE CAIRN, TAKING
CARE AS I THREAD BETWEEN SLIPPERY ROCKS.
AIM FOR A CLEAR TRACK LEADING TO CARROCK BECK.
I'M RUNNING AT A GOOD PACE AGAIN AS THE PATH
LEVELS AND TURNS EAST OVER SHORT GRASS AND
BRACKEN DIRECTLY TO THE CAR, WHERE I LOOK BACK
AND SEE THE SUMMIT OF HIGH PIKE FOR THE FIRST TIME
~ SHOULD HAVE SET OFF NOW!

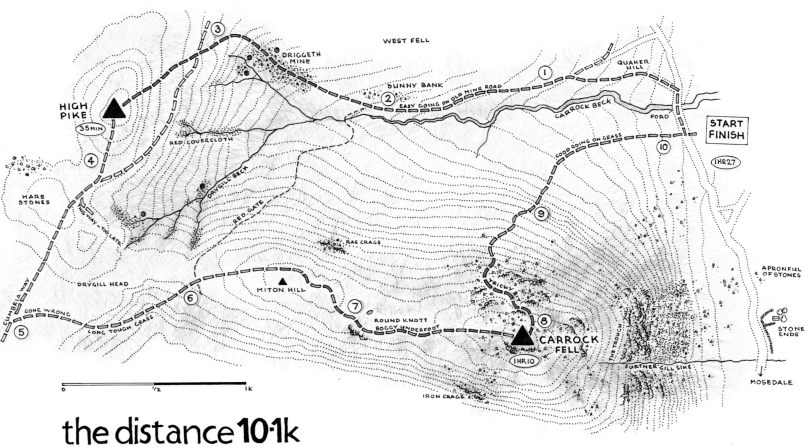

the distance **10·1**k
the time **1**hr**27**mins
the ascent **1,650**ft

RUNNING TOTAL	
DISTANCE	159·65 K
TIME	25 HRS 36 MINS
ASCENT	28,615 FT
SUMMITS	30

the **EASTERN** fells

ON ROAD - OFF ROAD
Great
Mell Fell

LAST WEEKEND AT THE SITE BEFORE IT CLOSES
FOR WINTER. THE WEATHER IS AWFUL AGAIN -
THE WORST SUMMER FOR 200 YEARS SEEMS
DETERMINED TO CONTINUE INTO AUTUMN.

A LOW-LEVEL WALK ON FRIDAY GAVE US SLEET, HAIL,
RAIN, SNOW, STRONG WINDS - AND A RAINBOW. MOST OF
THE HIGH TOPS WERE SPRINKLED WITH SNOW. SATURDAY
BROUGHT MORE SNOW TO THE FELLS - GREAT TO LOOK
AT, BUT NOT GOOD FOR FELL RUNNING.
SUNDAY MORNING WE WOKE TO BLUE SKY AND A HARD FROST.
DECIDED IT WOULD BE FOOLISH TO GO ON THE TOPS, SO DID
A ROAD RUN WITH JANICE AROUND PENRUDDOCK. STUNNING
VIEWS OF BLENCATHRA AND THE NORTHERN FELLS, PLUS A BONUS -

A LARGE FLOCK OF FIELDFARES FEEDING IN THE
FIELDS AT MOTHERBY.

RETURNED TO THE CARAVAN NICELY WARMED UP.
DECIDED TO JUMP IN THE CAR AND NIP DOWN THE ROAD TO
TICK OFF GREAT MELL FELL...

distance 5k
time 50mins
ascent 860ft

RUNNING TOTAL	
DISTANCE	164·65K
TIME	26HRS 26MINS
ASCENT	29,415 FT
SUMMITS	31

THE RUN.
SET OFF STRAIGHT INTO A QUAGMIRE
OF REEDS AND MOSS, WARM DRY FEET
FROZEN BY HOOF HOLES OF WATER, THE
TOPS COVERED BY A THIN LAYER OF ICE.
MOVE OVER TO A MOUND OF SOIL CARRYING
A BROKEN WALL... NO GOOD... STONES
TOO SLIPPERY, SO IT'S BACK TO FROZEN
FEET. SOON REACH THE BOUNDARY
FENCE AND GO STRAIGHT UP THE
STEEPEST POINT LEADING DIRECTLY
TO THE SUMMIT FOR FANTASTIC VIEWS.
SET OFF EAST, DUCKING MY WAY UNDER
TREES 'TIL I PICK UP THE BOUNDARY
TRACK AND CONTOUR ROUND TO
THE START OF THE ASCENT. OVER THE
FENCE AND THEN ANOTHER AND ANOTHER...
AND ANOTHER... ALL TOPPED WITH
BARBED WIRE - NICE! SOON BACK TO THE
CAR. ANOTHER ONE BITES THE DUST.

the NORTH WESTERN fells

First run of the New Year

takes me over OUTERSIDE and CAUSEY PIKE

ARRIVE AT THE COTTAGE IN BRAITHWAITE FOR A FULL WEEK AND AM GREETED BY BLUE SKY AND FREEZING TEMPERATURES.

JUST THE ONE TODAY...

WAKE SUNDAY MORNING TO A HEAVY FROST AND BRIGHT SKY. SO HAVE BREAKFAST AND HEAD OUT THE DOOR FOR MY FIRST FELL RUN SINCE LAST NOVEMBER. OUTERSIDE'S MY OBJECTIVE, SO HEAD THROUGH THE VILLAGE AND ONTO THE TRACK LEADING TO STILE END. BEAR RIGHT AND ONTO OUTERSIDE ON A GOOD GRASSY PATH. A FEW STIFF CLIMBS LEAD TO THE SUMMIT.

NOW IT'S TWO...

THAT WAS SUPPOSED TO BE IT, BUT CAUSEY PIKE LOOKS SO INVITING I HAVE TO CARRY ON. DOWN I GO TO THE MINE ROAD, THEN GET WET FEET CROSSING THE BOG BEFORE CLIMBING DIAGONALLY TOWARDS THE PEAK OF CAUSEY PIKE.

SHOULD HAVE BEEN THREE...

BRILLIANT VIEWS IN ALL DIRECTIONS WITH THE TOPS DUSTED IN SNOW. STAND AWHILE THEN, WITHOUT THINKING, RETURN TO THE MINE ROAD WHEN WITHOUT TOO MUCH EFFORT I COULD HAVE CONTINUED OVER SCAR CRAGS. NEVER MIND: BACK TO BRAITHWAITE FOR A HOT SHOWER –

BLISS

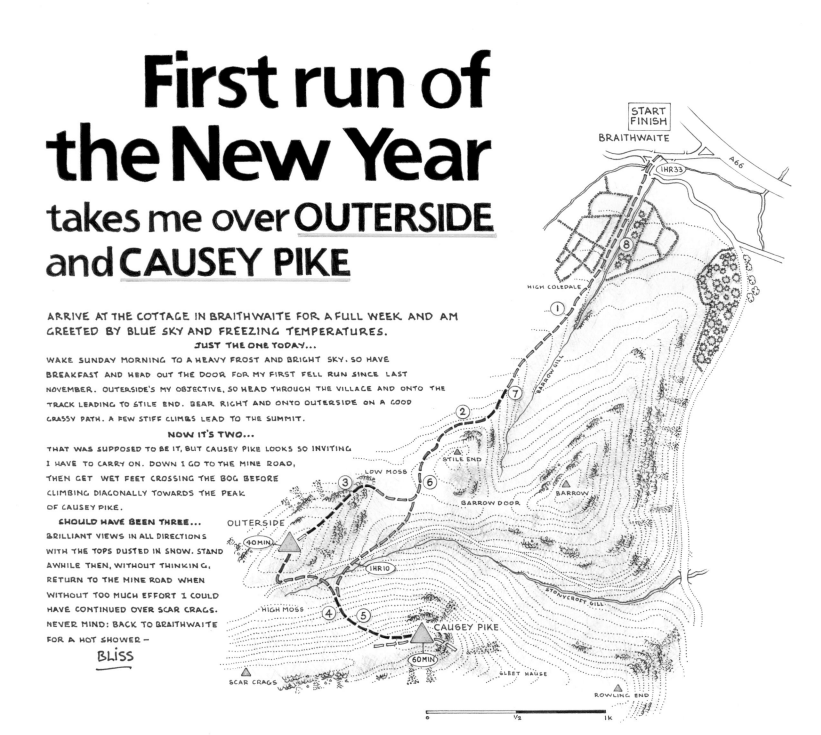

LOOKING TOWARDS SCAR CRAGS FROM THE SUMMIT OF A COLD AND FROSTY CAUSEY PIKE – BRRRING ON THE HOT PORRIDGE!

RUNNING TOTAL	
DISTANCE	173·4K
TIME	27HRS 59MINS
ASCENT	31,700 FT
SUMMITS	33

the distance
8·75k

the time
1hr 33mins

the ascent
2,285ft

the NORTH WESTERN fells

Rawsome!

SALE FELL, LING FELL, GRAYSTONES, BROOM FELL, LORD'S SEAT AND BARF – and it's -14°c

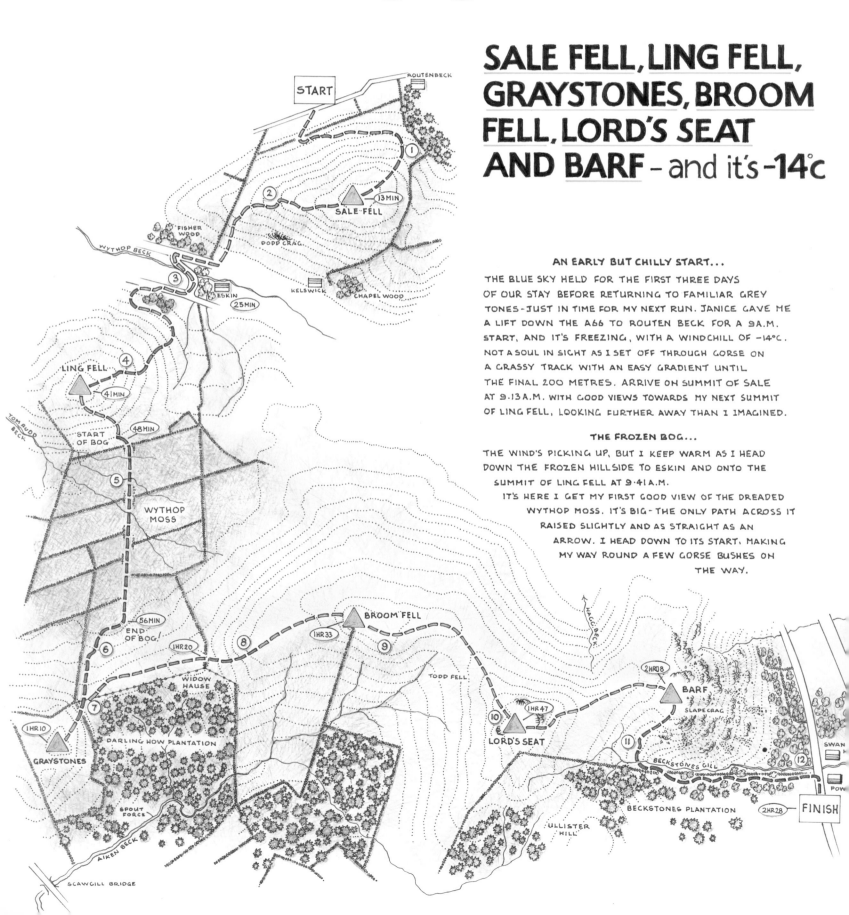

AN EARLY BUT CHILLY START...

THE BLUE SKY HELD FOR THE FIRST THREE DAYS OF OUR STAY BEFORE RETURNING TO FAMILIAR GREY TONES - JUST IN TIME FOR MY NEXT RUN. JANICE GAVE ME A LIFT DOWN THE A66 TO ROUTEN BECK FOR A 9A.M. START, AND IT'S FREEZING, WITH A WINDCHILL OF -14°C. NOT A SOUL IN SIGHT AS I SET OFF THROUGH GORSE ON A GRASSY TRACK WITH AN EASY GRADIENT UNTIL THE FINAL 200 METRES. ARRIVE ON SUMMIT OF SALE AT 9.13 A.M. WITH GOOD VIEWS TOWARDS MY NEXT SUMMIT OF LING FELL, LOOKING FURTHER AWAY THAN I IMAGINED.

THE FROZEN BOG...

THE WIND'S PICKING UP, BUT I KEEP WARM AS I HEAD DOWN THE FROZEN HILLSIDE TO ESKIN AND ONTO THE SUMMIT OF LING FELL AT 9.41 A.M.

IT'S HERE I GET MY FIRST GOOD VIEW OF THE DREADED WYTHOP MOSS. IT'S BIG - THE ONLY PATH ACROSS IT RAISED SLIGHTLY AND AS STRAIGHT AS AN ARROW. I HEAD DOWN TO ITS START, MAKING MY WAY ROUND A FEW GORSE BUSHES ON THE WAY.

THE WYTHOP VALLEY LOOKING TOWARDS SKIDDAW

HERE GOES...

ON THE RAISED PATH, EVERYWHERE IS
FROZEN SOLID - A GOOD DAY TO CROSS A BOG!
KEEP GOING DEAD STRAIGHT, WIND BLOWING UP NOW
AND TURNING COLD. NEARLY REACH THE FAR SIDE
WITH DRY FEET, BUT NOT QUITE... WITH ABOUT
50 METRES TO GO... CRACK...! RIGHT THROUGH
THE FROZEN CRUST INTO ICE-COLD SLUDGE. PUSH ON
TO SOLID GROUND AS MY FEET BECOME NUMB.
CLIMB UP TO GRAYSTONES. IT'S NOW 10-10 A.M.
I'VE BEEN ON THE RUN FOR SEVENTY MINUTES.

TIME FOR ANOTHER LAYER...

A SHORT, TRICKY DESCENT DUE TO FROZEN FEET
AND GROUND BRINGS ME ONTO A GOOD LEVEL PATH
LEADING TO BROOM FELL. ARRIVE AT 10-33 A.M. I'M

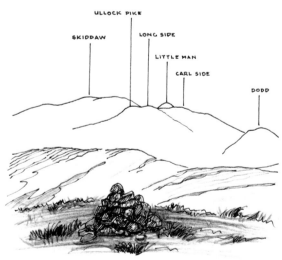

VIEW FROM THE FIRST SUMMIT - SALE FELL

SO COLD I HAVE TO PUT
ON MY RAB VAPOUR RISE
JACKET - THAT'S THREE LAYERS
NOW - AND EAT SOME JELLY BABIES.
REVIVED I STRIDE OUT TOWARDS LORD'S SEAT,
AT 1,811 FEET THE HIGHEST FELL ON THIS RUN.
IT'S NOW 10-47 A.M. AND I MEET THE FIRST
WALKERS OF THE DAY.

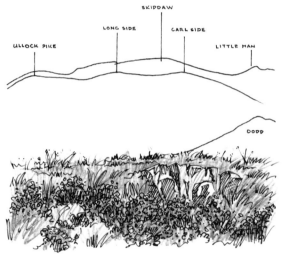

VIEW FROM THE LAST SUMMIT - BARF

BEST SUMMIT, BEST VIEW, WORST DESCENT...

JUST THE ONE SUMMIT TO GO - BARF - AND I SET OFF ON
A GOOD TRACK, FEELING SOFTER UNDERFOOT DUE TO
ITS PEATY NATURE. THE ROCKY SUMMIT HAS GOOD
VIEWS ACROSS TO THE SKIDDAW GROUP. IT'S 11-08 A.M.
AS I START MY DESCENT TO THE FINISH.
MEET A FAMILY STRUGGLING UP AND THEY WARN ME
THE PATH IS A SHEET OF ICE - A FROZEN STREAM WITH
NASTY PROTRUDING ROCKS. IT'S TOO IFFY TO
RISK, SO I ABANDON THE PATH AND PUSH MY WAY
THROUGH SAPLINGS, WHICH GIVES ME SOMETHING
TO GRASP HOLD OF ON WHAT'S BEGINNING TO PROVE
A TRICKY DESCENT.

RELIEF...

ARRIVE ON A WIDER, FLATTER PATH AND MEET
MORE WALKERS STARTING THEIR DAY OUT.
GOOD LUCK TO THEM AS I REACH THE ROAD WITH
RELIEF THAT THE ONLY MISHAP I ENCOUNTERED
WAS COLD FEET WHEN BROKEN BONES AND
HYPERTHERMIA COULD HAVE BEEN ON THE MENU.
GIVE JANICE A RING TO PICK ME UP AND
TAKE ME BACK TO THAT HOT SHOWER! OH YES

the distance 12k

the time 2h 28min

the ascent 3,290ft

RUNNING TOTAL	
DISTANCE	185.4K
TIME	30HRS 27MINS
ASCENT	34,290 FT
SUMMITS	39

the **CENTRAL** fells

Low altitude, low temperature, but high spirits on...

HIGH RIGG

FIRST TIME BACK IN THE CARAVAN. IT'S EASTER, IT'S FREEZING, AND THE A66 IS CLOSED DUE TO TEN FOOT SNOWDRIFTS. IT HAS BEEN THE COLDEST MARCH FOR TWO HUNDRED YEARS; WALKED FROM ROSTHWAITE TO GRASMERE THROUGH TWO FEET OF SNOW ON GREENUP EDGE. ALL THE HIGH TOPS ARE OUT OF BOUNDS FOR FELL RUNNING, SO I HAVE TO CHOOSE FROM A HANDFUL OF SNOW-FREE TOPS.

TWISTS AND TURNS...

STRAIGHT OVER A STILE ON A GOOD PATH, FROZEN SOLID, WITH BIG PATCHES OF SNOW BUT NO REAL PROBLEMS UNDERFOOT AS THE PATH TWISTS, DIPS AND TURNS ITS WAY TOWARDS THE SUMMIT, WITH GOOD VIEWS OF A SNOW-COVERED BLENCATHRA.
ARRIVE IN TWENTY EIGHT MINUTES BUT DON'T HANG ABOUT AS THE WIND CHILL STARTS TO BITE. HEAD DOWN TO THE CHURCH-YOUTH CENTRE ONTO A LANE LEADING ROUND TO SHAW BANK, THEN BACK ON A GOOD FOOTPATH THROUGH FIELDS TO THE A591.

A CHANGE OF PLAN...

GETTING COLDER AND COLDER AND LEGS STARTING TO COMPLAIN! THE PLAN WAS TO RUN OVER TO RAVEN CRAG FOR A QUICK UP-AND-DOWN, BUT IT'S TOO COLD TO ATTEMPT, SO I STICK TO THE A591 FOR ANOTHER TWO KILOMETRES AND AM PLEASED I'VE CHANGED MY MIND AS I ARRIVE AT THE FINISH FROZEN STIFF BUT HAPPY TO HAVE KNOCKED OFF ANOTHER SUMMIT.

RUNNING TOTAL

DISTANCE	193·9K
TIME	31 HRS 29 MINS
ASCENT	34,900 FT
SUMMITS	40

the distance 8·5k

the time 62mins

the ascent 610ft

the EASTERN fells

Circumnavigation and ascent
of LITTLE MELL FELL

LOW CLOUD AND THE PROMISE OF RAIN AT ANY TIME PERSUADE ME TO TACKLE A LOW FELL, SO I TALK JANICE INTO A RUN CIRCUMNAVIGATING LITTLE MELL FELL. SHE'S RUNNING WELL AT THE MOMENT AND HIGHLY MOTIVATED DUE TO SATURDAY MORNING PARK RUNS.

ON WITH THE ROAD SHOES...

IT'S A SHORT DRIVE TO NAB END THEN OFF WE GO. THE FIRST HUNDRED YARDS BRING A SHORT CLIMB. THE UNDULATING ROAD CONTINUES TOWARDS LOWTHWAITE AND THEN ONTO THE HAUSE. I WAIT FOR JANICE THEN HEAD OVER A STILE, THROUGH A MUDDY REED BED AND ONTO A PERMISSIVE PATH LEADING TO THE SUMMIT, WITH GREAT VIEWS DOWN TO ULLSWATER. AN EASY DESCENT LEADS BACK TO THE HAUSE AND TARMAC.

FROGSPAWN GALORE...

BACK ON A BRIDLEWAY FOR THE NEXT TWO KILOMETRES AND WAITING FOR JANICE I TAKE A QUICK LOOK IN THE DITCH RUNNING ALONGSIDE ME AND FIND IT FULL OF FROGSPAWN - BUCKETS OF IT! GOOD LUCK GUYS... HOPE YOU MAKE IT. AN EASY JOG CARRIES US ALL THE WAY BACK TO THE CAR. WELL DONE JANICE.

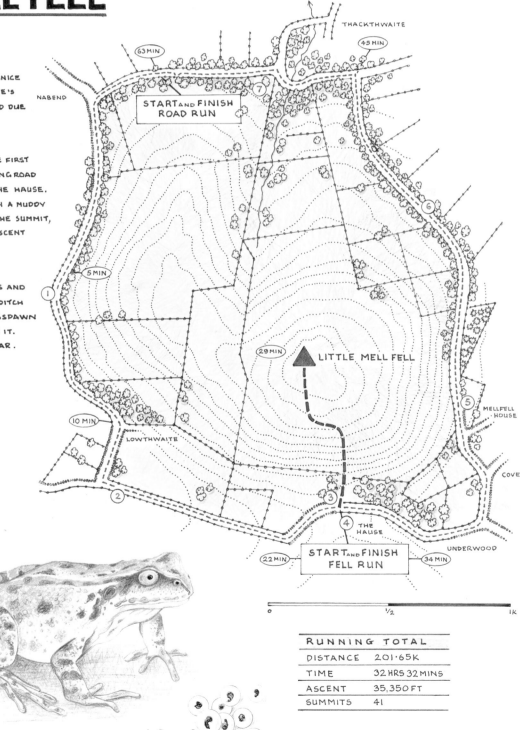

the distance
7·75k

the time
63mins

the ascent
450ft

RUNNING TOTAL	
DISTANCE	201·65K
TIME	32 HRS 32 MINS
ASCENT	35,350 FT
SUMMITS	41

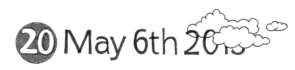

the **EASTERN** fells

ouch!

That really hurt...

as I take a tumble between CATSTYCAM and BIRKHOUSE MOOR

WITH THE PROMISE OF BETTER WEATHER TO COME I POP DOWN TO
GLENRIDDING BEFORE NOON FOR A MULTI-SUMMIT RUN OF
CATSTYCAM · BIRKHOUSE MOOR · ST SUNDAY CRAG ·
BIRKS AND ARNISTON CRAG.

HOW MUCH ...

PULL INTO A VERY BUSY CAR PARK AND PAY MY
DUES · £5 FOR 4 HOURS! SET OFF INTO THE
VILLAGE AND PICK UP THE ROAD LEADING
TO THE YOUTH HOSTEL.

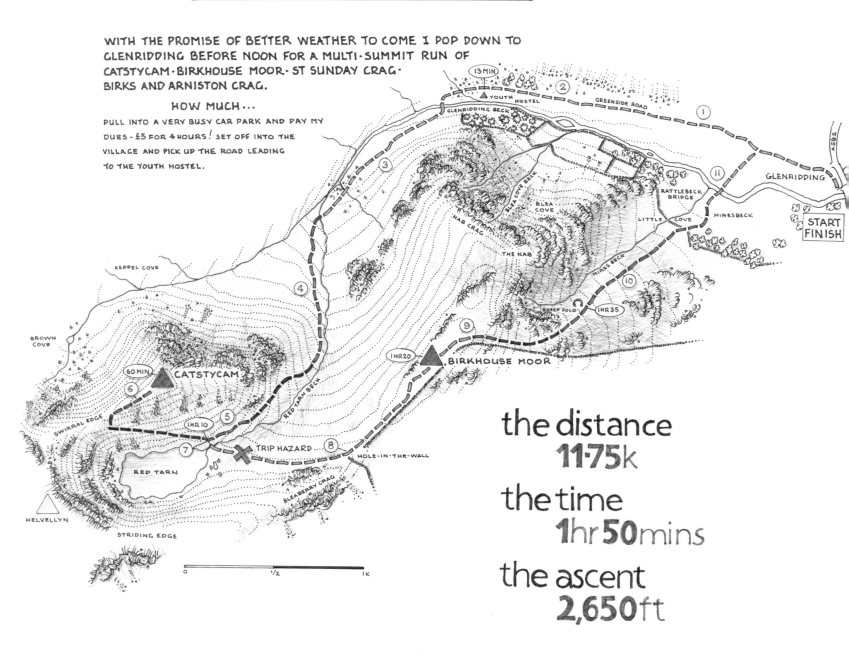

the distance
11·75k

the time
1hr **50**mins

the ascent
2,650ft

NO SIGN OF GOOD WEATHER YET.

GOOD GRADIENT FOR RUNNING AS I PASS A FEW
WALKERS. THE CLOUD THICKENS AS I REACH AND
PASS THE YOUTH HOSTEL AND CROSS THE BECK ONTO
THE FOOTPATH HEADING TO RED TARN.
LOADS OF HELICOPTER BAGS AT SIDE OF PATH AS THE
GRADIENT BEGINS TO STEEPEN. THEY MUST BE
REDOING THE PATH. I BEAR RIGHT AT A HUGE
CAIRN AS THE PATH STEEPENS AGAIN AND BEGINS
TO DETERIORATE - A BIT LIKE MY RUNNING! SLOW
TO HANDS-ON-KNEES PACE UP TO THE RIDGE. THE CLOUDS
ARE STILL LOW AND DENSE - SO MUCH SO I CAN'T SEE
EITHER HELVELLYN OR CATSTYCAM AS I TURN AND RUN
THE RIDGE TO THE SUMMIT OF CATSTYCAM. THE CLOUD'S
SO THICK I RUN ON AND DESCEND JUST TO MAKE SURE I'VE
REACHED THE SUMMIT. CHECK THE TIME AND HEAD BACK
DOWN TO THE BIG CAIRN AND ONTO THE OUTFLOW OF
RED TARN. SPOT HALF A DOZEN WALKERS TAKING A
BREAK BETWEEN SOME BIG BOULDERS.

NEARLY A BAD BREAK OF MY OWN.

NOW RUNNING AT A GOOD PACE ON A FLATISH, WIDE
WELL-MADE SECTION OF PATH
WHEN I TAKE A BAD TUMBLE,
BANGING MY RIGHT HIP, ELBOW
AND, WORST OF ALL, MY KNEE. I SIT
THERE FOR A MINUTE, DAZED AND HURTING, THEN CHECK
AROUND TO MAKE SURE NO ONE SAW AN OLD MAN MAKE AN
IDIOT OF HIMSELF; THICK MIST DOES HAVE ITS BENEFITS...

CHECK FOR DAMAGE...

MY ELBOW AND HIP ARE NOT TOO BAD, BUT MY KNEE'S
BLEEDING AND MY LEGGINGS ARE RIPPED AND TORN. MOVE MY
LEG, IT'S O.K. SO I STAND UP GINGERLY AND SET OFF TOWARDS
THE HOLE-IN-THE-WALL AND BIRKHOUSE MOOR. RUNNING
PACE STILL GOOD AS I HIT THE HIGH SPOT OF 2,350 FEET.

A WISE DECISION...

HAD PLANNED TO DOUBLE BACK TO
THE HOLE-IN-THE-WALL AFTER VISITING
BIRKHOUSE MOOR THEN DROP DOWN
INTO GRISEDALE, UP TO THE TARN AND
THEN ACROSS TO AND UP ST SUNDAY CRAG,
TICKING OFF BIRKS AND ARNISON CRAG
ON THE DESCENT TO THE FINISH.
AFTER TAKING THE EARLY FALL I
DECIDED TO CUT IT SHORT AND WITH
THE ONSET OF BLISTERS IT PROVED
TO BE THE RIGHT DECISION.

A PAINFUL DESCENT...

OFF I GO ON A MAN-MADE PATH ON THE LONG DESCENT TO
GLENRIDDING WHEN I START TO DEVELOP WHOPPING BIG
BLISTERS ON THE SOLES OF MY HEELS - WHAT NEXT? I THINK.
I ABANDON THE PATH FOR THE GRASS VERGE, TAKING
EXTRA CARE WITH MY FOOT PLACEMENT... CAN'T AFFORD
ANOTHER TUMBLE - TOO MANY PEOPLE ABOUT NOW, AND
NO MIST COVER EITHER, JUST CLEAR BLUE SKIES AT LAST!

FLAT GROUND HERE I COME...

BLISTERS ARE HURTING MORE THAN MY KNEE NOW,
SO I'M RELIEVED TO REACH GILLSIDE AND FLAT TARMAC
FOR THE FINAL RUN DOWN THROUGH THE VILLAGE
TO THE CAR PARK. RELIEF!

RUNNING TOTAL	
DISTANCE	213.4K
TIME	34 HRS 32 MINS
ASCENT	38,000FT
SUMMITS	43

the FAR EASTERN fells

At last...
sunshine!

As I stride out over BONSCALE PIKE, ARTHUR'S PIKE, LOADPOT HILL, WETHER HILL, STEEL KNOTTS and finally HALLIN FELL...

TWO DAYS OF GALE FORCE WINDS, RAIN AND LOW TEMPERATURES... YES, IT'S SPRING BANK HOLIDAY, AND IT'S BEEN THE COLDEST ON RECORD SINCE 1976. WHAT A RELIEF, THEN, AS SATURDAY BRINGS WALL-TO-WALL SUNSHINE AND NO WIND.

OFF I GO DOWN TO POOLEY BRIDGE AND ON TO HOWTOWN, PASSING HUNDREDS OF TENTS ON THE LAKESIDE CAMP-SITES. WITH THE WINDOW DOWN I GET A LOVELY WHIFF OF BACON AND EGGS SIZZLING AWAY ON GAS STOVES. RESIST THE TEMPTATION TO STOP, AND CARRY ON TO HOWTOWN TO PARK UP, GET MY BEARINGS AND SET OFF...

FANTASTIC VIEWS...
...THROUGH THE GATE PAST CLUMPS OF BLUEBELLS; THROUGH ANOTHER GATE AND ONTO THE GRASSY SIDE OF BONSCALE PIKE. FORCED TO WALK AS THE SLOPE STEEPENS BEFORE PICKING UP A GENTLER PATH ACROSS THE BREAST OF THE FELL. SOON STANDING ON THE SUMMIT WITH FANTASTIC VIEWS OF THE HELVELLYN RANGE. DOWN NOW ACROSS COTTON GRASS AND MOSS TO A RUIN AND ONTO A PEATY PATH LEADING TO ARTHUR'S PIKE.

DRIPPING IN SWEAT...
INTO A STEADY PACE HEADING TOWARDS LOADPOT HILL AS THE SUN BECOMES HOTTER - AND IT'S NOT EVEN 10 A.M. YET. DRIPPING IN SWEAT I REACH THE SUMMIT AND SPEND FIVE MINUTES TAKING ON FLUIDS AND SOAKING UP THE BRILLIANT VIEWS OF FAIRFIELD AND ST SUNDAY CRAG.

CARRIED AWAY...
NO CLOUDS AND STILL NO PEOPLE IN SIGHT AS A WIDE TRACK LEADS THE WAY TO WETHER HILL. IT'S SO EASY I GET CARRIED AWAY AND CONTINUE OVER THE SO-CALLED SUMMIT AND ONTO RED CRAG... LOOK AROUND AND REALISE I'VE GONE TOO FAR! I DOUBLE BACK TO GOWK HILL AND CONTINUE ON A LOVELY PATH FULL OF TWISTS AND TURNS, UPS AND DOWNS. PASS THE FIRST WALKERS OF THE DAY AS I REACH THE SUMMIT ROCKS OF STEEL KNOTTS AND SPEND FIVE MINUTES EATING MY HOME-MADE LARDY CAKE.

the distance
17k

the time
2hrs **49**mins

the ascent
3,150ft

RUNNING TOTAL	
DISTANCE	230·4K
TIME	37 HRS 21 MINS
ASCENT	41,150 FT
SUMMITS	49

BONSCALE PIKE LOOKING TOWARDS HELVELLYN

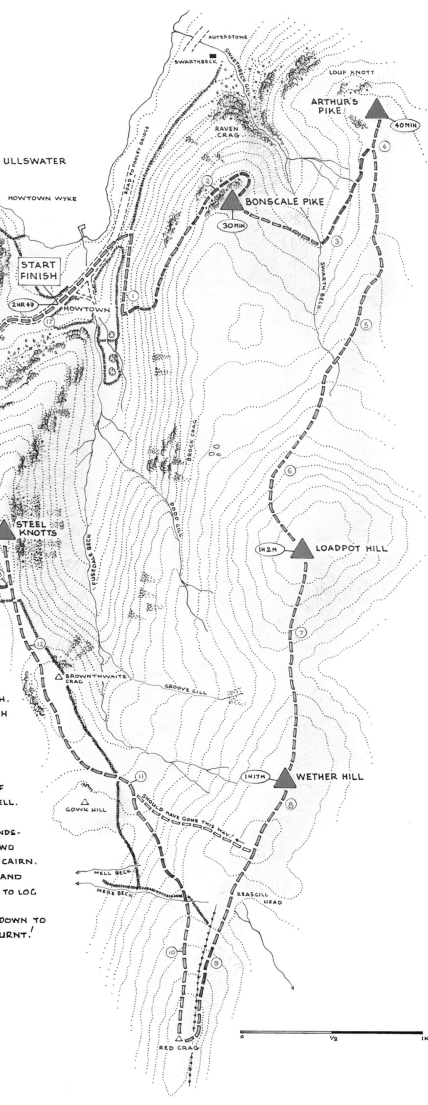

HOME STRETCH...

RETRACE MY STEPS AND DROP DOWN
ACROSS THE SIDE OF THE FELL ONTO A
GOOD PATH LEADING TO THE OLD CHURCH.
SOON ON THE PATH FOR THE NEW CHURCH
WITH LOADS OF PEOPLE, AND CARS
PARKED ALL OVER THE PLACE.

FEELING GOOD...

STILL VERY HOT AND SUNNY AS I SET OFF
TOWARDS THE LAST SUMMIT, HALLIN FELL.
LEGS AND LUNGS FEEL GOOD, BUT THE
INCREASING GRADIENT DEMANDS A HANDS-
ON-KNEES, HEAD-DOWN SLOG, THEN A TWO
HUNDRED YARD RUN TO THE SUMMIT CAIRN.
PLENTY OF FOLK ENJOYING THE VIEWS AND
GLORIOUS SUNSHINE. BORROW A PEN TO LOG
THE TIME - LOST MINE SOMEWHERE.
LAST DESCENT OF THE DAY TAKES ME DOWN TO
THE CAR IN GOOD SPIRITS... AND SUNBURNT!

the **EASTERN** fells

This must be as good as it gets...

as I tackle St SUNDAY CRAG, BIRKS and ARNISON CRAG on a glorious summer day...

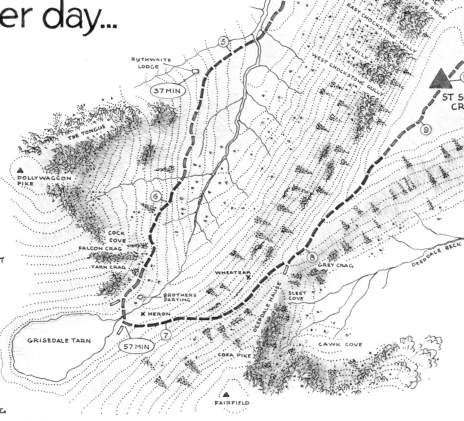

I DRIVE TO PATTERDALE AND THERE'S NOT A CLOUD IN THE SKY. FIND SOMEWHERE TO PARK AND SET OFF UP THE ROAD. TURNING LEFT ONTO THE LANE LEADING TO HELVELLYN AND GRISEDALE IN ANTICIPATION...

CAN'T BELIEVE THE WEATHER AS I LEAVE THE HELVELLYN TRACK AND CARRY STRAIGHT ON TO GRISEDALE TARN. THIS IS A GREAT PATH TO RUN ON AND I DON'T HIT THE FIRST TOUGH GRADIENT UNTIL JUST BEFORE RUTHWAITE LODGE. CHECK TIME: ONLY THIRTY SEVEN MINUTES FROM THE SCHOOL AT PATTERDALE.

TWO GREAT BIRDS, ONE AFTER THE OTHER...
THE PATH DETERIORATES UNDERFOOT AS IT TWISTS AND TURNS UP THE VALLEY TOWARDS GRISEDALE TARN. REACH THE TARN AS THE WIND PICKS UP AND CLOUD BEGINS TO FORM OVER THE HIGH TOPS. HALF A DOZEN WALKERS ARE DESCENDING DOLLYWAGGON PIKE AS I CROSS THE OUTLET STREAM AND TIPTOE THROUGH THE BOG TOWARDS THE START OF THE FINE TRACK CROSSING THE FLANK OF ST SUNDAY CRAG. HERE I SPOT A HERON OUT OF THE CORNER OF MY EYE STANDING MOTIONLESS ON ONE LEG, EYEBALLING ME AS IF TO SAY: 'WHAT ARE YOU DOING HERE?'
THIS IS A GREAT PATH, RUNABLE VIRTUALLY ALL THE WAY TO THE MAIN RIDGE. IT'S HERE I SPOT THE NEXT BIRD: A WHEATEAR NOT MORE THAN SIX FEET AWAY BEAUTIFUL.

IT CAN'T GET BETTER THAN THIS...
THE VIEW ACROSS TO NETHERMOST PIKE AND HELVELLYN IS VERY IMPRESSIVE AS THE CLOUDS FLOAT BY, THEN AS I REACH THE MAIN RIDGE THE CRAGS OF FAIRFIELD AND HART CRAG COME INTO VIEW AND I THINK TO MYSELF IT DOESN'T GET BETTER THAN THIS, ANYWHERE.

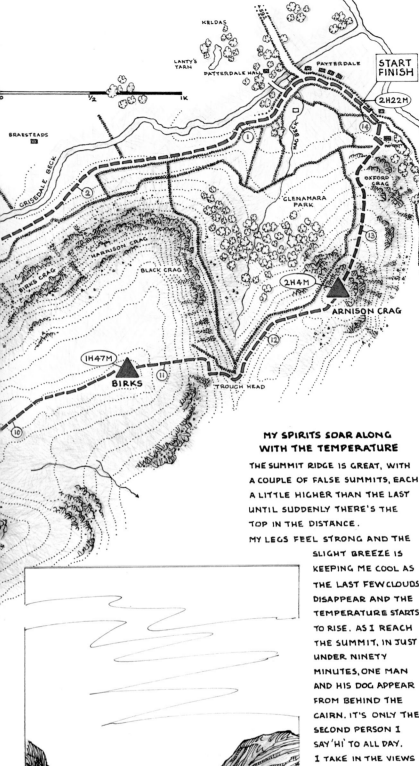

DAY TRIPPERS

SPOT TWO GUYS ON THE SUMMIT AS I REACH THE BOTTOM OF THE LITTLE ROCKY PEAK. I CHAT TO THEM AS I PAT THE SUMMIT CAIRN. THEY'VE DRIVEN UP FOR THE DAY FROM BRADFORD AND ARE ON THEIR WAY TO ST SUNDAY CRAG. BEST OF LUCK LADS - NOT MY CHOICE OF ROUTE MIND.

DOWN TO THE PUB

STEADY OFF THE TOP - DON'T WANT TO TRIP AT THE VERY END... THE FOOTPATH TAKES ME DOWN TO THE REAR OF THE PATTERDALE HOTEL NOT A HUNDRED YARDS FROM WHERE I PARKED THE CAR. JOG PAST ALL THE WALKERS STARTING THEIR DAY ON THE FELLS AS I'M FINISHING MINE. BACK TO A BAKING CAR AND A WELCOME DRINK OF WARM SQUASH. WISH THE PUB WAS OPEN! A GREAT RUN ON A GREAT DAY - ONE OF THE BEST SO FAR.

the DISTANCE
14k

the TIME
2hrs 22mins

the ASCENT
2,395ft

MY SPIRITS SOAR ALONG WITH THE TEMPERATURE

THE SUMMIT RIDGE IS GREAT, WITH A COUPLE OF FALSE SUMMITS, EACH A LITTLE HIGHER THAN THE LAST UNTIL SUDDENLY THERE'S THE TOP IN THE DISTANCE.
MY LEGS FEEL STRONG AND THE SLIGHT BREEZE IS KEEPING ME COOL AS THE LAST FEW CLOUDS DISAPPEAR AND THE TEMPERATURE STARTS TO RISE. AS I REACH THE SUMMIT, IN JUST UNDER NINETY MINUTES, ONE MAN AND HIS DOG APPEAR FROM BEHIND THE CAIRN. IT'S ONLY THE SECOND PERSON I SAY 'HI' TO ALL DAY. I TAKE IN THE VIEWS AND SPOT MY NEXT TWO SUMMITS, BIRKS AND ARNISON CRAG, THEN SET OFF DOWN A TRICKY PATH FULL OF BEANS.

ST SUNDAY CRAG
FROM GRISEDALE TARN

RUNNING TOTAL	
DISTANCE	244·4K
TIME	39HRS 43MINS
ASCENT	43,545 FT
SUMMITS	52

MY FIRST BIT OF GRASS

I'M SOON DOWN TO A GRASSY PLATEAU LEADING TO BIRKS. IT'S PLAIN SAILING NOW AS I REACH THE LITTLE STONE CAIRN ON THE GRASSY SUMMIT. NOT TOO SURE WHERE THE BEST LINE OF DESCENT IS AS I HEAD FOR THE NEXT LANDMARK, TROUGH HEAD. SPOT A GUY WALKING UP IN THE DISTANCE SO HEAD OVER AND SEE THE GRASS TROD LEADING DIRECTLY TO WHERE I WANT TO BE. STILL FEELING GOOD, AND LEGS STRONG, SO PUSH ON TO ARNISTON CRAG.

SUMMIT, ARNISON CRAG

the **CENTRAL** fells

Share a view with

Falco Peregrinus

on my way over
**HELM CRAG, GIBSON KNOTT,
CALF CRAG** and **STEEL FELL**

THE SUMMIT OF STEEL FELL

SUMMIT CRAGS - CALF CRAGS

THERE'S BRILLIANT SUNSHINE
AGAIN AS I DRIVE TOWARDS GRASMERE
WITH THE TEMPERATURE READING 22° -
AND IT'S NOT EVEN NINE O'CLOCK YET. PARK
THE CAR ON THE A591, CROSS THE ROAD AND SET
OFF DOWN A SINGLE LANE TRACK AND TURN OFF,
RIGHT, TO PASS AN INDEPENDANT YOUTH HOSTEL
WITH PLENTY OF ACTIVITY IN THE CAR PARK.
INTO MY STRIDE NOW AS I JOIN THE MAIN PATH FROM
GRASMERE. IT'S BEEN **ALL TARMAC SO FAR** AND THE
OLD LEGS ARE NOT FEELING TOO GREAT - HOPE THEY IMPROVE -
AND QUICKLY !

the DISTANCE **11**k the TIME **2**hrs**8**mins the ASCENT **2,550**ft

GIBSON KNOTT FROM HELM CRAG

I TURN OFF FOR **HELM CRAG** AS THE MAIN PATH CONTINUES UP THE VALLEY TO FAR EASEDALE AND EASEDALE TARN. NOW THE CLIMBING STARTS AND I'M **REDUCED TO JOGGING AND WALKING** MY WAY UP TO THE SUMMIT. TRY TO CLIMB TO THE TOP OF THE ROCK OUTCROP IN VAIN AS THE HARD STUDS ON MY TRAINERS PROVIDE NO GRIP ON THE SMOOTH ROCK.

RUNNING TOTAL	
DISTANCE	255.4 K
TIME	41 HRS 51 MINS
ASCENT	46,095 FT
SUMMITS	56

AS I SET OFF FOR **GIBSON KNOTT** I'M SET UPON BY A **HUGE SWARM OF FLIES,** ALL INTENT ON STICKING TO MY HOT, WET HEAD. MY WHOLE BODY IS HEATING UP AS I PICK MY WAY DOWN THE RIDGE PATH AND DECIDE I MUST PUT MY CAP ON WHEN I REACH THE SUMMIT. MY LEGS FEEL A LOT BETTER AS I REACH THE SUMMIT, WHERE I SPOT A **PEREGRINE FALCON PERCHED ON A ROCK NO MORE THAN TEN FEET AWAY.** IT'S THE FIRST TIME I'VE SEEN ONE IN THE WILD. HIS HEAD TURNS TO GIVE ME A STARE BEFORE LAUNCHING HIMSELF INTO FAR EASEDALE. BRILLIANT.

HAVE A DRINK, WIPE HEAD, PUT ON SUN CAP AND LOOK OVER TO MY NEXT PORT OF CALL, **CALF CRAG.** IT LOOKS A LONG WAY OFF AND I'M BECOMING **HOTTER AND HOTTER BY THE MINUTE.** SET OFF ON A CLEAR PATH THAT FADES THEN REAPPEARS ON THE OPPOSITE SIDE OF A **BOG** AND I SOON END UP WITH **BLACK OOZE UP TO MY KNEES.** NOT TO WORRY; I'LL SOON DRY IN THIS HEAT. SO ON I GO, UP AND DOWN, IN AND OUT, BEFORE I SPOT THE SUMMIT CAIRN PERCHED ON A ROCKY TOP.

I ARRIVE AT THE SUMMIT DRENCHED IN SWEAT, SO GRAB A DRINK, REMOVE MY T-SHIRT AND **WRING OUT THE SWEAT – BUT THERE'S NO BREEZE TO DRY ME OFF OR COOL ME DOWN!** IT'S DOWNHILL NOW ON SPONGY GRASS ALL THE WAY TO THE TARN AND FROM THERE UPHILL TO **STEEL FELL'S** SUMMIT.

AFTER THE SUMMIT THERE'S A TRICKY ROCKY SECTION TO NEGOTIATE BEFORE THE PATH RETURNS TO GRASS. THE LONG DESCENT MAKES MY KNEES ACHE, THEN CREATES **HOT SPOTS ON MY FEET,** AND WITH MY HOLIDAY STILL TO ENJOY I DECIDE TO SLOW RIGHT DOWN SO AS NOT TO DEVELOP BLISTERS AND GIVE ME ANOTHER CHANCE OF A FELL RUN BEFORE HEADING HOME. ONCE ON THE FLATISH TARMAC IT'S BUSINESS AS USUAL, AND IN NO TIME AT ALL I'M BACK AT THE CAR AND THE SANCTUARY OF SHADE.

THE TEMPERATURE HAS NOW **RISEN TO 27°C** – BUT I DON'T KNOW THE TEMPERATURE OF MY HEAD. I RECKON **YOU COULD FRY AN EGG ON IT!!!**

the NORTH WESTERN fells

A great run over

old favourites

ROBINSON, HINDSCARTH, DALE HEAD, HIGH SPY, MAIDEN MOOR and CATBELLS

I DRIVE DOWN TO NEWLANDS VALLEY, PASSING BLENCATHRA BEING TEASED BY CLOUDS AS THE EARLY MORNING SUN BURNS AWAY THE REMAINDER OF YESTERDAY'S THICK GREY CLOUDS. LOOKS PROMISING...

THE KESWICK VALLEY IS FULL OF LOW CLOUD AS I DRIVE THROUGH PORTINSCALE AND HEAD FOR THE SMALL CAR PARK AT **LITTLE TOWN**. THEY WANT **£3 TO PARK THE CAR** BUT I ONLY HAVE £1, SO I OWE 'EM £2.! THE CLOUD IS BREAKING UP AS I SET OFF PAST THE CHURCH ON A NARROW LANE, THEN TURN LEFT ONTO A TRACK LEADING TO **LOW HIGH SNAB**. I PASS A COUPLE OF HOUSES, HEAD THROUGH A GATE, THEN THE CLIMBING BEGINS UP **HIGH SNAB BANK**. IT'S A HANDS-ON-KNEES JOB TO REACH THE RIDGE, THEN I CAN RUN AT A GOOD PACE ON A GRASSY PATH ALL THE WAY TO THE FIRST ROCK TOWER. IT'S BACK TO HANDS-ON-KNEES TO THE SUMMIT PLATEAU.
THE **CLOUDS ARE ALL BUT GONE** AS I CROSS TO THE CAIRN - WIND SHELTER, ADMIRE THE VIEW THEN HEAD OFF.

A PATH HEADS SOUTH TO THE MAIN RIDGE AND I'M SOON INTO A **GOOD PACE**. THE PATH DIPS DOWN SLIGHTLY, THEN STEEPLY, BEFORE HEADING AWAY FROM THE MAIN RIDGE AND ACROSS THE SIDE OF **HINDSCARTH**, RISING AGAIN TOWARDS THE SUMMIT. I TOUCH THE CAIRN. THE **VIEW DOWN NEWLANDS** IS AWESOME, BUT WHEN I RETURN TO THE MAIN RIDGE THE **BUTTERMERE** VALLEY IS **TOTALLY CLOAKED IN THICK CLOUD**, NOT A LAKE OR FELL TO BE SEEN.

DALE HEAD NOW LOOKS IMPRESSIVE, WITH RUGGED ROCK OUTCROPS SILHOUETTED AGAINST THE THICK WHITE CLOUD OF BUTTERMERE. THE TEMPERATURE CONTINUES TO RISE AND I'M SWEATING BUCKETS. **HOPE THE DRINK LASTS TO THE END!**

I OWE LITTLE TOWN CAR PARK £2

I REACH THE SUMMIT OF **DALE HEAD** WITH LESS EFFORT THAN I THOUGHT. JUST ONE GUY'S ON TOP, STOOD NEXT TO A **FIRST CLASS CAIRN** AT LEAST SIX FEET TALL. HAVE A QUICK WORD ABOUT THE WEATHER - AS YOU DO - BEFORE A PAINFUL DESCENT TO **DALE HEAD TARN**. PAINFUL BECAUSE THE SOLES OF MY HEELS ARE **RED HOT AND BLISTERING**; EVERY STEP DOWN IS UNPLEASANT. I'M GLAD TO REACH THE TARN AND LEVEL RUNNING (NOT FOR LONG) TO TAKE SOME OF THE PRESSURE OFF THOSE BLISTERS. NOT GOOD.

IT'S UPHILL NOW ALL THE WAY TO **HIGH SPY** AND ANOTHER **PERFECT CAIRN**. I POUR MORE DRINK DOWN MY THROAT AND WIPE SWEAT FROM MY EYES THEN ATTACK **MAIDEN MOOR** - FULL STEAM AHEAD ON THE WIDE TRACK FOR TWO KILOMETRES TO ARRIVE IN FIFTEEN MINUTES. I'M MEETING LOTS OF PEOPLE NOW AS I CONTINUE TO MY LAST SUMMIT OF THE DAY, **CATBELLS**.

THE DESCENT FROM **MAIDEN MOOR** IS NOT SO STEEP AS TO PUT PRESSURE ON MY HEELS, AND I KEEP A GOOD PACE ALL THE WAY TO THE SUMMIT, **SPURRED ON BY THE NOW FREQUENT WALKERS** ON THE RIDGE.

SWEAT!

CATBELLS' SUMMIT IS **HEAVING WITH FOLK** SITTING, STAGGERING, POSING, POINTING, EATING AND DRINKING. I GRAB A DRINK - **THE LAST DROP** - BEFORE RETRACING MY STEPS TO MART BIELD, WHERE I DROP DOWN INTO **YEWTHWAITE COMB** ACROSS SCREE AND ROCKS. IT'S ANOTHER PAINFUL DESCENT DUE TO THE BLISTERS. **ALL IN ALL, THOUGH, A GREAT RUN OVER SOME OLD FAVOURITES.**

FIRST UP...
ROBINSON

4·5 KILOMETRES FROM THE CAR PARK AT LITTLE TOWN AND 2000 FT OF ASCENT TAKES ME 46 MIN TO SUMMIT.

NEXT UP...
HINDSCARTH

2 KILOMETRES AWAY FROM ROBINSON AND WITH 500 FT OF ASCENT TAKES ME 22 MIN TO REACH THE SUMMIT.

NEXT IN LINE...
DALE HEAD

1·5 KILOMETRES AWAY AND 330 FT OF ASCENT TAKES ME JUST 17 MIN.

A NEW RIDGE TO...
HIGH SPY

2 KILOMETRES FROM DALE HEAD AND 550 FT OF ASCENT TAKES ME 28 MIN.

PLAIN SAILING TO...
MAIDEN MOOR

JUST OVER 2 KILOMETRES FROM HIGH SPY WITH ONLY 100 FT OF ASCENT TAKES ME 15 MIN.

NOW FOR THE LAST ONE...
CATBELLS

JUST UNDER 2 KILOMETRES FROM MAIDEN MOOR WITH 310 FT OF ASCENT - 19 MIN.

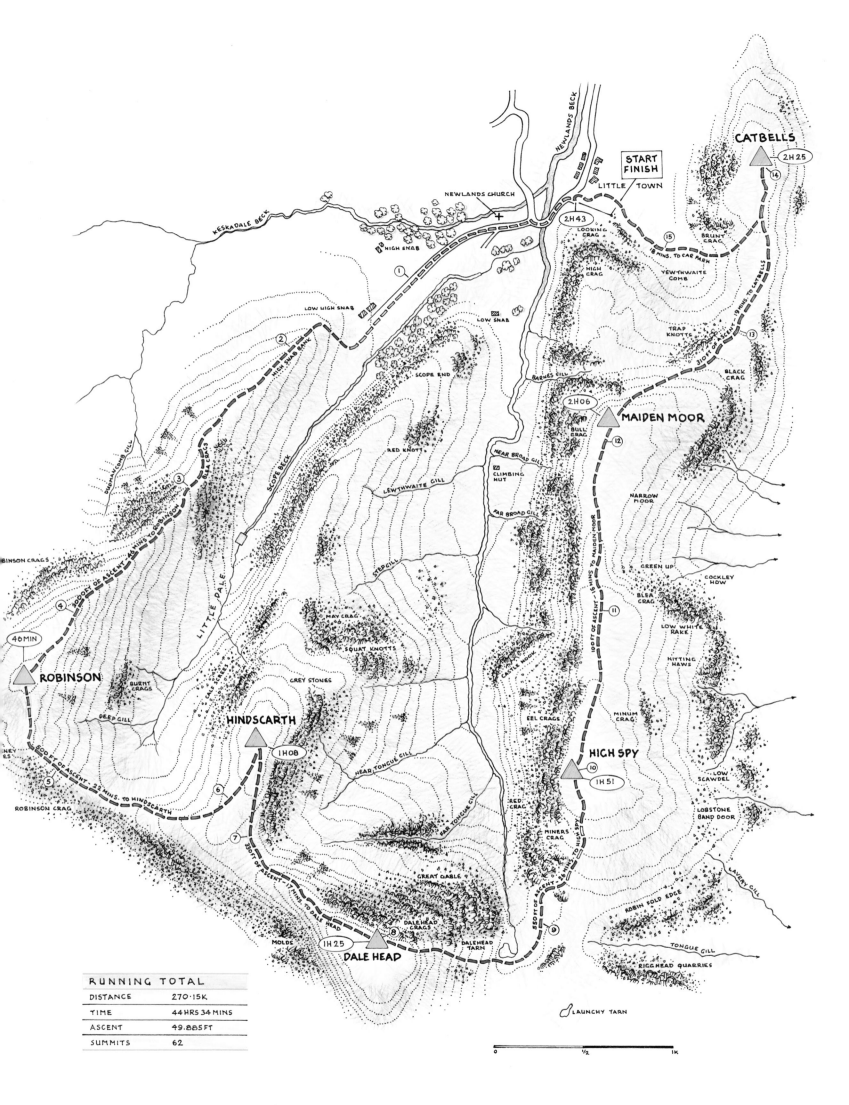

the distance 15·75k the time 2hrs 43mins the ascent 3,790ft

the NORTHERN fells

BAKESTALL?

It has to be done...
even though it's not a summit!

IT'S OUR SECOND TIME BACK IN THE LAKES SINCE MY LAST RUN ON 11th JULY. FIRST TIME BACK THE WEATHER WAS SO BAD NO RUNNING WAS POSSIBLE, AND THIS TIME IT'S NOT MUCH BETTER. BUT HERE GOES...

HEAVY RAIN FRIDAY AND SATURDAY, BUT THERE'S NO RAIN TODAY SO I HEAD TO THRELKELD TO KNOCK OFF A SUMMIT THAT'S NOT A SUMMIT. CLOUDS LIE HIGH ABOVE SKIDDAW AS I LEAVE THE CAR PARK AT THE FOOT OF BLEASE FELL. TRAFFIC SIGNS ALERT ME TO THE RISK OF BEING RUN OVER BY CONSTRUCTION TRAFFIC BUILDING A HYDROELECTRIC STATION AT ROUGHTEN BECK.

CONDITIONS ARE IDEAL UNDERFOOT, WITH NO BIG INCLINES - JUST A LONG TRAIL RUN ALL THE WAY TO THE GATE AT DASH FALLS. THROUGH THE GATE AND ONTO THE OPEN FELL. I'M FORTY NINE MINUTES FROM THRELKELD AND HAVE ONLY SEEN TWO PEOPLE, ONE RUNNING IN THE OPPOSITE DIRECTION, THE OTHER, A GUY WITH A DOG, TURNING OFF TOWARDS MUNGRISDALE AND GREAT CALVA.

SO FAR BOTH FEET HAVE STAYED DRY - BUT NOT FOR MUCH LONGER! THE FIRST FEW YARDS ARE FINE, THEN THE PATH BECOMES A QUAGMIRE WITH NO WAY ROUND. I HAVE WET FEET NOW, AND IT'S SLOW PROGRESS - HANDS ON KNEES - ALL THE WAY UP BIRKETT EDGE, TAKING SHORT BREAKS TO ADMIRE THE FINE ROCK ARCHITECTURE OF DEAD CRAGS. THERE'S SWEAT DRIPPING OFF MY NOSE AS I CUT ACROSS TO A CAIRN AND ADMIRE THE VIEW OVER GREAT COCKUP TO THE SOLWAY FIRTH AND DUMFRIESHIRE.

SUMMIT CAIRN

CONTINUE UP TO THE SUMMIT - HA HA - NINETEEN MINUTES UP FROM THE BRIDLEWAY AND TWELVE MINUTES DOWN. BACK ON THE BRIDLEWAY I PUSH ON AT A STEADY PACE AND ARRIVE BACK AT THE CAR IN FIFTY FIVE MINUTES, PLEASED TO HAVE GOT AT LEAST A SORT OF FELL RUN IN BEFORE HEADING HOME.

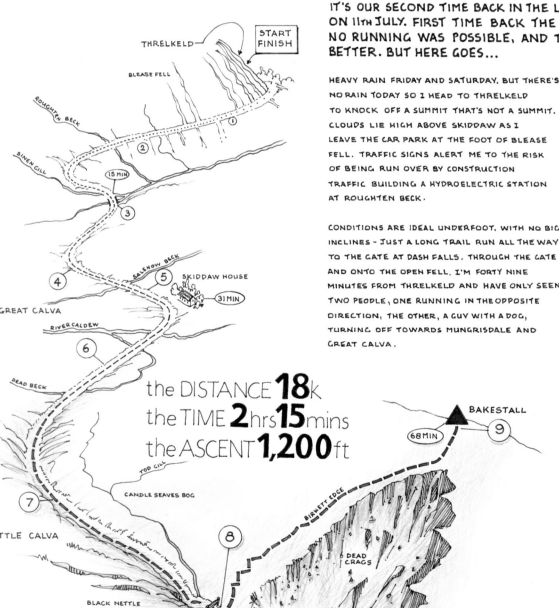

the DISTANCE **18**k
the TIME **2**hrs**15**mins
the ASCENT **1,200**ft

RUNNING TOTAL	
DISTANCE	289·15K
TIME	46 HRS 49 MINS
ASCENT	51,085 FT
SUMMITS	63

the **NORTHERN** fells

Great Calva-
but more like Great Cockup!

the DISTANCE **16**k
the TIME **1**hr**54**mins
the ASCENT **1,400**ft

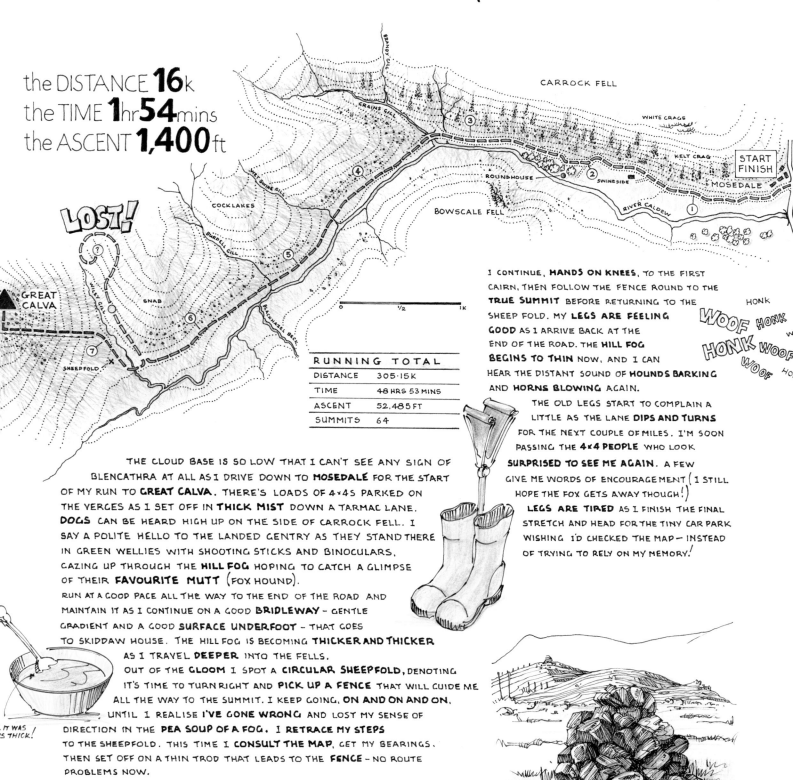

LOST!

GREAT CALVA

SHEEPFOLD

CARROCK FELL
WHITE CRAGS
KELT CRAG
START FINISH
MOSEDALE
SWINESIDE
ROUNDHOUSE
BOWSCALE FELL
RIVER CALDEW
MOSEDALE BRIDGE
GRAINS GILL
COCKLAKES
SNAB

WOOF HONK WOOF HONK HONK WOOF WOOF HONK WOOF

RUNNING TOTAL	
DISTANCE	305.15K
TIME	48 HRS 53 MINS
ASCENT	52,485 FT
SUMMITS	64

I CONTINUE, **HANDS ON KNEES**, TO THE FIRST CAIRN, THEN FOLLOW THE FENCE ROUND TO THE **TRUE SUMMIT** BEFORE RETURNING TO THE SHEEP FOLD. MY **LEGS ARE FEELING GOOD** AS I ARRIVE BACK AT THE END OF THE ROAD. THE **HILL FOG BEGINS TO THIN** NOW, AND I CAN HEAR THE DISTANT SOUND OF **HOUNDS BARKING** AND **HORNS BLOWING** AGAIN.

THE OLD LEGS START TO COMPLAIN A LITTLE AS THE LANE **DIPS AND TURNS** FOR THE NEXT COUPLE OF MILES. I'M SOON PASSING THE **4×4 PEOPLE** WHO LOOK **SURPRISED TO SEE ME AGAIN.** A FEW GIVE ME WORDS OF ENCOURAGEMENT (I STILL HOPE THE FOX GETS AWAY THOUGH!)

LEGS ARE TIRED AS I FINISH THE FINAL STRETCH AND HEAD FOR THE TINY CAR PARK WISHING I'D CHECKED THE MAP – INSTEAD OF TRYING TO RELY ON MY MEMORY.

THE CLOUD BASE IS SO LOW THAT I CAN'T SEE ANY SIGN OF BLENCATHRA AT ALL AS I DRIVE DOWN TO **MOSEDALE** FOR THE START OF MY RUN TO **GREAT CALVA**. THERE'S LOADS OF 4×4S PARKED ON THE VERGES AS I SET OFF IN **THICK MIST** DOWN A TARMAC LANE. **DOGS** CAN BE HEARD HIGH UP ON THE SIDE OF CARROCK FELL. I SAY A POLITE HELLO TO THE LANDED GENTRY AS THEY STAND THERE IN GREEN WELLIES WITH SHOOTING STICKS AND BINOCULARS, GAZING UP THROUGH THE **HILL FOG** HOPING TO CATCH A GLIMPSE OF THEIR **FAVOURITE MUTT** (FOX HOUND).
RUN AT A GOOD PACE ALL THE WAY TO THE END OF THE ROAD AND MAINTAIN IT AS I CONTINUE ON A GOOD **BRIDLEWAY** – GENTLE GRADIENT AND A GOOD **SURFACE UNDERFOOT** – THAT GOES TO SKIDDAW HOUSE. THE HILL FOG IS BECOMING **THICKER AND THICKER** AS I TRAVEL **DEEPER** INTO THE FELLS.
OUT OF THE **GLOOM** I SPOT A **CIRCULAR SHEEPFOLD**, DENOTING IT'S TIME TO TURN RIGHT AND **PICK UP A FENCE** THAT WILL GUIDE ME ALL THE WAY TO THE SUMMIT. I KEEP GOING, **ON AND ON AND ON**, UNTIL I REALISE **I'VE GONE WRONG** AND LOST MY SENSE OF DIRECTION IN THE **PEA SOUP OF A FOG**. I **RETRACE MY STEPS** TO THE SHEEPFOLD. THIS TIME I **CONSULT THE MAP**, GET MY BEARINGS, THEN SET OFF ON A THIN TROD THAT LEADS TO THE **FENCE** – NO ROUTE PROBLEMS NOW.

...ES IT WAS ...HIS THICK!

WHAT THE VIEW FROM THE SUMMIT WOULD HAVE LOOKED LIKE IF I COULD HAVE SEEN MORE THAN FOUR FEET IN FRONT OF ME. THIS IS WHAT I ACTUALLY SAW.

the EASTERN fells

a fair day
ON THE
horseshoe

DISTANCE **14·25**k
TIME **2**hrs**35**mins
ASCENT **3,500**ft

RUNNING TOTAL	
DISTANCE	319·40 K
TIME	51 HRS 28 MINS
ASCENT	55,985 FT
SUMMITS	72

the NORTH WESTERN fells

A double whammy!

a sore calf and wet, wet snow
on WHINLATTER...

FIRSTLY, A VERY SORE LEFT CALF MUSCLE HAS MEANT **NO RUNNING** FOR A COUPLE OF WEEKS, AND ALTHOUGH WE HAD A REALLY GOOD WALK YESTERDAY MY CALF MUSCLE WAS STILL SORE WHEN I WOKE THIS MORNING, SO I DON'T WANT TO RISK A LONG HARD RUN. **SECONDLY,** THE WETTEST WINTER SINCE RECORDS BEGAN MEANS THERE'S **WATERLOGGED** LAND EVERYWHERE. TO MAKE MATTERS WORSE LAST NIGHT IT **SNOWED,** SO ALL THE TOPS, EVEN TINY BARROW, HAVE A GOOD COVERING, MAKING CONDITIONS UNDERFOOT **TREACHEROUS.** MY ONLY OPTION IS WHINLATTER JUST UP THE ROAD FROM THE COTTAGE.

I DRIVE UP THE PASS AND PARK THE CAR ON THE GRASS VERGE PAST THE VISITOR CENTRE. I SET OFF ON A FOREST ROAD MADE OF SLATE AT A GOOD GRADIENT INTO THE SILENT DEPTHS OF THE FOREST. THINGS HAVE CHANGED SINCE WAINWRIGHT'S WANDERINGS, WITH MOUNTAIN BIKE TRAILS CRISS-CROSSING EVERYWHERE. JUST FOR FUN I TURN LEFT ONTO A CYCLE TRACK BUILT LIKE THE 'CRESTA' BOBSLEIGH RUN THAT TWISTS AND TURNS IN AND OUT OF THE FOREST ALL COVERED IN SOFT WET SNOW - FUN, FUN, FUN!
BACK ON THE FOREST ROAD I HEAD OVER A STILE ONTO THE OPEN FELL THEN USE THE CUT-OUT FOOTSTEPS AT THE EDGE OF THE FOREST FENCE TO CONTINUE OVER THE RIDGE. THERE'S NO SNOW ON THIS SECTION, THANK GOODNESS, AS THE OVERHANGING BRANCHES PREVENT PENETRATION TO GROUND LEVEL. EVERYTHING CHANGES AS I REACH THE RIDGE, WHERE THERE'S A THICK COVERING OF WET SNOW. WITH MY CALF MUSCLE REALLY HURTING I SHOULD HAVE THE SENSE TO STOP AND WALK BACK DOWN, BUT I DON'T, AND INSTEAD ARRIVE AT THE SUMMIT IN NO TIME WITH COLD, WET FEET! THE VIEWS OVER TO GRISEDALE PIKE AND HOPEGILL HEAD ARE ALPINE, WITH BOTH PEAKS CLOAKED FROM TOP TO BOTTOM IN SNOW. BRILLIANT - I SHOULD HAVE BROUGHT A CAMERA.
I RETRACE MY FOOTSTEPS TO THE FOREST, BYPASSING THE BOGGY BITS THIS TIME. BACK DOWN THE SLOPE I GO, USING THE WIRE FENCE AS A HANDRAIL, THEN OVER THE STILE AND ONTO TERRA FIRMA. AT A GOOD PACE NOW, BUT WITH MY CALF REALLY HURTING I'M RELIEVED TO REACH THE CAR.
LET'S HOPE IT GETS BETTER SOON - LOTS MORE TO DO YET!

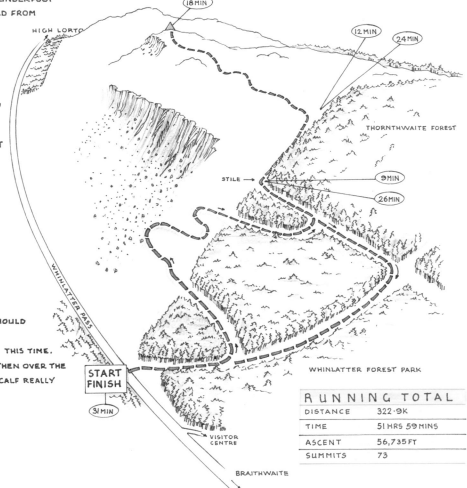

RUNNING TOTAL	
DISTANCE	322·9K
TIME	51 HRS 59 MINS
ASCENT	56,735 FT
SUMMITS	73

the DISTANCE **3·5**k the TIME **31**mins the ASCENT **750**ft

the FAR EASTERN fells

a pedestrian-free HIGH STREET...

including THE KNOTT, RAMPSGILL HEAD, HIGH RAISE, KIDSTY PIKE, THORNTHWAITE CRAG and GRAY CRAG

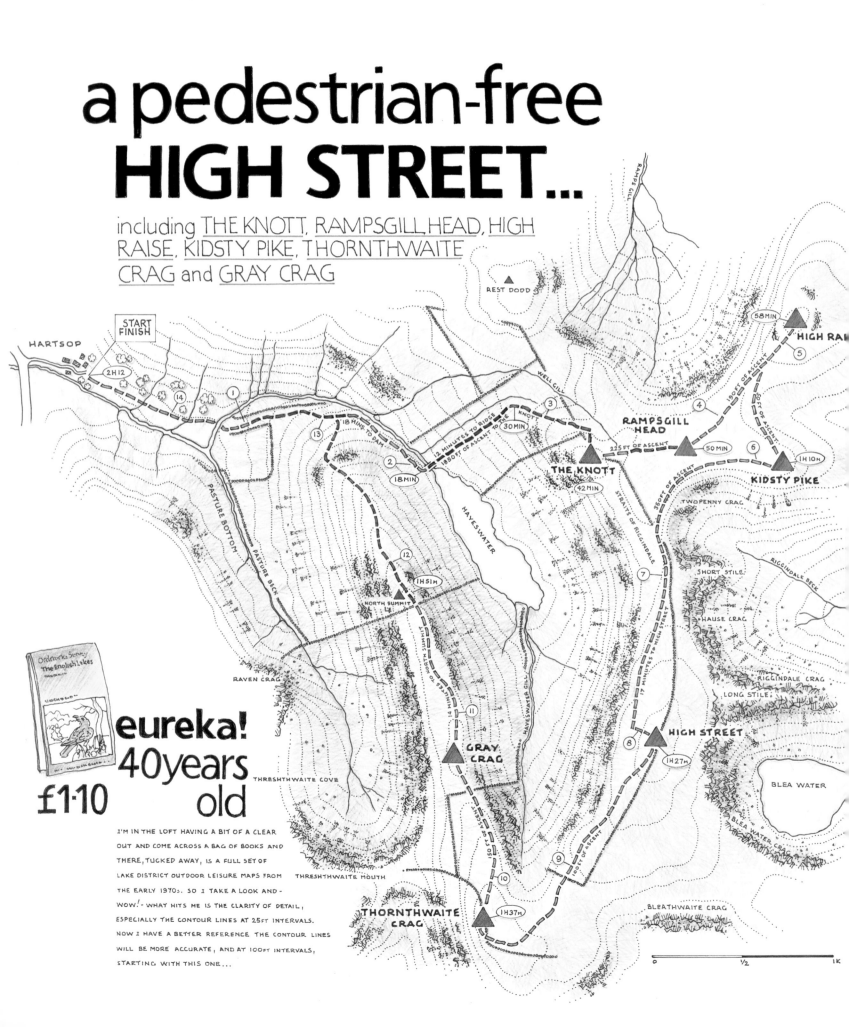

eureka!
40 years old

£1·10

I'M IN THE LOFT HAVING A BIT OF A CLEAR
OUT AND COME ACROSS A BAG OF BOOKS AND
THERE, TUCKED AWAY, IS A FULL SET OF
LAKE DISTRICT OUTDOOR LEISURE MAPS FROM
THE EARLY 1970s. SO I TAKE A LOOK AND -
WOW! - WHAT HITS ME IS THE CLARITY OF DETAIL,
ESPECIALLY THE CONTOUR LINES AT 25FT INTERVALS.
NOW I HAVE A BETTER REFERENCE THE CONTOUR LINES
WILL BE MORE ACCURATE, AND AT 100FT INTERVALS,
STARTING WITH THIS ONE...

IT'S **EASTER MONDAY** IN THE LAKES AND TIME FOR ANOTHER FELL RUN.
HARTSOP'S THE START SO I HEAD DOWN TO ULLSWATER NICE AND EARLY. IT'S
LOOKING BEAUTIFUL IN THE EARLY MORNING SUNSHINE - YES - **SUNSHINE!** I'M THE
FIRST CAR IN THE SMALL CAR PARK AT THE TOP OF THE VILLAGE. I POP A COUPLE
OF QUID IN THE BOX, CHECK MY WATCH - IT'S EIGHT FIFTEEN - THEN OFF I GO.

THERE'S NO TROUBLE ROUTE-FINDING TODAY, WITH NOT A CLOUD IN THE SKY AND
A SLIGHT **GROUND FROST** THAT SOON MELTS AWAY. I ARRIVE AT **HAYESWATER** NOT
FEELING TOO GREAT - **PUFFING** AND **PANTING LIKE AN OLD MAN** (OH DEAR, I AM),
WITH LEGS AS HEAVY AS CONCRETE. LOOK UP TO THE KNOTT: IT'S A STEEP
SLOG, SO I RUN **HANDS-ON-KNEES** ALL THE WAY TO THE RIDGE FROM REST
DODD THEN ONTO THE KNOTT'S SUMMIT.

ALL THE SUMMITS LOOK CLOSER TO EACH OTHER THAN I EXPECTED AS I SET OFF
ACROSS THE **SMALL DEPRESSION** TO RAMPSGILL HEAD. AFTER LEAVING THE
SUMMIT MY LEGS **FEEL A LOT BETTER**, AND I EVENTUALLY GET INTO SOME
SORT OF RHYTHM ON MY WAY TO HIGH RAISE. FROM HERE I HEAD STRAIGHT TO
KIDSTY PIKE ON A **DISTINCT PATH** WITH **HARDLY ANY ASCENT OR DESCENT**.
I STAY A WHILE TO ADMIRE THE VIEW DOWN INTO RIGGINGDALE - THE STRAITS
OF RIGGINDALE **LOOK IMPRESSIVE** - AND OVER TO HIGH STREET. WITH MY LEGS
FEELING BETTER BY THE MINUTE I SET OFF AT A GOOD PACE TOWARDS THE HIGH
STREET TRIG POINT.

the DISTANCE
14·5k
the TIME
2hrs 12mins
the ASCENT
2,940ft

I'VE **NOT SEEN A SOUL** ALL
MORNING, AND THERE'S NO
SIGN OF LIFE ON HIGH STREET
EITHER AS I ARRIVE AT THE
TRIG POINT ALL ALONE. A BIT OF
BREEZE GETTING UP AS I HEAD
SOUTH TO THE LANDMARK OF
THORNTHWAITE CRAG'S CAIRN.
GOOD CONDITIONS UNDERFOOT
MEAN I SOON ARRIVE AT THE
HUGE CAIRN AND SUMMIT WALL.

TIME FOR A QUICK DRINK AND A
COUPLE OF BISCUITS...

AN **ENJOYABLE RUN ALONG THE RIDGE** TO GRAY CRAG IS ONLY SPOILT BY A STRONG
SIDE-WIND WHICH STARTS TO CHILL THE BODY. I STOP TO PULL ON MY WINDPROOF
TOP AND NOTE THE **GOOD VIEWS DOWN TO HAYESWATER**.

I'VE JUST RUN VIRTUALLY NON-STOP FROM RAMPSGILL HEAD TO GRAY CRAG WITH NO
PROBLEMS, BUT NOW AS I START MY DESCENT THE SOLES
OF MY FEET START TO OVERHEAT. THE DESCENT OFF
GRAY CRAG LOOKED **STEEP** WHEN I SET OFF FROM
HARTSOP CAR PARK AND I WASN'T WRONG! IT'S NOT
LONG BEFORE I DEVELOP TWO HUGE BLISTERS ON
MY HEELS, MAKING THE DESCENT REALLY PAINFUL, AND

RUNNING TOTAL	
DISTANCE	337·4 K
TIME	54 HRS 11 MINS
ASCENT	59,675 FT
SUMMITS	80

I'M RELIEVED TO REACH THE FOOTPATH BACK TO THE CAR PARK.
IT'S NEARLY TEN THIRTY WHEN I COME ACROSS THE FIRST SIGNS OF LIFE: ABOUT A
DOZEN MOUNTAIN BIKERS PUSHING THEIR BIKES! SAY HI AND PUSH-ON (NOW ON
TIPTOES) TO THE CAR PARK TO FIND IT NEARLY FULL. **IT'S BEEN A GOOD RUN**
SPOILT ONLY BY THE PAINFUL DESCENT OF GRAY CRAG. HOPE THE **BLISTERS**
HEAL IN TIME FOR MY NEXT RUN AT **THE END OF THE WEEK**.

ABOVE: HIGH STREET FROM KIDSTY PIKE

the **NORTHERN** fells

Through the woods for
a **DODDle** of a run...
...sort of !

MY FEET HAVE RECOVERED ENOUGH TO RISK ANOTHER FELL RUN. BUT I'VE DECIDED ON **A CHANGE OF FOOTWEAR**. SO IT'S OFF WITH MY FELL RUNNING TRAINERS AND ON WITH A PAIR OF **APPROACH SHOES** THAT HAVE A LOT MORE CUSHIONING UNDER THE HEEL. LET'S SEE HOW WE GET ON...

I START AT **DODD WOOD CAR PARK**. IT'S CLOUDY IN PENRUDDOCK, BUT BRIGHTER HERE IN THE WEST. I PAY MY CAR PARK DUES THEN HEAD NORTH ON A FOREST TRAIL BESIDE THE A591. PERFECT CONDITIONS UNDERFOOT AND GENTLE GRADIENTS MAKE FOR AN **EASY** AND **ENJOYABLE** START. THE TRAIL STEEPENS BEFORE BREAKING OUT ONTO THE OPEN FELL AT RAVENSTONE HOTEL. THEN HEADING UPHILL TO THE INVITING RIDGE TO ULLOCK PIKE'S SUMMIT. IT'S A GREAT PATH, BUT STEEP. I ALTERNATE BETWEEN HANDS-ON-KNEES AND SLOW RUNNING, MY **FEET NOT COMPLAINING** YET! I GLANCE BEHIND FOR GREAT VIEWS ACROSS TO THE **SOLWAY FIRTH**.

AS I ARRIVE AT THE SUMMIT SKIDDAW IS VIRTUALLY FREE OF CLOUD. IT'S **EASY RUNNING** NOW TO LONG SIDE AND I'M SOON ON MY WAY OVER THE SUMMIT ONTO THE GRASSY DOME OF CARL SIDE.

MY **FEET FEEL FINE** AND LEGS TOO, BUT THE STEEP DESCENT OFF CARL SIDE WILL TEST THEM BOTH. I DROP DOWN VIA WHITE STONES TO THE COL AND OVER THE WALL ONTO A FOREST ROAD AND MOUNTAIN BIKE TRAIL THAT LEADS TO THE TOP OF DODD. IT'S GOOD TO GET BACK INTO A RUN AFTER THE CARL SIDE DESCENT. I ADMIRE THE VIEW FROM THE SUMMIT, NOW DEVOID OF TREES, RETRACE MY FOOTSTEPS OFF THE SUMMIT AND MEET MY **FIRST WALKERS OF THE DAY**. CONTINUE ON A FOREST ROAD AT A GOOD PACE ALL THE WAY BACK TO THE CAR PARK WITH NO BLISTERS - BUT ALSO NO SIGHT OF AN OSPREY EITHER.

RUNNING TOTAL	
DISTANCE	346·9K
TIME	55 HRS 58 MINS
ASCENT	62,235 FT
SUMMITS	84

the DISTANCE **9·5**k the TIME **1**hr **47**mins the ASCENT **2,560**ft

the **NORTH WESTERN** fells

A big run

over HOPEGILL HEAD, WHITESIDE, GRASMOOR, WANDOPE, EEL CRAG, SAIL and SCAR CRAGS...

WHITESIDE RIDGE LOOKING TOWARDS HOPEGILL HEAD

I HEAD TO BRAITHWAITE TO REVISIT OLD WAYS: THE FIRST LAKES FELLS I WALKED WAY BACK IN THE **LATE SIXTIES!** THE WEATHER IS BEING KIND AGAIN AS I LEAVE THE SMALL PULL-IN CAR PARK AT THE START OF THE ROAD LEADING TO **FORCE CRAG MINE**, WHERE I PASS A COUPLE OF EARLY MORNING DOG WALKERS. I'M SOON INTO A REASONABLE PACE, WHICH I MAINTAIN ALL THE WAY TO THE FORD AT COLEDALE BECK. FIRST BIT OF GRADIENT NOW AS THE PATH BECOMES STONY AND **CLIMBS GRADUALLY** TO **COLEDALE HAUSE**. NO NEED FOR MAP READING TODAY AS I CONTINUE STRAIGHT ON TO SAND HILL, CROSSING THE LOOSE SCREE SLOPE ALONG A FAINT ZIG-ZAG PATH TO THE TOP.

THERE'S NO TIME TO STOP AS THE **FIRST SUMMIT OF THE DAY**, HOPEGILL HEAD, **COMES INTO VIEW**. CAN'T SEE ANYONE NEARBY, BUT SPOT A COUPLE ON THE SUMMIT OF GRISEDALE PIKE. REACH THE SUMMIT IN NO TIME AND PICK MY WAY DOWN THE ROCKY TRACK ONTO THE **SUBLIME RIDGE** LEADING TO WHITESIDE. IT'S A GREAT PATH - TOO ROCKY IN PLACES FOR FULL-ON RUNNING, BUT THERE ARE GREAT VIEWS TO COMPENSATE, AND I GET TO DO IT TWICE. AS I REACH THE SUMMIT OF WHITESIDE THE **WIND PICKS UP**, SO I PULL ON MY WINDPROOF, CLOCK THE TIME AND HEAD BACK TO HOPEGILL HEAD. MY LEGS AND BODY FEEL **OUT OF SORTS** AS I GAZE OVER TO DOVE CRAGS AND GRASMOOR, MY NEXT PORT OF CALL. I WONDER IF I'LL HAVE TO SHORTEN MY ROUTE - ONLY TIME WILL TELL.

BACK ON HOPEGILL HEAD AND I SPOT THE TWO WALKERS IN THE MIDDLE DISTANCE ALONG THE EDGE OF HOBCARTON CRAG. I START THE DESCENT TO COLEDALE HAUSE. IT'S NOT AS BAD AS I THOUGHT, THE SCREE POSING NO PROBLEMS. BY THE TIME I HIT THE BOTTOM I'M **MORE OPTIMISTIC** ABOUT COMPLETING MY ORIGINAL ROUTE.

THE **MOTORWAY OF A PATH** LEADS ME TO GRASMOOR-IDEAL FOR RUNNING - AND IN NO TIME I'M ON THE PLATEAU HEADING TOWARDS THE SHELTER, WHERE I TAKE **TIME OUT** FOR A **DRINK** AND **CEREAL BAR**. IT'S MY FIRST STOP IN TWO HOURS AND I'M FEELING GOOD AS I LEAVE THE SHELTER FOR THE STRAIGHTFORWARD RUN OVER TO WANDOPE. THERE ARE **MORE WALKERS ABOUT NOW** AS I LEAVE WANDOPE'S SUMMIT AND HEAD NORTH TOWARDS EEL CRAG.

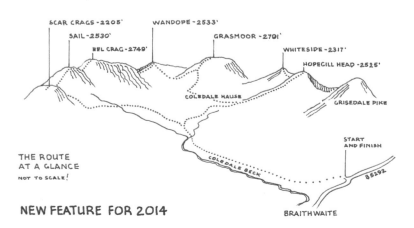

SCAR CRAGS -2205'
SAIL -2530'
EEL CRAG -2749'
WANDOPE -2533'
GRASMOOR -2791'
WHITESIDE -2317'
HOPEGILL HEAD -2525'
COLEDALE HAUSE
GRISEDALE PIKE
START AND FINISH
COLEDALE BECK
B5292
BRAITHWAITE

THE ROUTE AT A GLANCE NOT TO SCALE!

A LITTLE WORN AND WEARY - A BIT LIKE ME!

SIGG

NEW FEATURE FOR 2014

...requires
a big map!

HOBCARTON GILL

LADYSIDE PIKE

GRISE
P

PENN

COLD GILL

HOPE GILL

HOBCARTON CRAG

7

9

1H04

HOPEGILL HEAD

14 TO WHITESIDE AND 160FT OF ASCENT

15 MINUTES BACK TO HOPEGILL HEAD

350FT OF ASCENT

1H18m

ROCKY
IN PLACES

8

1H26

6

SAND HILL

WHITESIDE END

WHITESIDE

GRASS-
LOOSE
SCREE

FORCE
CRAG

BOAT CRAG

GASGALE CRAGS

HIGH
FORCE

MAN-MADE
STEPS-
NATURAL

ASCENT UP HIGH 600 FEET OF ASCENT

LIZA BECK

10

50 MIN

29 MINUTES TO THE HAUSE

WHIN BEN

GASGALE GILL

1H34

5

LEVEL
MAN-MADE
GRAVEL

ROCKY
IN
PLACES

LANTHWAITE

DOVE CRAGS

SCOTT C

2H40

THE SCAR

B 5289

GRASSMOOR END

GRASMOOR

11

31 MINS TO GRAS MOOR AND 850FT ASCENT

14

EEL CRAG

SCAR CRAG

2Hrs 5 min
plus
10 min BREAK

12

GOOD
NATURAL
PATH

15 MINS TO WANDOPE AND 130 FT ASCENT

TOUGH
OLD GRASS
NO PATH

NARROW
NATURAL
PATH

0 MINS TO EEL CRAG 360 FT ASCENT

ADDACOMB BECK

RED GILL

13

10 MINS TO EEL CRAG 360 FT ASCENT

2H30

WANDOPE

SAIL BECK

CRUMMOCK
WATER

CINDERDALE BECK

LAD HOWS

THIRDGILL
HEAD MAN

THIRD GILL

RANNERDALE
BRIDGE

SADDLE GATE

WHITELESS
PIKE

RANNERDALE BECK

RANNERDALE FARM

I IGNORE THE MOTORWAY PATH TO ITS SUMMIT FOR
THE ORIGINAL PATH ALONG THE EDGE OF ADDACOMB -
EASIER THAN IT LOOKED - AND TOUCH THE CAIRN
BEFORE HEADING OVER TO SAIL ON A **ROCKY PATH**
WITH GOOD VIEWS. TOUCH THE PILE OF STONES
ON THE SUMMIT AND COMMENCE THE DESCENT TO
SAIL PASS. I'M GREETED BY THE **WORST MAN-MADE
PATH** I'VE YET COME ACROSS: A RAISED PATH OF
STONE AND SOIL WITH A DITCH EITHER SIDE THAT
ZIG-ZAGS IN EQUAL LENGTHS.

I RUN A LENGTH OF ZIG
THEN DECIDE TO JUMP OFF
AND OVER THE DITCH TO
RUN ON HEATHER,
BILBERRY AND GRASS IN
A STRAIGHT LINE TO THE
PASS, NO PROBLEM!

LEFT: HOW IT IS - BORING.

FAR LEFT: HOW IT COULD HAVE BEEN - A LITTLE BIT MORE INTERESTING

SCAR CRAGS IS THE
LAST SUMMIT OF THE
DAY. IT'S A DELIGHT TO
RUN ON, ALTHOUGH I DO

CROSS SECTION OF PATH DUG OUT BY A JCB DIGGER!

MANAGE TO TRIP UP - NO ONE ABOUT TO SEE IT, THANK
GOODNESS. DO A U-TURN AT THE SUMMIT AND
RETURN TO SAIL PASS. SAY HI TO A LARGE PARTY OF
WALKERS STRUGGLING UP FROM BARROW THEN
DROP DOWN LEFT ON A FAINT TROD TO THE
FORCE CRAG MINE ROAD, MY LEGS ONLY NOW
STARTING TO COMPLAIN.

I PUSH ON AND I'M SOON BACK AT THE CAR,
WELL PLEASED WITH MYSELF, ESPECIALLY
CONSIDERING THAT AT ONE POINT I WAS
CONTEMPLATING CUTTING IT SHORT.

HAVE A PLAN AND STICK TO IT, I SAY!

the DISTANCE
20·75k

theTIME
3hrs**47**mins

theASCENT
3,790ft

FOUR MINUTES ADDED TO TOTAL TIME ON THE MAP
DUE TO MY POOR ADDITION ON THE WHITESIDE TO
HOPEGILL HEAD SECTION.

RUNNING	TOTAL
DISTANCE	367·65K
TIME	59HRS 45MINS
ASCENT	66,025 FT
SUMMITS	91

the FAR EASTERN fells

A late start thanks to England means I had
Beda geta move on
as I head down to Boredale

IT'S A LATER START THAN NORMAL TODAY DUE TO THE ENGLAND v ITALY WORLD CUP GAME NOT FINISHING 'TIL 1A.M. (WE LOST 2-1). IT'S JUST GONE 10A.M. AS I ARRIVE AT THE FARMSTEAD OF GARTH HEADS AT THE NORTH END OF THE BOREDALE VALLEY. I FIND A LITTLE SPOT TO PARK THE CAR, THEN IT'S **UPHILL FROM THE VERY START.** IT'S NOT LONG BEFORE I'M HOT AND SWEATY - THE WEATHER'S WARM AND MUGGY, WHICH DOESN'T HELP. I SOON REACH THE MAIN RIDGE TO FIND A METAL SEAT WITH GREAT VIEWS OVER TO ULLSWATER AND BEYOND,

NEW TRAINERS!
THEY'LL NOT STAY THIS COLOUR FOR LONG!

FAR RIGHT:-
BEDA FELL RIDGE LOOKING SOUTH TO ANGLETARN PIKES.

BUT IT'S TOO SOON FOR A REST. I'M INTO MY RUNNING STRIDE NOW ON A GOOD CLEAR PATH THROUGH FRESH BRACKEN, NOT YET FULLY OPEN, AND ROCKY OUTCROPS, THE FIRST BEING **WINTER CRAG.** WITH GOOD VIEWS ALL ROUND AND MY LEGS WARMING TO THE TASK I PRESS ON TO BEDA HEAD. I'M ENJOYING THE RUN SO FAR AND THE GENTILE INCLINES: IT'S JUST THE **STICKY HEAT** MAKING IT HARDER THAN IT SHOULD BE. I REACH THE SUMMIT IN NO TIME AND **RELISH** THE LOOK OF THE RIDGE LEADING ON TO BEDA FELL KNOTT.

A SHORT DESCENT FROM THE SUMMIT KEEPS THE PACE HIGH BEFORE A GENTLE ASCENT TO THE KNOTT. IN **RETROSPECT** I SHOULD HAVE CONTINUED ONTO ANGLETARN PIKES, BUT I TAKE THE **EASY OPTION** DOWN TO THE RIGHT ON A GOOD PATH ALL THE WAY TO BOREDALE HAUSE.

I'VE BEEN RUNNING NOW NON-STOP FOR OVER FORTY FIVE MINUTES, SO IT'S TIME FOR A DRINK AND BITE TO EAT AS A **FINE MIST ENGULFS THE SUMMIT OF PLACE FELL.** I HEAD UP, HANDS ON KNEES AND HEAD DOWN, FOR A FORCED WALK UP THE MAN-MADE ZIGZAG PATH THAT LEADS TO THE EDGE OF THE SUMMIT, SWEAT DRIPPING OFF MY NOSE NOW AS I GET BACK INTO MY

STRIDE, THIS TIME OVER SLABS OF ROCK AND OUTCROPS TO REACH THE TRIG POINT ON THE SUMMIT. I TOUCH THAT THEN GIVE THE CAIRN NOT MORE THAN TEN FEET AWAY A PAT.

THE MIST'S DISPERSED BUT THERE'S NO TIME TO STAND AND STARE AS I HEAD OFF FEELING GOOD APART FROM EYES BEING STUNG BY THE **COPIOUS AMOUNT OF SWEAT** RUNNING DOWN MY FOREHEAD!

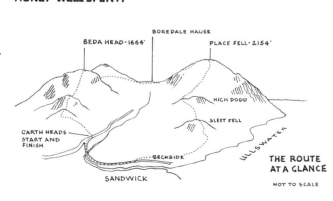

THERE'S A TRICKY FIFTY YARDS OR SO OFF THE SUMMIT AS THE PATH PICKS ITS WAY THROUGH ROCKY OUTCROPS BEFORE RETURNING TO GRASS. I THEN RUN THE LENGTH OF THE FELL, PASSING THE SHEEP FOLD AT LOW MOSS. I WAS GOING TO DROP DOWN TO NETTLESLACK AND FINISH, BUT I'M ENJOYING MYSELF SO MUCH I CARRY ON AROUND HIGH DODD AND ONTO SLEET HOW BEFORE DESCENDING TO THE ROAD, RUNNING THE LAST KILOMETRE BACK TO THE CAR FOR WHAT'S BEEN A **REALLY GOOD RUN** WITH GOOD VIEWS, LOADS OF RUNNING AND - BEST OF ALL - **NO BLISTERS** THANKS TO THE NEW PAIR OF TRAINERS I BOUGHT AFTER THE LAST COUPLE OF RUNS GAVE ME BIG BAD BLISTERS... **MONEY WELL SPENT!**

BOREDALE HAUSE
BEDA HEAD-1664'
PLACE FELL-2154'
HIGH DODD
SLEET FELL
CARTH HEADS START AND FINISH
BECKSIDE
ULLSWATER
SANDWICK

THE ROUTE AT A GLANCE

NOT TO SCALE

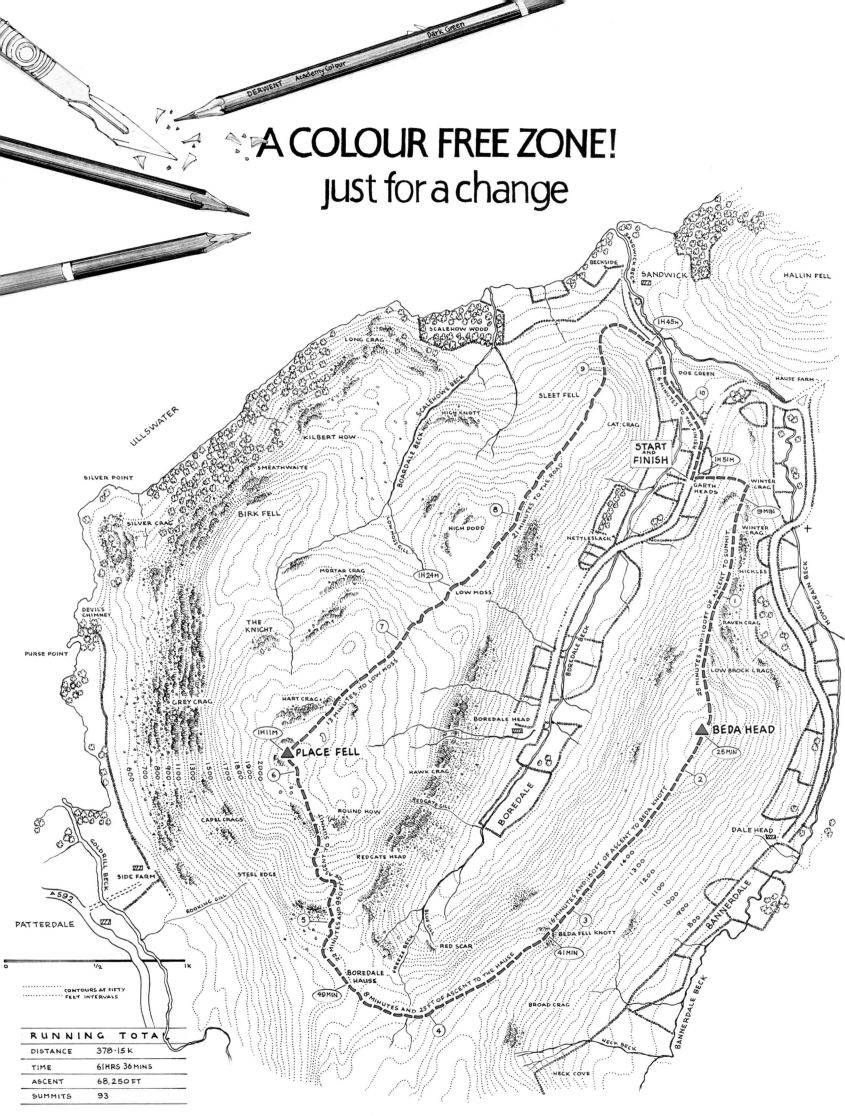

A COLOUR FREE ZONE!
just for a change

RUNNING TOTAL	
DISTANCE	378·15 K
TIME	61 HRS 36 MINS
ASCENT	68,250 FT
SUMMITS	93

the DISTANCE **10·5** k · the TIME **1** hr **51** mins · the ASCENT **2,225** ft

the **EASTERN** fells

Dramatic views quicken the Hart rate

as I tick off <u>HARTSOP ABOVE HOW</u>, <u>LITTLE HART CRAG</u> and <u>HIGH HARTSOP DODD</u>

IT'S THE DAY AFTER THE TOUR DE FRANCE GRAND DEPART FROM LEEDS. JANICE AND I SPENT THE PREVIOUS TWO DAYS IN THE DALES SLEEPING IN THE CAR IN A LAY-BY AT MUKER, ALONG WITH THOUSANDS OF OTHER LIKE-MINDED FOLK. YESTERDAY WAS SPENT WAKING UP, STRETCHING, BOILING WATER FOR COFFEE AND WALKING A FAIR DISTANCE TO THE SUMMIT OF BUTTERTUBS PASS. THE ATMOSPHERE WAS GREAT, WITH THOUSANDS STRUNG ALONG THE ROUTE. THE ONLY DOWNSIDE WAS THE COLD WIND AND FIVE HOUR WAIT FOR THE CYCLISTS TO APPEAR, ALONG WITH THEIR PROCESSION OF BACKUP VEHICLES, THE HELICOPTERS AND POLICE. IT'S A GOOD JOB WE DIDN'T BLINK; WHOOSH AND THEY WERE GONE! BACK TO MUKER FOR THE SLOW DRIVE UP TO PENRUDDOCK. HOPE MY LEGS ARE O.K. FOR TODAY'S RUN – I'M NOT GOOD AT STANDING STILL FOR HOURS ON END.

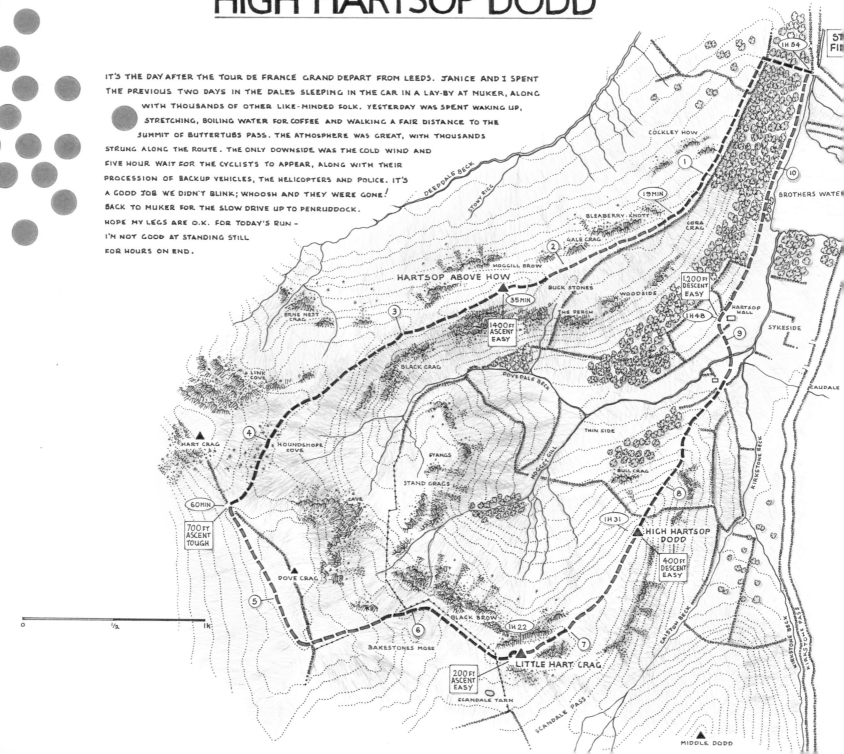

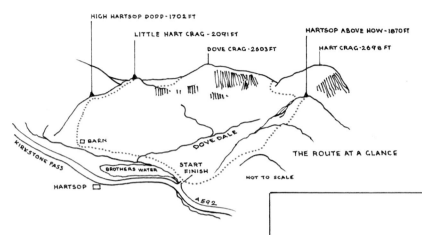

HIGH HARTSOP DODD · 1702 FT
LITTLE HART CRAG · 2091 FT
DOVE CRAG · 2603 FT
HARTSOP ABOVE HOW · 1870 FT
HART CRAG · 2698 FT
DOVE DALE
BARN
KIRKSTONE PASS
BROTHERS WATER
START FINISH
HARTSOP
A592
THE ROUTE AT A GLANCE
NOT TO SCALE

IT'S A PLEASANT MORNING AS I DRIVE TO THE CAR PARK AT COWBRIDGE. I'M NOT THE FIRST ONE THERE, WITH ONLY A COUPLE OF SPACES LEFT.

IT'S HARD GRAFT FROM THE OFF AS I HEAD STRAIGHT UP THE SIDE OF HARTSOP-ABOVE-HOW. IT'S STEEP, TREE ROOT-RIDDEN AND ENCLOSED BY SHOULDER-HIGH BRACKEN. WHEN I BURST OUT ONTO THE MAIN RIDGE I'M INTO MY RUNNING STRIDE. I FOLLOW THE PATH AS IT GENTLY HEADS UP TO BLEABERRY KNOTT THEN INCLINES ALL THE WAY TO THE SUMMIT OF HARTSOP ABOVE HOW.

GREAT VIEWS OPEN AHEAD OF CLIFFS AND CRAGS AS A GOOD, CLEAR PATH CONTINUES TOWARDS HART CRAG. THERE'S NO NEED TO CONTINUE UP - BEEN THERE, DONE THAT - SO I CONTOUR LEFT INTO HOUNDSHOPE COVE GIVING THE SUMMIT A MISS. THERE'S NO PATH HERE, ONLY **BOULDERS, ROCKS, GRASS AND ANKLE-BREAKING HOLES.** IT'S SLOW GOING, BUT I EVENTUALLY REACH THE COL BETWEEN HART AND DOVE CRAG WITHOUT BROKEN ANKLES. SAY HI TO THE FIRST WALKER OF THE DAY DESCENDING DOVE CRAG.

IT'S BECOMING **HOTTER NOW**, MY FACE FEELING THE MORNING SUN AS SWEAT DRIPS FROM MY BROW. I SPOT A TRACK THAT CIRCUMNAVIGATES THE SUMMIT OF DOVE CRAG - AGAIN, BEEN THERE DONE THAT. **IT'S VERY EASY RUNNING NOW** AS I TURN OFF THE MAIN PATH AND HEAD DOWN TO LITTLE HART CRAG.

HIGH HARTSOP DODD

WITH THE EXCEPTION OF HOUNDSHOPE COVE, SO FAR CONDITIONS UNDERFOOT HAVE BEEN EXCELLENT. BUT THAT IS ABOUT TO CHANGE FOR THE WORSE. A STEEPISH DESCENT ON LOOSE STONES LEVELS OFF AND TURNS INTO A BOG. I SPOT SCANDALE TARN WAY BELOW AS I HEAD FOR THE ROCKY OUTCROP OF LITTLE HART CRAG WITH GOOD VIEWS OVER RED SCREES AND NORTHWARDS TO ULLSWATER.

IT'S DOWNHILL ALL THE WAY NOW AS THE GRASSY TRACK HEADS NORTH ALONG THE RIDGE TO HIGH HARTSOP DODD. IT'S GREAT RUNNING, WITH VIEWS INTO DOVEDALE NOW BATHED IN BRIGHT SUNSHINE.

MY LEGS HAVE FELT GOOD ALL THE WAY ROUND AS I DESCEND OFF THE SUMMIT ON A STEEP PATH TO THE GREEN PASTURES BELOW. **JUST BEAUTIFUL.**

I REACH LEVEL FOOTING AT THE BARN. MY LEGS FEEL SUPER CHARGED, SO I PUSH HARD PAST HARTSOP HALL AND BROTHERS WATER TO COVER THE LAST ONE-AND-A-HALF KILOMETRES IN JUST OVER SIX MINUTES - PARK RUN PACE! I'M HAPPY WITH THAT. NOW FOR A SHOWER...

RUNNING TOTAL	
DISTANCE	388·75k
TIME	63 HRS 30 MINS
ASCENT	70,550 FT
SUMMITS	96

NO TOUR DE FRANCE BUT I FELT LIKE I WAS **KING OF THE MOUNTAINS TODAY**

HARTSOP ABOVE HOW

the DISTANCE **10·6**k · the TIME **1**hr**54**mins · the ASCENT **2,300**ft

the CENTRAL fells

Raven Crag
You're having a laugh!

HAD A BIG WALK YESTERDAY, SO IT'S A SHORT UP-AND-DOWN SINGLE-SUMMIT RUN TODAY: RAVEN CRAG - NOT EVEN A FELL IN MY OPINION, JUST A ROCKY OUTCROP, BUT HERE GOES... I PARK THE CAR IN THE SMALL CAR PARK AT THE BASE OF THE CRAG. JUST FIFTY YARDS DOWN THE LANE IS THE SIGN, AS PROMISED BY WAINWRIGHT, POINTING TO CASTLE CRAG FORT. THERE'S A GOOD TRAIL STRAIGHT AWAY, RUNABLE ALL THE WAY TO THE COL. I ONLY HAVE TO STOP NOW AND AGAIN TO NEGOTIATE FALLEN TREES - BEECH AND LARCH - LYING ACROSS THE PATH. CROSS A FOREST ROAD AND THROUGH A DOUBLE DEER GATE, STILL RUNNING ON A DISTINCY PATH, THEN HEAD THROUGH ANOTHER DOUBLE GATE AND BACK ACROSS THE FOREST ROAD.

THE TREES ARE THINNING OUT AS I REACH THE COL, BUT THERE'S NO CAIRN AND NO TREES: THEY'VE ALL BEEN FELLED AND CUT INTO PIECES ON THE GROUND TO TRIP RUNNERS UP! THERE'S A MAN-MADE WOODEN PATH HEADING OFF LEFT TO THE SUMMIT, SO OFF I TIPTOE THROUGH THE SUN-BLEACHED LOGS, BRANCHES AND TWIGS, BACK INTO DENSE TREES ON MORE MAN-MADE STEPS SURROUNDED BY A HUGE CLUSTER OF BEAUTIFUL FOXGLOVES IN FULL BLOOM.

I REACH THE SUMMIT BY A SHORT SCRAMBLE OVER MOSS-COVERED ROCKS AFTER SOMEHOW LOSING TRACK OF THE PATH AMONG ALL THE TREES. THE FULL VIEW OF THIRLMERE IS NO LONGER AVAILABLE DUE TO ENCROUCHING TREES. HEAD BACK DOWN, THIS TIME FOLLOWING THE WOODEN BOARDWALK - HOW DID I MISS THIS ON THE WAY UP? TOO BUSY ADMIRING FOXGLOVES! I RETRACE MY FOOTSTEPS 'TIL I REACH THE FOREST ROAD AND DECIDE TO USE THIS JUST FOR A CHANGE. BIG RUTS AND LOGS ALL OVER MAKE FOR SLOWER PROGRESS THAN I THOUGHT. AFTER ABOUT SIXTY YARDS, AT A BEND, I SPOT A SIGN AT A SMALL TRACK LEADING TO THE FACE OF RAVEN CRAG AND STOP FOR A QUICK READ, HMMM - INTERESTING. I CARRY ON TO THE DEER GATE THEN DROP BACK DOWN INTO THE TREES AND ONTO THE LANE. BEST BIT- THE FOXGLOVES.

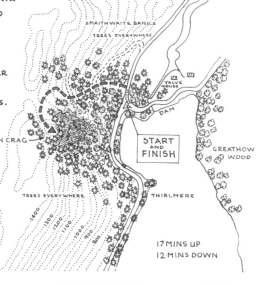

PEREGRINE FALCON NESTING SITE

NO CLIMBING DURING BREEDING SEASON

NO RAVENS HERE!

NO RAVENS THEN!

SMAITHWAITE BANKS
TREES EVERYWHERE
VALUE HOUSE
DAM
RAVEN CRAG
START AND FINISH
GREATHOW WOOD
TREES EVERYWHERE
THIRLMERE
17 MINS UP
12 MINS DOWN

0   1/2   1K

RUNNING TOTAL	
DISTANCE	390.75K
TIME	63 HRS 59 MINS
ASCENT	71,500 FT
SUMMITS	97

the DISTANCE **2**k the TIME **29** mins the ASCENT **950** ft

the FAR EASTERN fells

Route finding: easy peasy
Just follow the wall
between HARTSOP DODD and CAUDALE MOOR

GREAT WEATHER AGAIN! I'M NEARLY AT MY DESTINATION - HARTSOP VILLAGE - WHEN I COME ACROSS LOADS OF PEOPLE JOGGING UP AND DOWN, CARS PARKED IN FIELDS AND **SMALL TENTS** OF ALL **SHAPES** AND **COLOURS** PITCHED IN THE FIELDS. SOMETHING'S AFOOT! I SLOW DOWN AND ASK AN OFFICIAL (HE HAS A HIGH-VIS VEST ON) WHAT'S TAKING PLACE. APPARENTLY IT'S THE START OF **THE SAUNDERS LAKELAND MOUNTAIN MARATHON** STARTING IN DEEPDALE. GOOD LUCK TO THEM... I'VE GOT MY OWN RUN TO DO.

THE SMALL CAR PARK IS NEARLY FULL, BUT I MANAGE TO SNEAK IN. THIS TIME I'VE BROUGHT SOME CASH FOR THE HONESTY BOX SO I CAN **RUN WITH A CLEAR CONSCIENCE.** I START OVER THE BRIDGE, THEN HEAD STRAIGHT UP THE STEEP END OF HARTSOP DODD. I'M SOON PUFFING AND PANTING AS THE GRADIENT BECOMES TOO SEVERE TO RUN. IT'S A GOOD PATH THOUGH, THAT TAKES ME TO WHAT I THOUGHT WAS THE SUMMIT CAIRN ONLY TO FIND IT'S THE END OF A WALL! NO PROBLEM: THE TRUE SUMMIT IS ONLY A FEW FEET FURTHER ON.

I LOOK AT WHAT LIES AHEAD AND IT'S A **GRADUAL CLIMB ALONGSIDE A STONE WALL ALL THE WAY TO THE** SUMMIT OF CAUDALE MOOR. I HIT A GOOD PACE NOW AND ARRIVE AT THE SUMMIT IN ABOUT TWENTY MINUTES, THEN HEAD WEST ON A CLEAR PATH TO A GOOD SIZED CAIRN AND SAY HI TO A GUY TAKING IN THE VIEWS DOWN CAUDALE HEAD. MY LEGS ARE FEELING GOOD AS I **DROP DOWN ONTO ROUGH EDGE RIDGE** AND THE OLD QUARRY RUINS.

A **PATH CUT INTO A DYKE** TAKES ME DOWN THROUGH THE BRACKEN ON QUITE A STEEP GRADIENT, BUT THERE ARE NO COMPLAINTS FROM MY FEET: THE **NEW TRAINERS SEEM TO BE DOING THE TRICK!** THE PATH DELIVERS ME DIRECTLY TO CAUDALE BRIDGE AND THE A592. WITH NO FOOTPATH I FOLLOW THE ROAD ALL THE WAY BACK TO THE CAR OVER TWO KILOMETRES AWAY – WITH MOST OF IT UPHILL. STILL, MY LEGS FEEL GOOD AND IT ONLY TAKE TWELVE MINUTES. I ARRIVE BACK TO FIND **THE CAR PARK CHOCK-A-BLOCK,** WITH A COUPLE OF WHITE VANS UNLOADING MOUNTAIN BIKES FOR A LARGE GROUP OF BYSTANDERS. I WAIT 'TIL THEY FINISH, THEN SQUEEZE PAST AND MAKE MY WAY BACK TO THE CARAVAN. A GOOD DAY, WITH NON-STOP RUNNING FROM THE SUMMIT OF HARTSOP DODD TO THE FINISH BACK AT THE CAR PARK. WELL DONE.

A RUSH OF BLOOD OR A GUILTY CONSCIENCE ANSWERS ON A POSTCARD PLEASE

HON BOX HARTSOP

CAUDALE MOOR AND THE WAY DOWN ALONG ROUGH EDGE

HARTSOP

START FINISH

1HR 22

WALKER BRIDGE

7

1400 FT ASCENT HARD

1

RUNNING TOTAL

DISTANCE	398·75K
TIME	65 HRS 21 MINS
ASCENT	73,520 FT
SUMMITS	99

HARTSOP DODD 25 MIN

6

CAUDALE BRIDGE

1HR 10

PASTURE BECK

2

THE TONGUE

CAUDALE BECK

RAVEN CRAG

THRESHTHWAITE COVE

5

OLD QUARRY

ROUGH EDGE

620 FT ASCENT EASY

2000 FT DESCENT EASY-ISH

CAUDALE HEAD

3

THRESHTHWAITE MOUTH

4

CAUDALE MOOR

45 MIN

MONUMENT

the DISTANCE **8**k·theTIME **1**hr**22**mins·the ASCENT **2,020**ft

the **CENTRAL** fells

nine out of ten for the LANGDALE PIKES and a few others

TARN CRAG ✓

SERGEANT MAN ✓

HIGH RAISE ✓

THUNACAR KNOTT ✓

PIKE O' STICKLE ✓

LOFT CRAG ✓

HARRISON STICKLE ✓

PAVEY ARK ✓

BLEA RIGG ✓

SILVER HOW ✗

RUNNING TOTAL	
DISTANCE	418·50K
TIME	69 HRS 20 MINS
ASCENT	77,120 FT
SUMMITS	108

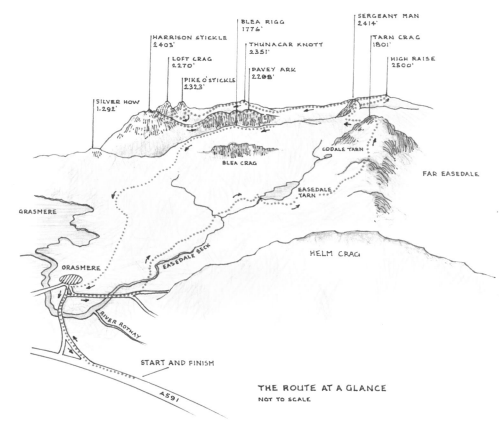

THE ROUTE AT A GLANCE
NOT TO SCALE

the DISTANCE **19·75**k · the TIME **3**hrs**59**mins · the ASCENT **3,600**ft

IT'S A BEAUTIFUL MORNING AS I PULL INTO THE A591 LAY-BY ON THE OUTSKIRTS OF GRASMERE; NO WIND, BLUE SKY, PLENTY OF SUNSHINE, AND A SPRING IN MY STEP. I'VE BEEN LOOKING FORWARD TO THIS FOR SOME TIME - TEN SUMMITS IN ONE RUN - THE MOST I'VE ATTEMPTED SO FAR.

I SET OFF INTO GRASMERE VILLAGE AND TURN RIGHT ONTO THE EASEDALE ROAD THEN OFF AT THE BECK TOWARDS THE TARN. IT'S BEEN TARMAC ALL THE WAY SO FAR, BUT NOW I JOIN THE WORST MAN-MADE PATH IN THE DISTRICT: YOU CAN'T RUN - OR EVEN WALK - ON IT, AS TRACKS IN THE

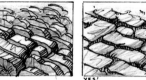

GRASS EITHER SIDE BEAR WITNESS. THERE ARE A FEW WALKERS ABOUT NOW AS THE PATH REVERTS TO ITS NATURAL STATE AND STARTS TO CLIMB TOWARDS THE TARN AT A GOOD INCLINE FOR RUNNING. I SOON ARRIVE, WITH VERY LITTLE EFFORT. TIME FOR **A DRINK.**

I CROSS THE OUTLET STREAM AND HEAD TO THE OPPOSITE SHORE TO TRY AND LOCATE A NARROW PATH UP THE SIDE OF TARN CRAG. NO LUCK, SO I JUST PICK A SENSIBLE LINE THROUGH THE WAIST-HIGH BRACKEN UP TO THE RIDGE. IT'S SLOW GOING, BUT ONCE ON THE TOP I'M BACK TO RUNNING, THIS TIME WITH A PLETHORA OF NARROW TRACKS AND TRODS TO CHOOSE FROM, MOST OF THEM LEADING IN THE GENERAL DIRECTION OF TARN CRAG'S SUMMIT AND MY NEXT TARGET, SERGEANT MAN.

ON TARN CRAG'S SUMMIT I CHECK THE TIME, HAVE **A DRINK** THEN MOVE ON, THE PATH BECOMING INTERMITTENT AS IT CLIMBS THEN LEVELS OFF. AS I TURN THE CORNER SERGEANT MAN COMES INTO VIEW FOR THE FIRST TIME LIKE A SMALL PYRAMID IN THE DISTANCE. I APPROACH THREE GUYS CHECKING A MAP. THEY ASK ME IF IT'S SERGEANT MAN'S SUMMIT THEY'RE POINTING TO AND I CONFIRM IT IS - THEY'RE ON THEIR WAY TO BOWFELL. SOON SUMMIT THE 'MAN' AND HEAD NORTH ON A DISTINCT PATH ACROSS A PLATEAU - HARDLY ANY GRADIENT TO SPEAK OF OR EFFORT REQUIRED.

MY LEGS ARE FEELING GOOD AS I ADMIRE THE VIEW OVER EAGLE AND SERGEANT'S CRAG FROM THE SURVEY COLUMN ON HIGH RAISE. HAVE **A DRINK** THEN MY EYES TURN SOUTHWARDS TO THUNACAR KNOTTS AND THE LANGDALE PIKES. EASY RUNNING ON A WIDE PATH WITH GOOD GOING UNDERFOOT ENABLES A FAST PACE ALL THE WAY TO THE ROCKY OUTCROP THAT IS THUNACAR KNOTT. PIKE O'STICKLE LOOKS IMPRESSIVE FROM THIS SIDE, EVEN THOUGH THERE'S ONLY A COUPLE OF HUNDRED FEET ON SHOW. HAVE A QUICK **SWIG** THEN HEAD DOWN ON A CLEAR PATH TO HARRISON COMBE AND UP THE OTHER SIDE ON GRASS THEN STONES THEN ROCK AS THE PATH PICKS ITS WAY TO THE TOP OF THE STICKLE, WHERE I CHECK THE TIME, TAKE ANOTHER **SWIG** OF WATER AND TAKE IN THE AMAZING VIEW OVER BOWFELL AND CRINKLE CRAGS.

I TAKE IT STEADY OFF THE TOP AND JOIN THE LOFT CRAG PATH, A FEW WALKERS MEANDERING OVER THE PIKES AND MAKING THE MOST OF THE WEATHER. I'M FEELING GOOD AS I REACH LOFT CRAG'S SUMMIT, BUT IT'S HEATING UP BY THE MINUTE AND THERE'S STILL NO BREEZE, EVEN UP HERE, TO COOL ME DOWN. HAVE ANOTHER **SWIG** OF WATER AND SAY HI TO A COUPLE OF WALKERS ON MY WAY DOWN TO THE DEPRESSION BEFORE STARTING THE ASCENT OF HARRISON STICKLE.

MAN-MADE STEPS LEAD ME DIRECTLY TO THE SUMMIT, WHERE A FEW PEOPLE ARE ADMIRING THE VIEWS. I PAUSE FOR ANOTHER **DRINK**. THERE'S NOT MUCH LEFT NOW - AND STILL A FAIR WAY TO GO. I PUSH ON TO PAVEY ARK ON A PATH THAT TURNS OUT NOT TO BE GREAT FOR RUNNING - TOO MANY ROCK STEPS AND STONES TO NEGOTIATE. I PEER DOWN JACK'S RAKE - THERE'S NO ONE ON THEIR WAY UP - AND CONTINUE ROUND TO THE SUMMIT. I NOTE THE TIME, NIBBLE A FRUIT BAR AND TAKE A **SWIG**, THEN CONTINUE ALONG THE EDGE TO THE TOP OF NORTH GULLY, MY WAY DOWN TO STICKLE TARN.

IT'S BUSY NOW, WITH LOTS OF WALKERS STRUGGLING UP THE GULLY, SO I MAKE A SLOWISH DESCENT, TAKING CARE NOT TO DISLODGE ANY STONES OR ROCKS ONTO THE ASCENDING HORDES - DON'T WANT TO HAVE ANY INJURED WALKERS ON MY CONSCIENCE! I HEAD DOWN THE GULLY, CROSS BRIGHT BECK (BIG MISTAKE) AND CARRY ON PAST THE TARN TO PICK UP THE PATH FOR MY NINTH SUMMIT OF THE DAY, BLEA RIGG. IT'S A SLOG UP TO THE RIDGE AS MY LEGS START TO FEEL THE STRAIN. EVENTUALLY THE PATH LEVELS OFF AND I FIND THE TOP WITH EASE.

DRINK THE LAST DROP OF WATER. I SHOULD HAVE FILLED UP AT THE STREAM WHILE I HAD THE CHANCE, BUT IT'S TOO LATE NOW, AND DOUBTS START TO CREEP IN ABOUT MAKING THE TENTH SUMMIT, SILVER HOW. I SET OFF SOUTH, MY LEGS STARTING TO COMPLAIN; THERE'S STILL A LOT OF RUNNING TO GET FIRST TO SILVER HOW AND THEN BACK TO THE CAR ON THE A591.

I CHECK THE MAP FOR AN EARLY ROUTE OFF THE RIDGE DOWN TO GRASMERE AND FIND - SHOCK HORROR! - THAT I'VE RUN OFF THE MAP. THERE'S A WALKER APPROACHING AND I ASK TO HAVE A QUICK LOOK AT HIS. I WORK OUT WHERE I WANT TO BE, SAY CHEERS MATE, DROP DOWN A NARROW PATH LEADING TO BLINDTARN MOSS, THEN TRAVERSE RIGHT OFF LANG HOWE TO ALLAN BANK AND GRASMERE.

THE BOULDERY LITTLE LANE TURNS TO TARMAC AND GUIDES MY WEARY, HOT, PARCHED, ACHING BODY BACK TO CIVILISATION AND THE CAR. I GULP DOWN THE WARM WATER LEFT BEHIND IN THE CAR - IT STILL TASTES GREAT - AND AS I EASE MY WRECKED BODY INTO THE DRIVING SEAT I THINK **NINE OUT OF TEN AIN'T BAD.**

...gging for a drink and not a drop left and no sign of a stream anywhere

THE LAST DROP

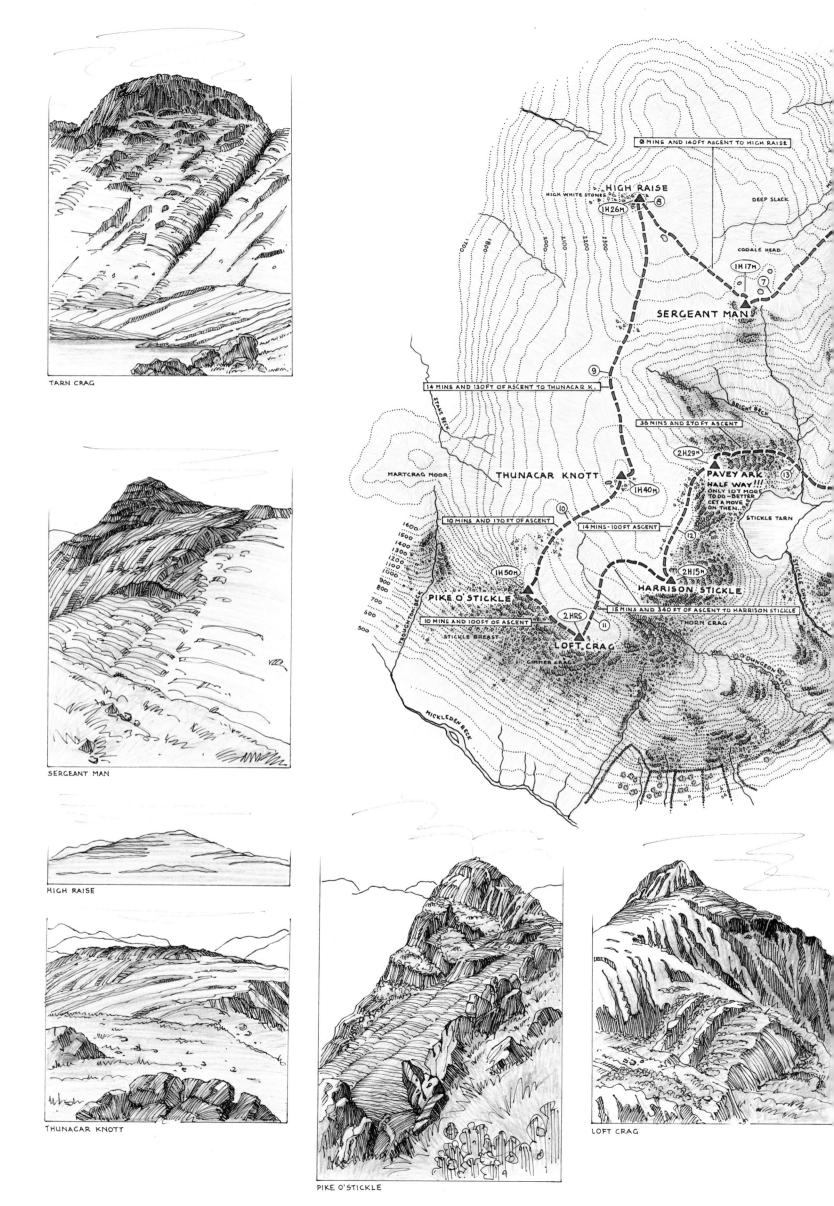

TARN CRAG

SERGEANT MAN

HIGH RAISE

THUNACAR KNOTT

PIKE O'STICKLE

LOFT CRAG

8 MINS AND 140FT ASCENT TO HIGH RAISE

HIGH RAISE

HIGH WHITE STONES

1H26M

8

DEEP SLACK

CODALE HEAD

1H17M

7

SERGEANT MAN

9

14 MINS AND 130FT OF ASCENT TO THUNACAR K.

STAKE BECK

MARTCRAG MOOR

THUNACAR KNOTT

BRIGHT BECK

36 MINS AND 270 FT ASCENT

2H29M

PAVEY ARK

HALF WAY!!!
ONLY 10% MORE
TO DO - BETTER
GET A MOVE
ON THEN...

13

STICKLE TARN

1H40M

10

10 MINS AND 170 FT OF ASCENT

14 MINS - 100 FT ASCENT

12

1600
1400
1300
1200
1100
1000
900
800
700
600
500

1H50M

PIKE O STICKLE

2H15M

HARRISON STICKLE

TROUGH TON BECK

10 MINS AND 100FT OF ASCENT

STICKLE BREAST

2 HRS

11

LOFT CRAG

15 MINS AND 340 FT OF ASCENT TO HARRISON STICKLE

THORN CRAG

STICKLE GHYLL

GIMMER CRAG

DUNGEON GHYLL

MICKLEDEN BECK

MOOR
MOSS

DEER BIELDS

FAR EASEDALE GILL

STYTHWAITE
STEPS

HELM CRAG

49 MIN

5

13 MINS AND 900 FT ASCENT TO TARN CRAG

TARN CRAG

GREATHEAD CRAG

STENNERS CRAG

26 MIN

COCKLY
CRAG

ECTON
CRAG

26 MINS AND 750 FT ASCENT TO EASEDALE TARN

WHITE CRAG

CODALE TARN

EASEDALE TARN

4

SOUR MILK GILL

BRINHOWE
CRAG

3

JACKDAW
CRAG

LANCRIGG

START
FINISH

3H 59 M

SWAN HOTEL

A591

BELLES
KNOTT

EAGLE CRAG

LITTLE BRINHOWE GILL

LOOKING
HOWE

YEW CRAG

BLINDTARN GILL

EASEDALE BECK

COAL BECK

2

EASEDALE ROAD

B5287

14

3H 5M

BLEA CRAG

BLEA RIGG

GREAT CASTLE
HOWE

BLIND TARN
MOSS

ALLAN
BANK

17

18

19

GRASMERE

15

LITTLE CASTLE
HOWE

84 MINS AND 1600 FT DESCENT TO CAR

BROAD CRAG

SWINESCAR PIKE

16

LANG HOWE

WRAY GILL

KELBARROW

B5287

WHITEGILL
CRAG

RAW PIKE

1300

1200

GRASMERE

WINE
KNOTT

SCOUT
CRAG

1100
1000
900
800

BRIGSTONE MOSS

GREEN
HOWE

700
600
500

400

SILVER HOW

B5345

LONG
HOUSE

ELLERS

BOOTH GILL

GREAT LANGDALE BECK

½   1k

HARRISON STICKLE

PAVEY ARK

BLEA RIGG

the **EASTERN** fells

STONE ARTHUR via Greenhead Gill
awful, don't do it, ever!

I SET OFF ON A TARMAC LANE NEXT TO THE SWAN HOTEL ON AN EASY GRADIENT, WHICH BECOMES HARDER AS I TURN RIGHT ON A LANE SIGNPOSTED ALCOCK TARN. SOON REACH A WOODEN GATE AND THE START OF THE OPEN FELL. HERE THE PATH DIVIDES INTO THREE. ONE FORK GOES LEFT FOLLOWING A WALL; ONE GOES STRAIGHT ON; AND THE THIRD TURNS RIGHT FOR ALCOCK TARN. I CHOOSE STRAIGHT ON. IT'S NOT A GOOD DECISION. I SHOULD HAVE GONE VIA THE WALL, BUT I DIDN'T BRING A MAP AND AM RELYING ON MEMORY - ANOTHER BAD DECISION. I CARRY ON REGARDLESS, BUT IT CAN'T BE RIGHT, SO I BITE THE BULLET AND BEAR LEFT STRAIGHT UP THE FELL AND INTO A WALL OF HEAD - HIGH BRACKEN!

IT'S HORRENDOUS. THERE'S NO ESCAPE AS I PULL MYSELF UP THE FELLSIDE, NOT KNOWING WHERE I'M GOING TO END UP. I SPOT WALKERS HIGH ABOVE ME SO KNOW THERE MUST BE A PATH SOMEWHERE. WHAT SEEMS LIKE HOURS LATER I REACH A PATH THAT TAKES ME OUT OF THE BRACKEN (AT LAST) AND ONTO THE OPEN FELL. HEAD TOWARDS THE SUMMIT... BUT IS IT? THERE BELOW ME IS THE TRUE SUMMIT WITH A COUPLE OF WALKERS ON TOP ENJOYING THE VIEW. SO I FOLLOW A PATH DOWN TO THE SUMMIT, CHECK THE TIME, THEN HEAD DOWN, DOWN, DOWN ON THE PATH I SHOULD HAVE USED ON ASCENT. THERE ARE GOOD CONDITIONS UNDERFOOT BEFORE IT DETERIORATES INTO A RIVER OF STONES THEN REACHES A MAN-MADE STONE PATH THAT'S GREAT FOR WALKING UP, BUT RUBBISH FOR RUNNING DOWN. BACK THROUGH THE GATE ONTO TARMAC AND I'M AT THE FINISH. I LOOK DOWN. MY LEGS ARE ALL BLOODY WITH CUTS AND SCRATCHES FROM THE BRACKEN. SERVES ME RIGHT. I SHOULD HAVE GONE TO SPECSAVERS AND TAKEN A MAP - NO EXCUSE!

Up to my eyes in the bloody stuff!

RUNNING TOTAL	
DISTANCE	422·50k
TIME	70 HRS 17 MINS
ASCENT	78,470 FT
SUMMITS	109

the DISTANCE **4**k· the TIME **57** mins· the ASCENT **1,350** ft

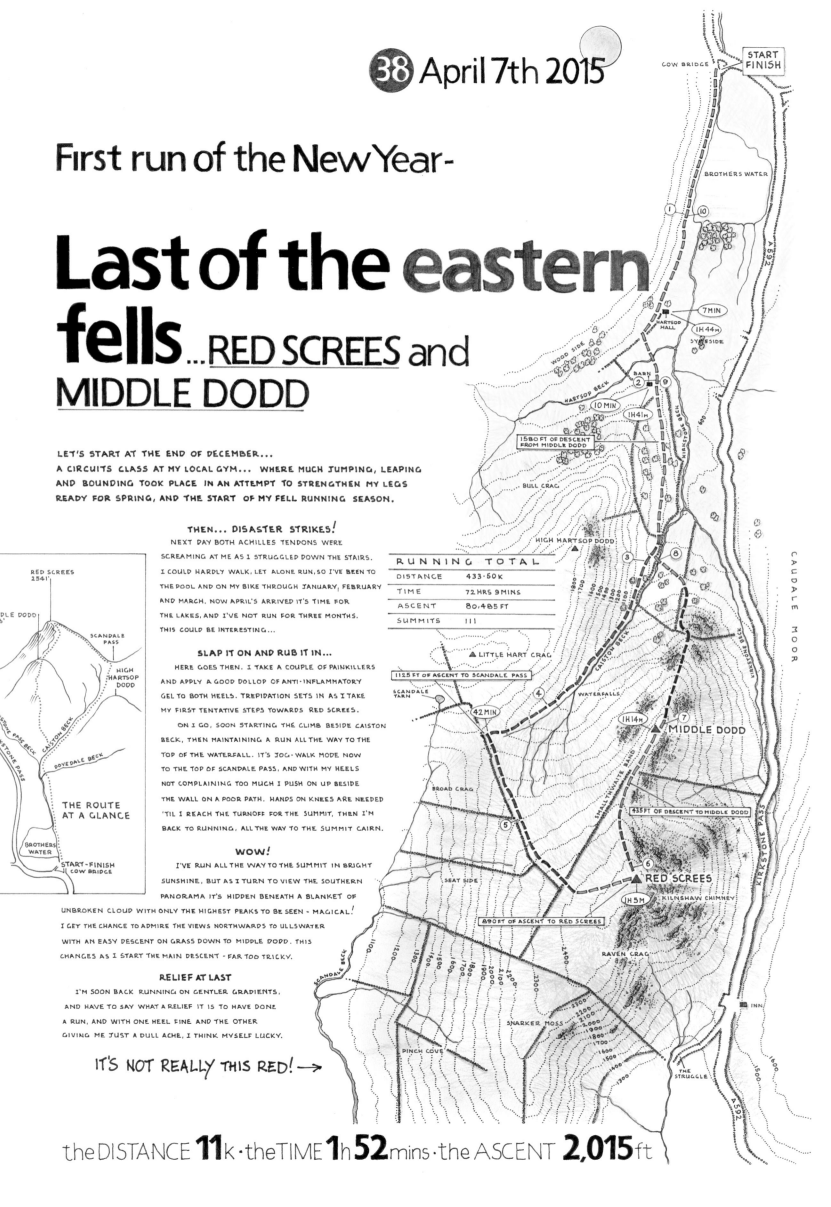

First run of the New Year-

Last of the eastern fells... RED SCREES and MIDDLE DODD

LET'S START AT THE END OF DECEMBER...
A CIRCUITS CLASS AT MY LOCAL GYM... WHERE MUCH JUMPING, LEAPING AND BOUNDING TOOK PLACE IN AN ATTEMPT TO STRENGTHEN MY LEGS READY FOR SPRING, AND THE START OF MY FELL RUNNING SEASON.

THEN... DISASTER STRIKES!
NEXT DAY BOTH ACHILLES TENDONS WERE SCREAMING AT ME AS I STRUGGLED DOWN THE STAIRS. I COULD HARDLY WALK, LET ALONE RUN, SO I'VE BEEN TO THE POOL AND ON MY BIKE THROUGH JANUARY, FEBRUARY AND MARCH. NOW APRIL'S ARRIVED IT'S TIME FOR THE LAKES, AND I'VE NOT RUN FOR THREE MONTHS. THIS COULD BE INTERESTING...

SLAP IT ON AND RUB IT IN...
HERE GOES THEN. I TAKE A COUPLE OF PAINKILLERS AND APPLY A GOOD DOLLOP OF ANTI-INFLAMMATORY GEL TO BOTH HEELS. TREPIDATION SETS IN AS I TAKE MY FIRST TENTATIVE STEPS TOWARDS RED SCREES.
ON I GO, SOON STARTING THE CLIMB BESIDE CAISTON BECK, THEN MAINTAINING A RUN ALL THE WAY TO THE TOP OF THE WATERFALL. IT'S JOG-WALK MODE NOW TO THE TOP OF SCANDALE PASS, AND WITH MY HEELS NOT COMPLAINING TOO MUCH I PUSH ON UP BESIDE THE WALL ON A POOR PATH. HANDS ON KNEES ARE NEEDED 'TIL I REACH THE TURNOFF FOR THE SUMMIT, THEN I'M BACK TO RUNNING, ALL THE WAY TO THE SUMMIT CAIRN.

WOW!
I'VE RUN ALL THE WAY TO THE SUMMIT IN BRIGHT SUNSHINE, BUT AS I TURN TO VIEW THE SOUTHERN PANORAMA IT'S HIDDEN BENEATH A BLANKET OF UNBROKEN CLOUD WITH ONLY THE HIGHEST PEAKS TO BE SEEN - MAGICAL! I GET THE CHANCE TO ADMIRE THE VIEWS NORTHWARDS TO ULLSWATER WITH AN EASY DESCENT ON GRASS DOWN TO MIDDLE DODD. THIS CHANGES AS I START THE MAIN DESCENT - FAR TOO TRICKY.

RELIEF AT LAST
I'M SOON BACK RUNNING ON GENTLER GRADIENTS, AND HAVE TO SAY WHAT A RELIEF IT IS TO HAVE DONE A RUN, AND WITH ONE HEEL FINE AND THE OTHER GIVING ME JUST A DULL ACHE, I THINK MYSELF LUCKY.

IT'S NOT REALLY THIS RED! →

THE ROUTE AT A GLANCE
RED SCREES 2541'
MIDDLE DODD 2106'
SCANDALE PASS
HIGH HARTSOP DODD
KIRKSTONE PASS BECK
CAISTON BECK
DOVEDALE BECK
BROTHERS WATER
START-FINISH COW BRIDGE

RUNNING TOTAL	
DISTANCE	433.50K
TIME	72 HRS 9 MINS
ASCENT	80,485 FT
SUMMITS	111

1580 FT OF DESCENT FROM MIDDLE DODD

1125 FT OF ASCENT TO SCANDALE PASS

435 FT OF DESCENT TO MIDDLE DODD

890 FT OF ASCENT TO RED SCREES

HIGH HARTSOP DODD
LITTLE HART CRAG
SCANDALE TARN
BROAD CRAG
SEAT SIDE
MIDDLE DODD
WATERFALLS
SMALLTHWAITE BAND
RED SCREES
KILNSHAW CHIMNEY
RAVEN CRAG
SNARKER MOSS
PINCH COVE
SCANDALE BECK
CAISTON BECK
KIRKSTONE PASS
THE STRUGGLE
INN
CAUDALE MOOR
COW BRIDGE
START FINISH
BROTHERS WATER
HARTSOP HALL
WOOD SIDE
SYKESIDE
BARN
BULL CRAG
A592

7MIN · 1H44M
10MIN · 1H41M
42MIN
1H14M
1H5M

the DISTANCE **11**k · the TIME **1**h **52** mins · the ASCENT **2,015** ft

the **NORTHERN** fells

Knott great!...
...but no cockups either!

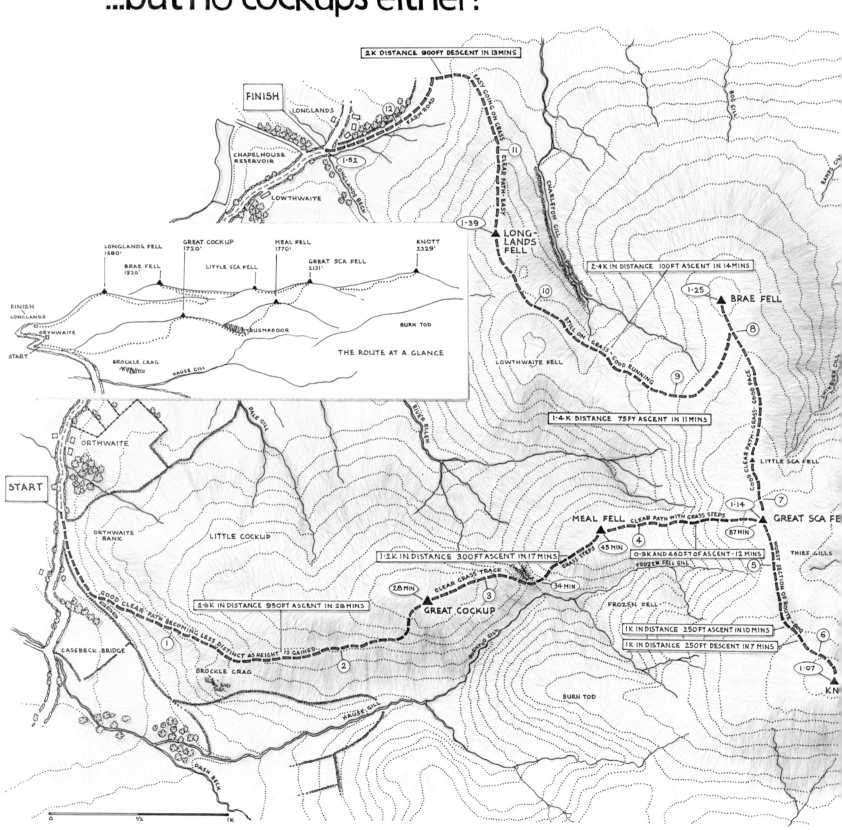

I'M STILL UNABLE TO RUN ON THE ROAD DUE TO
MY CONTINUING HEEL INJURY, SO I TAKE PLENTY OF
PAINKILLERS BEFORE DRIVING UP AND OVER TO ORTHWAITE
FOR A TENTATIVE RUN IN THE ULDALE FELLS.

THE BEST SUMMIT BY FAR - MEAL FELL

VIRGIN COUNTRY

THIS PART OF THE LAKES IS NEW TO ME; THE FELLS HAVE NEVER APPEALED TO MY
EYE WHEN SEEN FROM THE HEIGHTS OF SKIDDAW OR BLENCATHRA. I EVENTUALLY FIND
A SPOT TO PARK THE CAR. I START ON A NARROW LANE, THEN SET OFF ON THE BRIDLEWAY
SIGNED BURN TOD - ONE D. THE GOING'S EASY ON A GOOD GRASS SURFACE AS IT CLIMBS
THE FLANK OF GREAT COCKUP. I LEAVE THE EASY GRADIENT AND HEAD UP TOWARDS
THE SUMMIT CAIRN, WHERE I STOP AND ADMIRE THE VIEWS OF THE DUMFRIES
AND GALLOWAY HILLS ACROSS THE SOLWAY FIRTH FOR A COUPLE OF MINUTES.

SUMMITS - SO I NEED TO WORK OUT WHICH ONE'S WHICH. I'M SOON
SORTED AND FOLLOW A GOOD TRACK HEADING FOR TRUSMADOOR
AND ON TO MEAL FELL. WITH FINE WEATHER CONDITIONS
ROUTE FINDING WON'T BE A PROBLEM - HE SAYS WITH CONFIDENCE!
USE THE SOIL STEPS ALL THE WAY UP THE SIDE OF MEAL FELL. IT'S
A NICE SUMMIT, WITH A STONE WIND SHELTER, BUT THERE'S NO NEED
FOR IT TODAY; THE SUN'S STILL BRIGHT, WITH A COOL WIND PICKING
UP. A CLEAR PATH CONTINUES TO GREAT SCA FELL, ON GRASS, SO OFF I GO,
SLIGHTLY DOWNHILL AT FIRST BEFORE A LONG UPHILL SLOG. WITH HANDS
ON KNEES AND NOSE DRIPPING SWEAT I PRESS ON TO THE SUMMIT OF GREAT SCA
FELL - IF YOU CAN CALL IT A SUMMIT.

WHICH WAY NOW?

I TAKE ANOTHER MINUTE TO GET MY BEARINGS. THESE FELLS
ARE LIKE THE HOWGILLS - LOTS OF GRASS AND DOME-LIKE

KNOTT GREAT!

NEXT UP IS KNOTT, THE HIGHEST SUMMIT OF TODAY'S RUN, AND HOME TO THE WORST
BIT OF PATH OF THE DAY - FULL-ON BOG BEFORE IT REVERTS BACK TO THE GREEN STUFF.
ON THE SUMMIT I TAKE ON FLUID AND A CEREAL BAR BEFORE RE-TRACING MY STEPS
BACK TO GREAT SCA FELL AND BRAE FELL, WITH FINE VIEWS OVER TO BAKESTALL AND
DASH CRAGS.

THAT'S BETTER

SPOT THE FIRST WALKER OF THE
DAY IN THE DISTANCE AND WITH GOOD
CONDITIONS UNDERFOOT I CAN GAZE
UP TO THE HORIZON AND ADMIRE THE
DISTANT VISTA OF THE SCOTTISH HILLS.

POP ON MY WINDPROOF AT BRAE
FELL SUMMIT AS THE WIND BECOMES
COLDER AND THE RUNNING EASIER.
IT'S EASY GOING NOW ALL THE WAY TO
LONGLANDS SUMMIT AND DOWN TO
LONGLANDS VILLAGE - A VERY NICE
SPOT INDEED.

SKIDDAW FROM
GREAT COCKUP

THE WORST
SUMMIT BY
FAR - GREAT
SCA FELL

A STROLL

I'M BACK ON TARMAC FOR THE END OF MY RUN. MY HEELS ARE ACHING NOW, AND WITH THE CAR TWO
MILES DOWN THE ROAD I DECIDE TO WALK THE REST OF THE WAY - DON'T WANT TO PUSH MY LUCK.
IT'S A LOVELY LANE ENCLOSED BY BEECH YET TO SPRING INTO LIFE AND BRIGHT GREEN HAWTHORN THAT'S
HOME TO AN ABUNDANCE OF BIRD LIFE. IT ENDS A GOOD RUN OVER GRASSY HILLS, BUT I WON'T
BE GOING BACK... THE HILLS ARE NOTHING TO GET TOO EXCITED ABOUT...

RUNNING	TOTAL
DISTANCE	456·00K
TIME	74 HRS 1 MIN
ASCENT	82,620 FT
SUMMITS	117

THERE'S BETTER ONES OUT THERE !!!

the DISTANCE **12·5**k
the TIME **1**h **52** mins
the ASCENT **2,135** ft

OTHER GELS ARE AVAILABLE
AS THEY SAY

first visit to
the WESTERN fells

Give us a break heel!

as I struggle up and down
<u>MELLBREAK</u>

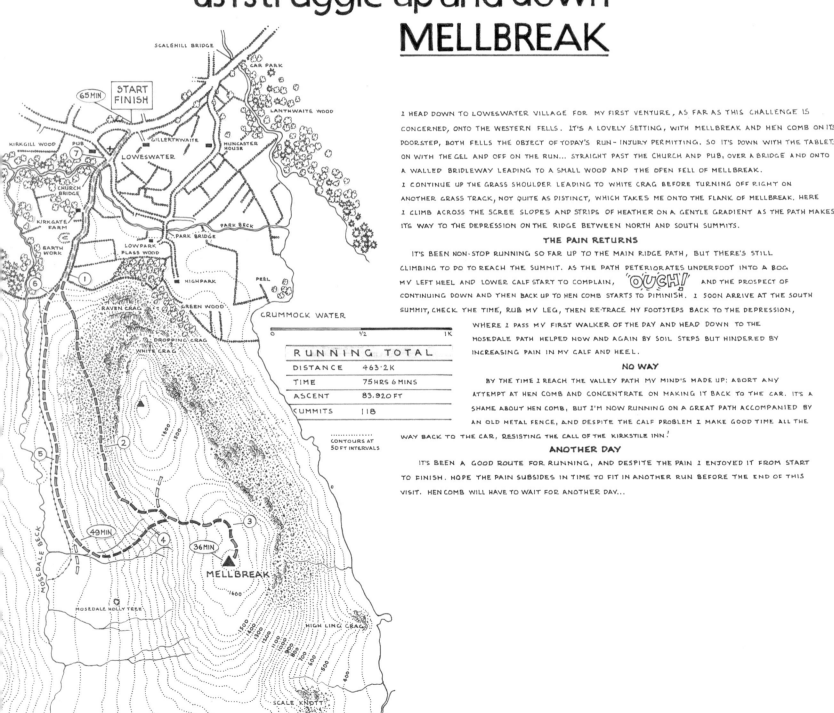

I HEAD DOWN TO LOWESWATER VILLAGE FOR MY FIRST VENTURE, AS FAR AS THIS CHALLENGE IS CONCERNED, ONTO THE WESTERN FELLS. IT'S A LOVELY SETTING, WITH MELLBREAK AND HEN COMB ON ITS DOORSTEP, BOTH FELLS THE OBJECT OF TODAY'S RUN- INJURY PERMITTING. SO IT'S DOWN WITH THE TABLETS, ON WITH THE GEL AND OFF ON THE RUN... STRAIGHT PAST THE CHURCH AND PUB, OVER A BRIDGE AND ONTO A WALLED BRIDLEWAY LEADING TO A SMALL WOOD AND THE OPEN FELL OF MELLBREAK.
I CONTINUE UP THE GRASS SHOULDER LEADING TO WHITE CRAG BEFORE TURNING OFF RIGHT ON ANOTHER GRASS TRACK, NOT QUITE AS DISTINCT, WHICH TAKES ME ONTO THE FLANK OF MELLBREAK. HERE I CLIMB ACROSS THE SCREE SLOPES AND STRIPS OF HEATHER ON A GENTLE GRADIENT AS THE PATH MAKES ITS WAY TO THE DEPRESSION ON THE RIDGE BETWEEN NORTH AND SOUTH SUMMITS.

THE PAIN RETURNS

IT'S BEEN NON-STOP RUNNING SO FAR UP TO THE MAIN RIDGE PATH, BUT THERE'S STILL CLIMBING TO DO TO REACH THE SUMMIT. AS THE PATH PETERIORATES UNDERFOOT INTO A BOG MY LEFT HEEL AND LOWER CALF START TO COMPLAIN, "OUCH!" AND THE PROSPECT OF CONTINUING DOWN AND THEN BACK UP TO HEN COMB STARTS TO DIMINISH. I SOON ARRIVE AT THE SOUTH SUMMIT, CHECK THE TIME, RUB MY LEG, THEN RE-TRACE MY FOOTSTEPS BACK TO THE DEPRESSION, WHERE I PASS MY FIRST WALKER OF THE DAY AND HEAD DOWN TO THE MOSEDALE PATH HELPED NOW AND AGAIN BY SOIL STEPS BUT HINDERED BY INCREASING PAIN IN MY CALF AND HEEL.

NO WAY

BY THE TIME I REACH THE VALLEY PATH MY MIND'S MADE UP: ABORT ANY ATTEMPT AT HEN COMB AND CONCENTRATE ON MAKING IT BACK TO THE CAR. IT'S A SHAME ABOUT HEN COMB, BUT I'M NOW RUNNING ON A GREAT PATH ACCOMPANIED BY AN OLD METAL FENCE, AND DESPITE THE CALF PROBLEM I MAKE GOOD TIME ALL THE WAY BACK TO THE CAR, RESISTING THE CALL OF THE KIRKSTILE INN!

ANOTHER DAY

IT'S BEEN A GOOD ROUTE FOR RUNNING, AND DESPITE THE PAIN I ENJOYED IT FROM START TO FINISH. HOPE THE PAIN SUBSIDES IN TIME TO FIT IN ANOTHER RUN BEFORE THE END OF THIS VISIT. HEN COMB WILL HAVE TO WAIT FOR ANOTHER DAY...

RUNNING TOTAL

DISTANCE	463·2K
TIME	75 HRS 6 MINS
ASCENT	83,920 FT
SUMMITS	118

CONTOURS AT 50 FT INTERVALS

7·2k-1h5mins-1,300ft

the NORTH WESTERN fells

Knott 'ard at all...
(EXCEPT FOR THE FIRST SIX MINUTES)

IT'S A MONTH FURTHER ON AND I'M STILL NOT RUNNING ON THE ROADS OF SCUNTHORPE, JUST SWIMMING AND CYCLING TO HOLD ONTO SOME FITNESS AND GIVE THE HEELS A CHANCE TO RECOVER. THEY'VE BEEN SO TENDER I'VE CUT THE BACKS RIGHT DOWN ON AN OLD PAIR OF TRAINERS JUST TO WALK AROUND PAIN-FREE. I'M DESPERATE FOR THEM TO SETTLE DOWN AS I'M HEADING TO THE ALPS WITH MY BROTHER PETER AT THE END OF JULY TO WALK FROM CHAMONIX TO ZERMATT. THE WAY THINGS ARE AT THE MOMENT IT'S NOT GOING TO HAPPEN.

I LEAVE JANICE IN THE CAR AT NEWLANDS HAUSE AND HEAD STRAIGHT UP ON A CLEAR GRASS PATH WITH LITTLE MUD STEPS. IT'S NOT LONG BEFORE I'M PUFFING AND BLOWING AS JANICE WATCHES FROM THE CAR, BEFORE SETTING OFF FOR OUR RENDEZVOUS POINT DOWN THE VALLEY.

THERE'S A PATH ALL THE WAY TO THE SUMMIT OF KNOTT RIGG, WITH GOOD VIEWS IN EVERY DIRECTION. A CLEAR PATH LEADS ON, DOWN SLIGHTLY AT FIRST BEFORE GAINING HEIGHT TOWARDS THE SUMMIT OF ARD CRAGS. IT'S IDEAL FOR RUNNING, AND CONTINUES IN THE SAME VEIN TO THE EAST SUMMIT. THE STEEP DESCENT NEEDS A BIT MORE CARE, WITH A TRICKY SECTION OVER AIKIN KNOTT SLOWING THE PACE BEFORE IT PICKS UP AGAIN ON THE SHORT GRASS AND GENTLER SLOPE TO BIRK RIGG. HERE I BEAR LEFT, DOWN AND

ACROSS RIGG BECK TO JOIN THE PATH FROM BUTTERMERE VIA SAIL BECK. THIS DELIVERS ME TO THE ROADSIDE AT RIGG BECK, WHERE JANICE IS WAITING.

THE GOOD NEWS IS MY HEELS ARE NO PROBLEM, AND CONSIDERING I'VE NOT RUN FOR WEEKS MY BREATHING AND LEGS AREN'T TOO BAD EITHER.

SPEND A COUPLE OF MINUTES LOOKING AT A BEAUTIFUL STONE-BUILT HOUSE JUST ACROSS THE ROAD. WHOEVER LIVES THERE MUST BE A VERY HAPPY CHAPPY INDEED.

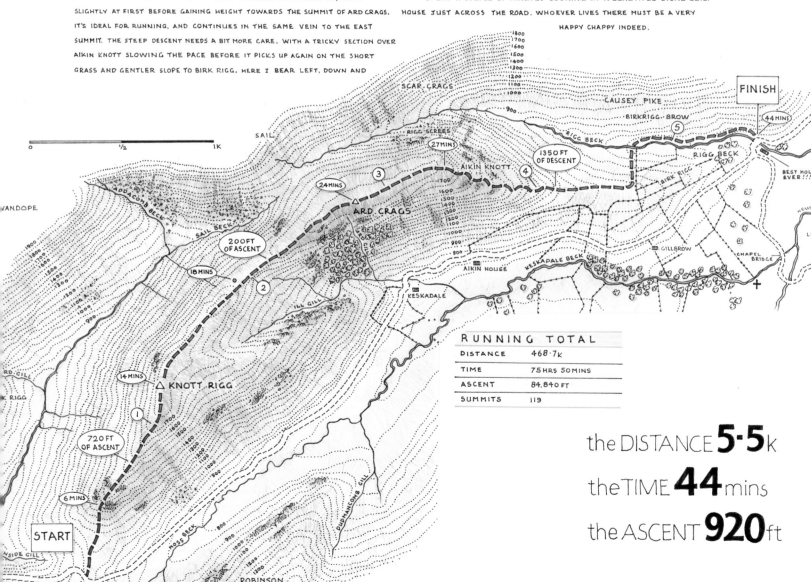

RUNNING TOTAL	
DISTANCE	468.7k
TIME	75 HRS 50 MINS
ASCENT	84,840 FT
SUMMITS	119

the DISTANCE **5·5**k

the TIME **44** mins

the ASCENT **920** ft

CONTOURS AT 50FT INTERVALS

the SOUTHERN fells

Old man running
on CONISTON OLD MAN

COMPLETED MY FIRST PARK RUN LAST WEEK SINCE THE END OF DECEMBER 2014 AND THE START OF MY TENDONITIS. FEEL READY FOR A STIFFER FELL RUN THIS TIME - BUT STILL VEERING ON THE SIDE OF CAUTION.

JANICE AND I DRIVE DOWN TO CONISTON FOR MY FIRST VENTURE ONTO THE SOUTHERN FELLS. IT'S BUSY IN TOWN BUT WE MANAGE TO PARK UP - HAVE TO PAY THOUGH! SOON LEAVE THE CROWDS BEHIND AS I HEAD OUT OF TOWN ON TARMAC LEADING TO THE WALNA SCAR ROAD AND THE OPEN FELL. THE STEEP START SOON HAS ME WARMED UP, AND BY THE TIME I REACH THE FELL - WHERE THERE'S A FREE CAR PARK - I'M DRIPPING WITH SWEAT.

THE 'ROAD' STRETCHES OUT LIKE A RIVER OF STONES INTO THE DISTANCE, CLIMBING AT A GENTLE GRADIENT ALL THE WAY TO WALNA SCAR AND THE TURNOFF FOR BROWN PIKE. IT'S HANDS-ON-KNEES FOR A WHILE NOW AFTER THE STEADY GRADIENT OF THE 'ROAD', THEN TAKE A QUICK DRINK ON THE SUMMIT, WITH PLENTY OF OTHER WALKERS ENJOYING THE EXPANSIVE VIEWS.

IT'S STILL SUNNY AS I SET OFF, BUT A STIFF, COOL BREEZE BLOWING UP MEANS IT'S ON WITH THE WINDPROOF. THE GRADIENTS ARE EASIER NOW, BUT CONDITIONS UNDERFOOT WORSEN WITH THE ARRIVAL OF ROCKS AND STONES PROTRUDING THROUGH GRASS AS I PICK MY WAY TO THE NEXT SUMMIT, BUCK PIKE, AND A LITTLE FURTHER ON MY FIRST WAINWRIGHT OF THE DAY, DOW CRAG.

A TIPTOE DESCENT DOWN TO GOATS HAUSE, THEN I'M RUNNING AGAIN, FULL STEAM AHEAD TRYING TO IMPRESS ALL THE WALKERS PASSING BY. ON THE FAR SIDE I TURN OFF LEFT ON A THIN TRACK HEADING AT A GOOD GRADIENT TOWARDS BRIM FELL.

I LEAVE THE TRACK AFTER A HUNDRED YARDS OR SO AND PUSH UPHILL, HANDS ON KNEES AGAIN, TO REACH THE RIDGE NOT TEN YARDS SHORT OF THE SUMMIT CAIRN.

IN NO TIME AT ALL I'M ON TOP OF THE OLD MAN. IT'S VERY BUSY, OF COURSE, SO I DON'T HANG ABOUT FOR LONG - HAVE A QUICK DRINK, A BITE TO EAT AND ADMIRE THE VIEWS, THEN I'M OFF DOWN THE TOURIST PATH BACK TO CONISTON VILLAGE...

A BIG
MISTAKE
IN ROUTE
CHOICE...

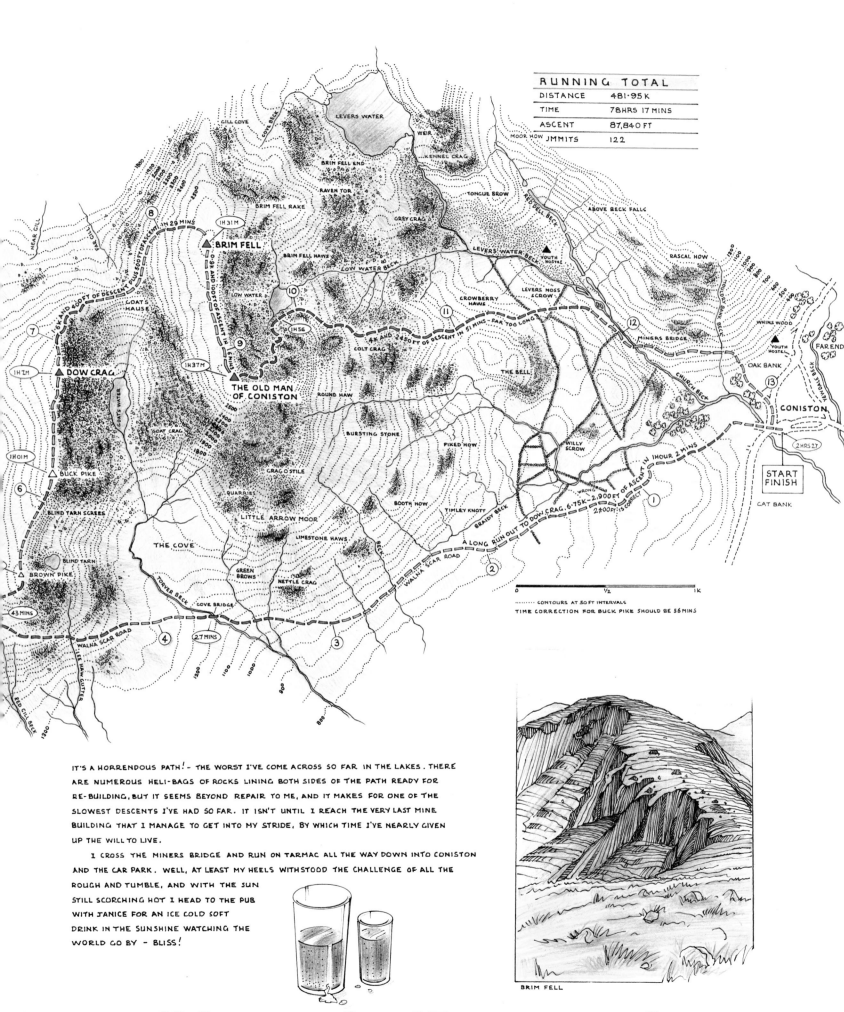

RUNNING TOTAL

DISTANCE	481·95 K
TIME	78 HRS 17 MINS
ASCENT	87,840 FT
SUMMITS	122

IT'S A HORRENDOUS PATH! - THE WORST I'VE COME ACROSS SO FAR IN THE LAKES. THERE
ARE NUMEROUS HELI-BAGS OF ROCKS LINING BOTH SIDES OF THE PATH READY FOR
RE-BUILDING, BUT IT SEEMS BEYOND REPAIR TO ME, AND IT MAKES FOR ONE OF THE
SLOWEST DESCENTS I'VE HAD SO FAR. IT ISN'T UNTIL I REACH THE VERY LAST MINE
BUILDING THAT I MANAGE TO GET INTO MY STRIDE, BY WHICH TIME I'VE NEARLY GIVEN
UP THE WILL TO LIVE.

I CROSS THE MINERS BRIDGE AND RUN ON TARMAC ALL THE WAY DOWN INTO CONISTON
AND THE CAR PARK. WELL, AT LEAST MY HEELS WITHSTOOD THE CHALLENGE OF ALL THE
ROUGH AND TUMBLE, AND WITH THE SUN
STILL SCORCHING HOT I HEAD TO THE PUB
WITH JANICE FOR AN ICE COLD SOFT
DRINK IN THE SUNSHINE WATCHING THE
WORLD GO BY - BLISS!

BRIM FELL

DISTANCE 13·25k TIME 2hrs27mins ASCENT 3,000ft

the **FAR EASTERN** fells

Oh dear, no deer
AS I NAB FOUR MORE SUMMITS...
REST DODD, THE NAB, BROCK CRAGS
and ANGLETARN PIKES

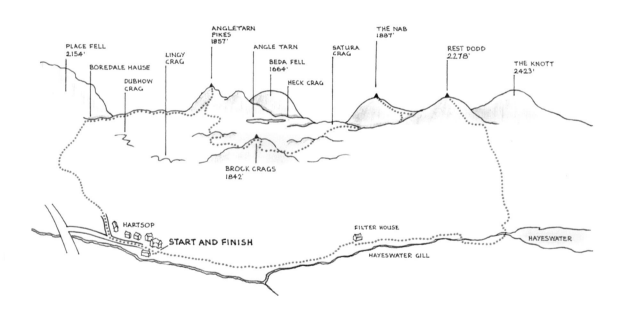

THERE'S BEEN NO REACTION FROM MY INJURIES, SO ANOTHER MULTI-SUMMIT RUN IS ON THE CARDS AND IT'S GRASS MOST OF THE WAY; I HAD ENOUGH ROCKS ON MY LAST RUN THANK YOU!

IT'S THE HOTTEST DAY OF THE YEAR FORECAST TODAY, 36°, SO I'M OFF EARLY FROM HARTSOP VILLAGE CAR PARK. I PAY MY DUES AT THE HONESTY BOX THEN SET OFF THROUGH THE GATE ON A TARMAC TRACK TO THE FILTER HOUSE. RUN OUT OF TARMAC ONTO GRASS AND ROCKS BESIDE THE BECK. IT'S DIFFICULT GOING; IN HINDSIGHT I SHOULD HAVE CHOSEN THE PATH ON THE FAR SIDE. NEVER MIND.

I REACH THE OUTLET OF HAYESWATER AND TAKE ONE OF THE MANY GRASS PATHS LEADING UP TO THE KNOTT. IT'S HANDS-ON-KNEES RUNNING NOW UNTIL THE MAIN RIDGE PATH IS CROSSED. I CONTINUE PUFFING AND BLOWING MY WAY TO THE SUMMIT OF REST DODD.

TAKE A QUICK DRINK BEFORE STARTING THE STEEP DESCENT TOWARDS THE NAB. THE TERRAIN IS NO PROBLEM AS I CROSS A WALL ONTO THE NAB. THE GRASS IS FINE AND THE PEAT HAGS ARE BONE DRY, WHICH MAKES FOR FAST AND EASY RUNNING ALL THE WAY.

BUT DEER... **NOT ONE GLIMPSE YET!**

AFTER A SHORT CLIMB I'M ON THE SUMMIT, WHERE I NOTE THE TIME. CHECK THE HORIZON FOR SIGNS OF LIFE - NO LUCK - SO I RETRACE MY STEPS BACK TO REST DODD. I'M STILL RUNNING AT A COMFORTABLE PACE AS I VEER OFF, RIGHT, ON THE FAINTEST OF TRACKS IN THE DIRECTION OF BUCK CRAG. CLIMB THE SHOULDER OF REST DODD ONTO A WELL DEFINED PATH MAKING ITS WAY DOWN, OVER AND BETWEEN NUMEROUS HILLOCKS TO THE MAIN ANGLE TARN PATH.

I SPY THE SMALL CAIRN ON BROCK CRAGS SILHOUETTED AGAINST CLEAR BLUE SKY IN THE DISTANCE. TURN OFF THE MAIN PATH BY THE WALL. I'M STILL ON GRASS, STILL RUNNING, AND IT'S STILL DELIGHTFUL, WITH LOVELY VIEWS OVER TO FAIRFIELD AND DOVEDALE FROM THE SUMMIT. THE PATH CONTINUES ITS GRASSY WAY ACROSS HILLOCKS AND ROCK OUTCROPS BEFORE REJOINING THE MAIN PATH AT THE FOOT OF ANGLETARN PIKES.

STILL NO SIGN OF ANY DEER

AS TIME STARTS TO RUN OUT...

the DISTANCE **14·75** k - the TIME **2**hrs **26** mins - the ASCENT **2,650** ft

ON THE NORTH SUMMIT OF THE PIKES I CHEW A TOFFEE, HAVE A DRINK,
THEN HEAD BACK DOWN TO THE MAIN BOREDALE HAUSE PATH, PASSING
QUITE A FEW WALKERS ON THEIR WAY UP AS I DROP DOWN, LEFT,
BACK TO HARTSOP VILLAGE AND THE FINISH. IT'S A GOOD PATH AFTER
THE INITIAL HUNDRED YARDS OF LOOSE GRAVEL, THAT KEEPS ME
RUNNING ALL THE WAY BACK TO THE CAR. IT
NOW FEELS LIKE THE HOTTEST DAY OF THE
YEAR, AND I'M PLEASED TO HAVE TAKEN
TWO BOTTLES OF WATER AS I DOWN THE
LAST DROP.

I'M ALSO PLEASED WITH THE
AMOUNT OF RUNNING ON THIS ROUTE.
BEST OF ALL, MY HEELS ARE FINE;
PROBLEM SOLVED I HOPE – AFTER SIX
MONTHS OF PAIN!

**SHAME
ABOUT THE DEER...**

RUNNING TOTAL	
DISTANCE	496·70 K
TIME	80 HRS 43 MINS
ASCENT	90,490 FT
SUMMITS	126

"Quick, hide,
here comes
a fell runner"

the CENTRAL fells

You've got to be quackers to do this one!

As I waddle over WALLA CRAG, BLEA-BERRY FELL, HIGH SEAT HIGH TOVE, ARMBOTH FELL and BRUND FELL

IT'S A GOOD START FROM THE EDGE OF KESWICK, THROUGH WOODS THEN OUT ONTO THE OPEN FELL ON A CLEAR PATH THAT'S RUNNABLE ALL THE WAY TO THE SUMMIT OF WALLA CRAG WITH ONLY ONE OR TWO STIFF LITTLE SECTIONS. THE PATH FROM THE WALL TO THE SUMMIT IS VERY PRETTY, TWISTING BETWEEN ROCKS, HEATHER AND THE OCCASIONAL TREE WITH OUTSTANDING VIEWS OVER THE LAKE AND THE NORTH WESTERN FELLS.

I TURN MY ATTENTION IN THE OPPOSITE DIRECTION AND MY NEXT OBJECTIVE, BLEABERRY FELL. A NEW PATH UNDER CONSTRUCTION OFFERS GOOD RUNNING, BUT AS I NEAR THE FINAL APPROACH STONE STEPS MEAN WALKING BECOMES A MUST.

I PUSH ON, HANDS ON KNEES, PAST A COUPLE OF HUGE CAIRNS TO THE SUMMIT WIND SHELTER.

A QUICK DRINK AND I'M SOUTHWARD-BOUND ON A WELL-DEFINED PATH HEADING FOR HIGH SEAT.

I MANAGE TO AVOID THE WORST OF THE PEAT BOGS, BUT NOT ALL OF THEM, AND AS IT CLIMBS TOWARDS THE SUMMIT THE PATH BECOMES INDISTINCT AND WETTER UNDERFOOT.

I ARRIVE WITH WET FEET ON THE SUMMIT, BUT MY LEGS FEEL GOOD AFTER THE FIRST HOUR SO I PUSH ON TO HIGH TOVE FULL OF BEANS. IT'S ALL NEW UP HERE FOR ME; I'VE NEVER WANDERED OVER THESE FELLS BEFORE. THERE'S NO REAL DISTINCT PATH EXCEPT BY THE FENCE, SO I DECIDE TO GO WITH IT, BUT IT'S NOT WORTH THE EFFORT: IT DISAPPEARS IN AND OUT OF PEAT BOGS, TAKES WIDE DIVERSIONS AND BECOMES WETTER, SPLASH WETTER AND WETTER. LET THE FUN BEGIN!

ROUTE AT A GLANCE
NOT TO SCALE

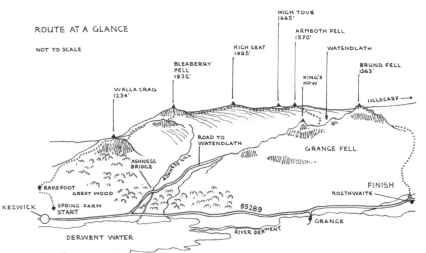

HIGH TOVE 1665'
ARMBOTH FELL 1570'
WATENDLATH
HIGH SEAT 1995'
BLEABERRY FELL 1932'
BRUND FELL 1363'
WALLA CRAG 1234'
KING'S HOW
ULLSCARF
ROAD TO WATENDLATH
GRANGE FELL
ASHNESS BRIDGE
ASHNESS GILL
FINISH
RAKE FOOT
GREAT WOOD
ROSTHWAITE
KESWICK
SPRING FARM START
B5289
GRANGE
RIVER DERWENT
DERWENT WATER

I'VE SOON HAD ENOUGH **SPLISH** AND ABANDON THE FENCE PATH, CROSS OVER ONTO ROUGH WET GRASS AND MAKE A BEELINE FOR THE CAIRN ON THE HORIZON WHICH I HOPE WILL BE HIGH TOVE. IT IS - WITH QUITE A FEW PEOPLE WALKING OVER FROM WATENDLATH, MOST WITH HUGE RUCKSACKS; MIGHT BE ON A D of E CHALLENGE.

I CONTINUE STRAIGHT ON TO MIDDLE CRAG TAKING WAINWRIGHT'S ADVICE, OF COURSE, THEN OVER TO ARMBOTH FELL IN THE HOPE OF MISSING THE WORST OF THE BOG. **SPLOSH!** NO CHANCE! I'M STILL SPLASHING ALONG HAVING A WONDERFUL TIME RIGHT UP TO THE SUMMIT OUTCROP. FROM THE SUMMIT CAIRN I CAN NOW SEE A CLEAR PATH DIRECTLY TO AND FROM HIGH TOVE'S SUMMIT, WHICH I COULD HAVE TAKEN INSTEAD OF THE DETOUR TO MIDDLE CRAG. NOT TO WORRY.

I HEAD STRAIGHT DOWN TO THE PATH, STRIDE OVER A STREAM AND UP TO HIGH TOVE FOR A SECOND TIME. THE SAME PEOPLE ARE STILL HANGING AROUND AS I HEAD DOWN IN THE DIRECTION OF WATENDLATH AND WHAT I HOPE WILL BE A DRIER PATH. WRONG! IT'S VERY WET **SPLISH!** UNDERFOOT, WITH WATER RUNNING OVER VERY SHORT GRASS - NOT GOOD. TERRA FIRMA ARRIVES IN THE SHAPE OF ENGINEERED ROCK STEPS FROM WATENDLATH - HURRAY!

THE VILLAGE IS BUSY WITH TOURISTS AND WALKERS CLICKING AWAY AS I CROSS THE TARN OUTLET AND PICK UP THE THIN TRACK, ON GRASS, HEADING TO JOPPLETY HOW AND MY FINAL SUMMIT OF THE DAY BRUND FELL (GRANGE FELL). THIS IS A BIT MORE LIKE IT! THE PATH TWISTS ITS WAY PAST OUTCROPS BEFORE CLIMBING TO THE ROCKY SUMMIT OF BRUND FELL.

LITTLE TRACKS LEAD IN VARIOUS DIRECTIONS OFF THE SUMMIT. I CHOOSE ONE THAT LOOKS LIKE IT MIGHT TAKE ME DOWN TO ROSTHWAITE. IT DOES, BUT ONLY FOR ABOUT A HUNDRED YARDS OR SO BEFORE BEING SWALLOWED UP BY A JUNGLE OF SHOULDER-HEIGHT BRACKEN. FLASHBACKS TO STONE ARTHUR ENTER MY MIND. AAAH!

I PUSH MY WAY THROUGH AND DOWN ONTO THE MAIN WATENDLATH TO ROSTHWAITE PATH - PLAIN SAILING NOW ALL THE WAY TO THE BUS STOP ON THE B5289 WHERE AFTER ONLY FIVE MINUTES OF KICKING MY WET HEELS A NUMBER **78** BUS PULLS UP. ON I JUMP, BUS PASS IN HAND AND HAPPY AS PUNCH, WET FEET AN'ALL!

RUNNING TOTAL

DISTANCE	512·60K
TIME	83HRS 28MINS
ASCENT	93,390FT
SUMMITS	132

the DISTANCE **15·9**k · the TIME **2**hrs **45**mins · the ASCENT **2,900**ft

And now for something completely different
CHAMONIX to ZERMATT TREK

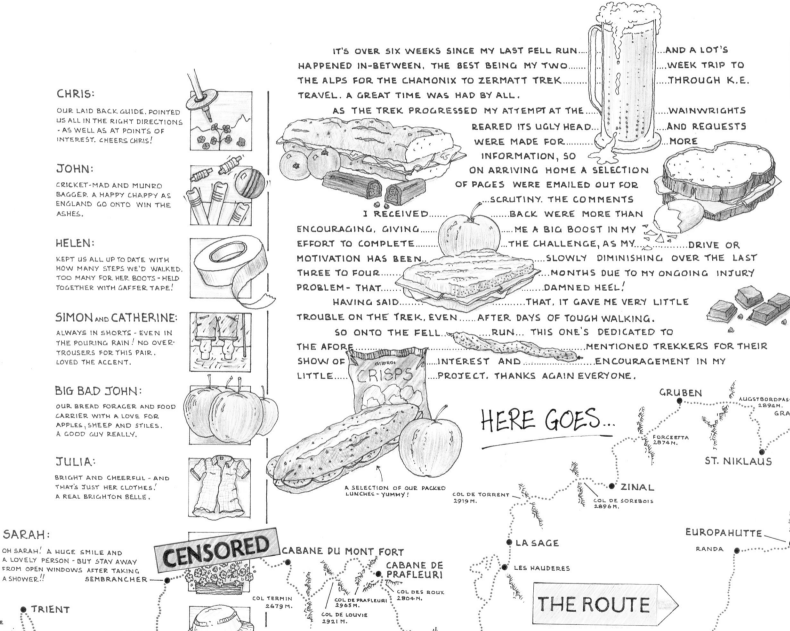

CHRIS: OUR LAID BACK GUIDE. POINTED US ALL IN THE RIGHT DIRECTIONS - AS WELL AS AT POINTS OF INTEREST. CHEERS CHRIS!

JOHN: CRICKET-MAD AND MUNRO BAGGER. A HAPPY CHAPPY AS ENGLAND GO ONTO WIN THE ASHES.

HELEN: KEPT US ALL UP TO DATE WITH HOW MANY STEPS WE'D WALKED. TOO MANY FOR HER BOOTS - HELD TOGETHER WITH GAFFER TAPE!

SIMON and CATHERINE: ALWAYS IN SHORTS - EVEN IN THE POURING RAIN! NO OVER-TROUSERS FOR THIS PAIR. LOVED THE ACCENT.

BIG BAD JOHN: OUR BREAD FORAGER AND FOOD CARRIER WITH A LOVE FOR APPLES, SHEEP AND STILES. A GOOD GUY REALLY.

JULIA: BRIGHT AND CHEERFUL - AND THAT'S JUST HER CLOTHES! A REAL BRIGHTON BELLE.

SARAH: OH SARAH! A HUGE SMILE AND A LOVELY PERSON - BUT STAY AWAY FROM OPEN WINDOWS AFTER TAKING A SHOWER!!

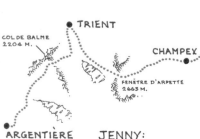

JENNY: A POCKET DYNAMO AND CONSTANT SUPPLIER OF COPIOUS AMOUNTS OF SUN LOTION. ALSO A BIG BELIEVER IN HAND-KERCHIEFS · NOT TISSUES. SHE'S ALSO MY FAVOURITE... JUST TO EMBARRASS HER · SORRY!

PETE:- MY TRIP SPONSOR AND A GREAT BROTHER · KEEP TAKING THE PICS.

IT'S OVER SIX WEEKS SINCE MY LAST FELL RUN.... HAPPENED IN-BETWEEN, THE BEST BEING MY TWO...... THE ALPS FOR THE CHAMONIX TO ZERMATT TREK.... TRAVEL. A GREAT TIME WAS HAD BY ALL. AS THE TREK PROGRESSED MY ATTEMPT AT THE.... REARED ITS UGLY HEAD... WERE MADE FOR...... INFORMATION, SO ON ARRIVING HOME A SELECTION OF PAGES WERE EMAILED OUT FOR ...SCRUTINY. THE COMMENTS I RECEIVED...... BACK WERE MORE THAN ENCOURAGING, GIVING..... ME A BIG BOOST IN MY EFFORT TO COMPLETE...... THE CHALLENGE, AS MY.... MOTIVATION HAS BEEN.... SLOWLY DIMINISHING OVER THE LAST THREE TO FOUR..... MONTHS DUE TO MY ONGOING INJURY PROBLEM- THAT...... DAMNED HEEL! HAVING SAID..... THAT, IT GAVE ME VERY LITTLE TROUBLE ON THE TREK, EVEN..... AFTER DAYS OF TOUGH WALKING. SO ONTO THE FELL..... RUN... THIS ONE'S DEDICATED TO THE AFORE..... MENTIONED TREKKERS FOR THEIR SHOW OF...... INTEREST AND...... ENCOURAGEMENT IN MY LITTLE..... PROJECT. THANKS AGAIN EVERYONE.

...AND A LOT'S ...WEEK TRIP TO ...THROUGH K.E. ...WAINWRIGHTS ...AND REQUESTS ...MORE ...DRIVE OR

HERE GOES...

A SELECTION OF OUR PACKED LUNCHES - YUMMY!

Map labels: GRUBEN · AUGSTBORDPASS 2894M · GRA · FORCLETTA 2874M · ST. NIKLAUS · ZINAL · COL DE SOREBOIS 2896M · COL DE TORRENT 2919M · LA SAGE · LES HAUDERES · EUROPAHUTTE · RANDA · THE ROUTE · CABANE DU MONT FORT · CABANE DE PRAFLEURI · COL DES ROUX 2804M · COL DE PRAFLEURI 2965M · COL DE LOUVIE 2921M · COL TERMIN 2679M · SEMBRANCHER · CENSORED · TRIENT · CHAMPEX · FENÈTRE D'ARPETTE 2665M · COL DE BALME 2204M · ARGENTIÈRE · START · AROLLA · COL DE RIEDMATTEN 2919M · ZERMATT · FINISH

SUN LOTION NEVER 56 xxx

STAGE ONE
ARGENTIÈRE TO TRIENT
DISTANCE 12K · ASCENT 953M · TIME 7HRS

STAGE TWO
TRIENT TO CHAMPEX
DISTANCE 15K · ASCENT 1450M · TIME 8HRS

STAGE THREE
CHAMPEX TO CABANE DU MONT FORT
DISTANCE 15K · ASCENT 400M · TIME 7HRS

STAGE FOUR
CABANE DU MONT FORT TO CABANE DE PRAFLEURI
DISTANCE 13K · ASCENT 885M · TIME 7HRS

STAGE FIVE
CABANE DE PRAFLEURI TO AROLLA
DISTANCE 16K · ASCENT 735M · TIME 8HRS

STAGE SIX
AROLLA TO LA SAGE
DISTANCE 18K · ASCENT 500M · TIME 6HRS

STAGE SEVEN
LA SAGE TO ZINAL
DISTANCE 25K · ASCENT 2000M · TIME 9HRS

STAGE EIGHT
ZINAL TO GRUBEN
DISTANCE 12K · ASCENT 300M · TIME 6HRS

STAGE NINE
GRUBEN TO ST. NIKLAUS
DISTANCE 16K · ASCENT 1070M · TIME 8HRS

STAGE TEN
ST. NIKLAUS TO EUROPAHUTTE
DISTANCE 10K · ASCENT 500M · TIME 7HRS

STAGE ELEVEN
EUROPAHUTTE TO ZERMATT
DISTANCE 12K · ASCENT 300M · TIME 6HRS

the DISTANCE **172**k · the ASCENT **10,500**m · the TIME **80**hrs · WEIGHT LOSS **2·5***k

* EAT BREAD · DRINK BEER AND LOOSE WEIGHT!

It's down to
Beautiful
BUTTERMERE...
not quite the Alps though!

Well, it has to be a rocky one to do them justice. I don't think they would be impressed if I chose Binsey! I decide on the Buttermere skyline as I remember it's stony and rocky underfoot, so I head down to Gatesgarth via Borrowdale and Honister Pass.

It's bright and early, and as I cross the car park, cash in hand (£4), a red squirrel bounds across the road and balances on a stone before skipping up the road and out of sight.

A good start, let's hope it continues...

HAYSTACKS FROM GAMBLIN END

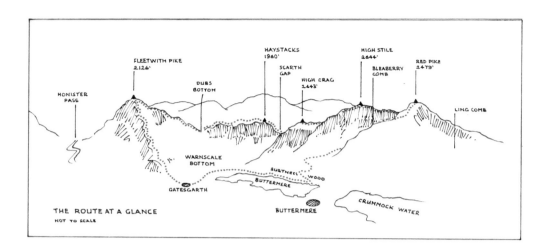

FLEETWITH PIKE 2126'
HONISTER PASS
DUBS BOTTOM
HAYSTACKS 1960'
SCARTH GAP
HIGH CRAG 2443'
HIGH STILE 2644'
BLEABERRY COMB
RED PIKE 2479'
LING COMB
WARNSCALE BOTTOM
GATESGARTH
BURTNESS WOOD
BUTTERMERE
BUTTERMERE
CRUMMOCK WATER

THE ROUTE AT A GLANCE
NOT TO SCALE

follow that squirrel

I FOLLOW THE SQUIRREL UP THE ROAD AND ONTO THE GRASSY FOOT OF FLEETWITH PIKE. WHAT A PATH - IT TURNS OUT TO BE THE BEST OF THE WHOLE RUN. IT'S HANDS-ON-KNEES AND SOMETIMES HANDS-ON-ROCKS AS HEIGHT IS GAINED AND THE PATH TWISTS ITS WAY UP THE WEST RIDGE DIRECTLY TO THE SUMMIT. I SCURRY UP AT A GOOD PACE, LEGS AND LUNGS NOT COMPLAINING YET. A QUICK LOOK BACK DOWN TO BUTTERMERE FROM THE CAIRN REMINDS ME HOW BEAUTIFUL IT IS.

I JOIN A FAINT TRACK, ONE OF THREE LEAVING THE SUMMIT, THAT HEADS DOWN TO DUBBS QUARRY. IT'S A GOOD GRADIENT FOR DOWN-HILL RUNNING, BUT A LITTLE DAMP IN PLACES, SO IT'S WET FEET TIME ALREADY (NO GOOD FOR YOU JENNY!) AS I DROP DOWN TO THE QUARRY AND THE MAIN PATH TO HAYSTACKS.

I'M INTO MY STRIDE AS THE PATH TAKES ME FIRST PAST BLACKBECK TARN AND THEN INOMMINATE TARN ON A GENTLE GRADIENT. WHEN CONDITIONS UNDERFOOT DETERIORATE I HAVE TO WATCH EVERY STEP. SPOT MY FIRST WALKER OF THE DAY HEADING TOWARDS HAYSTACKS' SUMMIT. SOON AFTER I ARRIVE AT THE SOUTH CAIRN AND TIPTOE FROM ONE BOULDER TO ANOTHER TO SAFELY ARRIVE AT THE NORTH CAIRN AND SUMMIT.

HIGH CRAG LOOKS A LONG WAY AWAY, WITH A TOUGH ASCENT UP GAMBLIN END. FIRST THOUGH THERE'S A TRICKY, SLOW DESCENT OVER ROCKS BEFORE CROSSING SCARTH GAP AND ASCENDING SEAT UP STONE STEPS. HERE I REACH GREEN GRASS AND A GENTLER GRADIENT STRETCHING TO THE FOOT OF GAMBLIN END. MY LEGS ARE STILL STRONG AS I CONTINUE RUNNING ALONG THE RIDGE WHILE WATCHING GUYS DESCENDING GAMBLIN END ON THEIR BACKSIDES! I'M HAVING TO CHECK MY STRIDE NOW AS STONES MAKE A REAPPEARANCE THROUGH THE GRASS.

AS I ARRIVE AT THE FOOT OF GAMLIN END A MAN-MADE ROCK STAIRCASE RUNNING ALONGSIDE THE SCREE THAT COVERS THIS SIDE OF HIGH CRAG COMES INTO VIEW. IT'S A HANDS-ON-KNEES JOB NOW; HEAD DOWN AND THINK OF ENGLAND - OR THE COL DE RIEDMATTEN ON THE WAY OVER TO AROLLA IN THE ALPS. I HEAD ONWARDS AS MY CALFS TELL ME THEY'VE HAD ENOUGH AND THE PATH BECOMES LOST BENEATH SHIFTING SCREE, MAKING THE FINAL PUSH TO HIGH CRAG'S SUMMIT TOUGH. I'M PLEASED TO REACH THE SUMMIT CAIRN AND FLAT GROUND.

TIME FOR A BITE TO EAT. NO JANICE BARS TODAY. THIS TIME IT'S BIG JOHN'S FRUIT AND NUT MIX, BROUGHT ALL THE WAY BACK FROM ZERMMAT. CHEERS JOHN, LOOKS GOOD, DOESN'T IT.

I CHECK THE TIME AND RAISE MY EYES TO HIGH STILE, LOOKING IMPRESSIVE IN THE DISTANCE. THERE'S NO PROBLEM ROUTE FINDING - JUST FOLLOW THE IRON POSTS. THE PROBLEM IS STONY UNDERFOOT CONDITIONS THAT REQUIRE FULL CONCENTRATION, ALL THE WAY TO THE SUMMIT CAIRN.

A MULTITUDE OF CAIRNS GREET ME - HOPE I CHOOSE THE RIGHT ONE. CHECK TIME AND SNATCH ANOTHER DRINK. COULD DO WITH YOUR '56' FACTOR SUN CREAM, JENNY, AS MY FACE BEGINS TO FEEL THE EFFECT OF THE LATE MORNING SUN.

RUNNING TOTAL	
DISTANCE	527.85K
TIME	86HRS 45 MINS
ASCENT	97,140 FT
SUMMITS	137

GARNIER AMBRE SOLAIRE

FACTOR 56 NEVER

ADVANCED UVA/UVB PROTECTION

DERMATOLOGICALLY TESTED ON BARRY

...quick!

THE SURROUNDING GROUND IS STILL CHOCK-A-BLOCK WITH ROCKS AND STONES, AND ALTHOUGH THE GRADIENT TO RED PIKE IS QUITE GENTLE, PROGRESS TO ITS SUMMIT IS ONLY STEADY.

I MEET THE SECOND AND THIRD WALKERS OF THE DAY ADMIRING THE VIEW FROM RED PIKE'S SUMMIT, WHERE I PAUSE TO PULL ON A WINDPROOF AS A CHILL WIND BLOWS ACROSS THE RIDGE. WHICH WAY NOW?, I ASK MYSELF. DO I CONTINUE ALONG THE RIDGE DOWN LINGCOMB EDGE TO SCALES? OR DO I HEAD DOWN THE SADDLE TO BLEABERRY TARN? (WHERE'S CHRIS THE GUIDE WHEN YOU NEED HIM?)

I OPT FOR BLEABERRY TARN, BUT IT'S UNBELIEVABLY BAD. EVERYTHING'S LOOSE AND DISINTEGRATING, AND WITH WALKERS NOW ASCENDING FROM BELOW EXTRA CARE AND DILIGENCE IS REQUIRED SO AS NOT TO DISLODGE ANY STONES.

EVENTUALLY I GET ONTO A STRETCH OF REAL SCREE AND SLIDE DOWN ONTO A MAN-MADE PATH LEADING TO THE TARN. SAY HI TO A NUMBER OF PEOPLE TAKING A BREAK ON THE WATER'S EDGE. IT'S 11.30 A.M NOW AND LOADS OF WALKERS ARE STILL ON THEIR WAY UP FROM BUTTERMERE AS I CONTINUE MY DESCENT TO BURTNESS WOOD. THE PATH'S NOT THAT GOOD, GOING FROM ROCK STEPS AND PEAT TO WET GRASS AND SCREE. BUT IT MAKES THINGS INTERESTING, AND I EVENTUALLY REACH THE GATE INTO THE GLOOM OF BURTNESS WOOD. THE PATH REVERTS BACK TO ROCK STEPS – NOW WET AND MOSS-COVERED IN PLACES – NOT GOOD FOR MY TRAINERS, WHICH DON'T GRIP WELL ON WET ROCK.

HOORAY! AT LAST I REACH THE LAKE SHORE FOOTPATH CIRCUMNAVIGATING BUTTERMERE. IT TOOK ME 37 MINUTES TO DESCEND FROM THE SUMMIT AND IT SEEMED NEVER ENDING.

THE WINDPROOF COMES OFF, I TAKE ANOTHER DRINK AND THEN RESUME RUNNING. IT'S A GREAT PATH, AND BUSY ALL THE WAY BACK TO THE FINISH AT GATESGARTH. TOWARDS THE END MY HEEL STARTS TO ACHE, AND MY THOUGHTS TURN TO YOU, HELEN, AND YOUR ACHILLES

TENDON PROBLEMS IN THE ALPS. HOPE THEY HAVE CLEARED UP AND THOSE NEW BOOTS ARE STILL NICE AND COMFY. THERE'S NO GLASS OF BEER WAITING FOR ME AS I FINISH BUT, DARE I SAY IT, BETTER, AN ICE CREAM CART. HOW GOOD IS THAT! SO WITH A SMILE NEARLY AS WIDE AS YOURS, SARAH, I PURCHASE A DOUBLE CORNET OF VANILLA LAKELAND ICE CREAM, SIT ON THE WALL AND DEVOUR IT IN SUPER-QUICK TIME - LIKE MY GLASS OF BEER! MANAGE TO END UP WITH THAT AWFUL HEADACHE THING WHEN YOU EAT SOMETHING COLD TOO QUICK- YOU KNOW WHAT I MEAN, RIGHT?

I STAND TO WALK BACK TO THE CAR AND MY LEGS ARE SO STIFF I COULD DO WITH YOUR MUSCLE ROLLER, JULIA, FOR A QUICK LEG MASSAGE. LITTLE JOHN: FOR THE FIRST TIME I TRIED RUNNING WITH MY MP3 PLAYER RINGING IN MY EARS, SO I HAD THE GOOD COMPANY OF CHRIS REA, NEIL YOUNG, EAGLES JETHRO TULL AND THE GREAT SAM COOKE. I'M SURE YOU'LL HAVE HEARD THEM ALL. FINALLY, TO COMPLETE THE TREKKERS ROLL CALL, SIMON AND CATHERINE, YOU'LL BE PLEASED TO KNOW THE WHOLE RUN WAS COMPLETED IN SHORTS, WITH NO OVER-TROUSERS REQUIRED!

THANKS AGAIN GUYS, AND CHEERS...

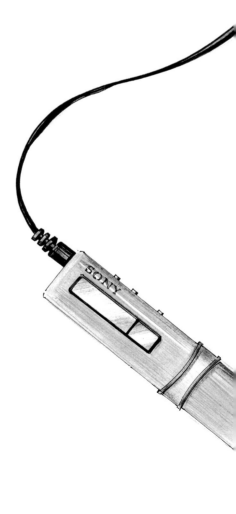

JETHRO TULL CHRIS REA
CHRIS NEIL YO SAM COOKE EAGLES NEIL YOUNG
SAM COOKE
TULL

SONY

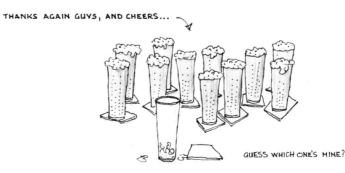

GUESS WHICH ONE'S MINE?

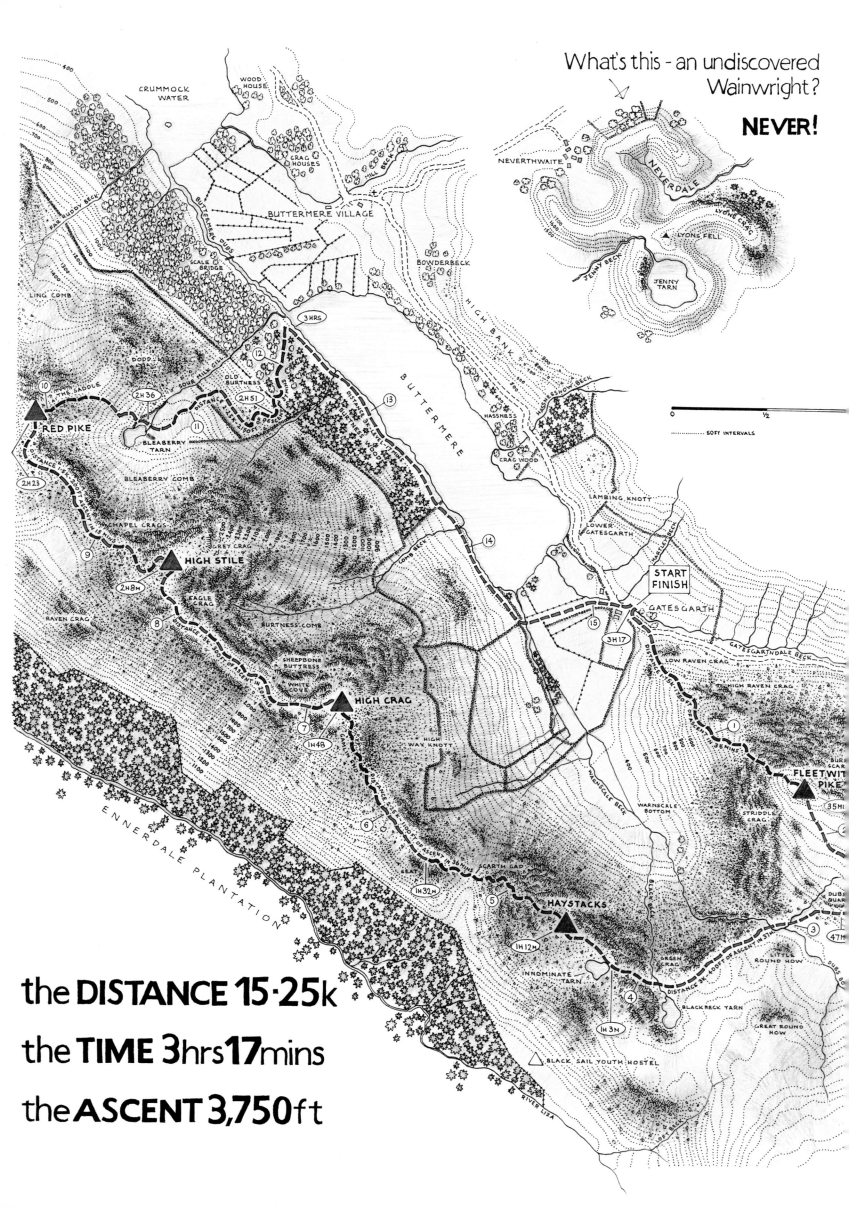

What's this - an undiscovered Wainwright?

NEVER!

the **DISTANCE 15·25**k

the **TIME 3**hrs**17**mins

the **ASCENT 3,750**ft

the CENTRAL fells

No escape this time for Silver How ...

SILVER HOW IS ONE THAT ESCAPED ME ON MY RUN OVER THE LANGDALE PIKES WHEN
I RAN OUT OF STEAM, WATER AND MAP, AND HAD NO CHOICE BUT TO ABORT THE FINAL
SUMMIT. THAT NOW MEANS IT HAS A RUN AND A FULL PAGE ALL TO ITSELF, LUCKY FELL!

I SET OFF FROM THE GARDEN CENTRE ON TARMAC FOR THE FIRST FEW
HUNDRED YARDS. IT'S NICE AND FAST, BUT NEED TO TAKE CARE DODGING THE
TOURISTS AND WALKERS. THROUGH A GATE AND I'M ON THE FELLSIDE,
CLIMBING BETWEEN MOSS-COVERED STONE WALLS LINED
BY TREES BEFORE HEADING ONTO THE
OPEN FELL. I'M RUNNING NICELY AS THE
PATH FOLLOWS THE WALL ONTO HIGHER
GROUND AND MY FRIEND BRACKEN. IT'S NOT A
PROBLEM, THOUGH, AS I TURN OFF RIGHT ON A
GRASS PATH LEADING TO THE FOOT OF A SMALL
SCREE GULLY, WHERE A GOOD STONE STEP
PATH HAS BEEN PUT IN PLACE LEADING
UP TO THE COL.

THE GOING'S EASY AND I'M ENJOYING
THE CHANCE TO ADMIRE THE VIEWS DOWN
TO GRASMERE AND BEYOND. FROM THE
COL A THIN TRACK LEADS UP LEFT,
BOUND FOR THE NEAT LITTLE SUMMIT.

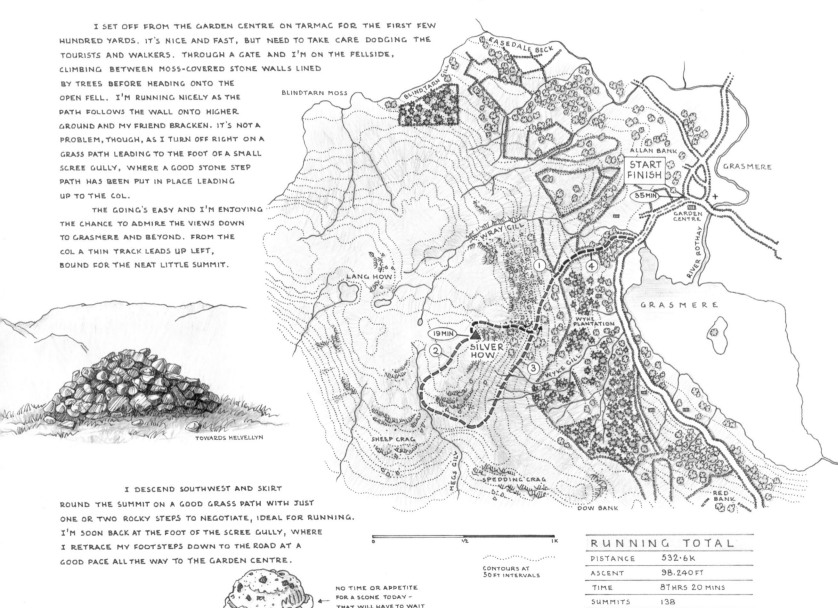

TOWARDS HELVELLYN

I DESCEND SOUTHWEST AND SKIRT
ROUND THE SUMMIT ON A GOOD GRASS PATH WITH JUST
ONE OR TWO ROCKY STEPS TO NEGOTIATE, IDEAL FOR RUNNING.
I'M SOON BACK AT THE FOOT OF THE SCREE GULLY, WHERE
I RETRACE MY FOOTSTEPS DOWN TO THE ROAD AT A
GOOD PACE ALL THE WAY TO THE GARDEN CENTRE.

NO TIME OR APPETITE
FOR A SCONE TODAY -
THAT WILL HAVE TO WAIT
FOR ANOTHER DAY!
I'LL BE BACK!

CONTOURS AT
50 FT INTERVALS

RUNNING TOTAL	
DISTANCE	532·6K
ASCENT	98,240 FT
TIME	87 HRS 20 MINS
SUMMITS	138

DISTANCE 4·75k ASCENT 11,000ft TIME 35mins

the **SOUTHERN** fells

SO IMPRESSIVE,

no, not me...

... as I take on **PIKE O' BLISCO,
COLD PIKE, CRINKLE CRAGS,
BOWFELL** and **ROSSETT PIKE**
while Esk Pike will have to wait
for another day...

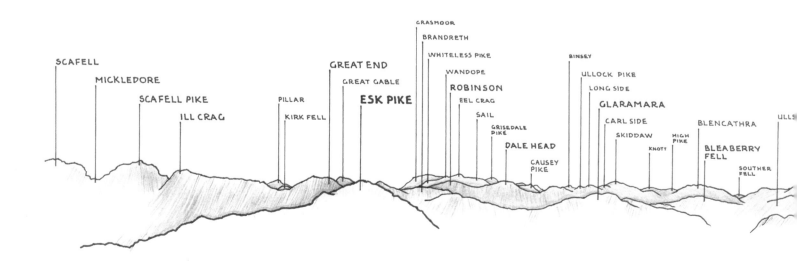

the views!

Into the Old Dungeon Ghyll Hotel. Not for a drink, but to pay for the car park... the drinks will have to wait. Back to the car and what a magnificent sight in front of me: the head of the Langdale Valley, rugged grey rock faces silhouetted against the cloudless blue sky - absolutely stunning.

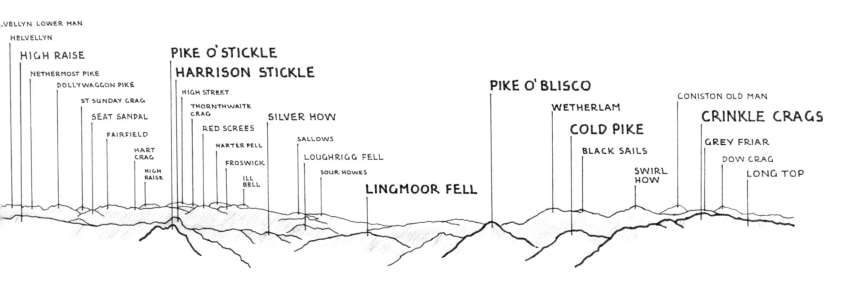

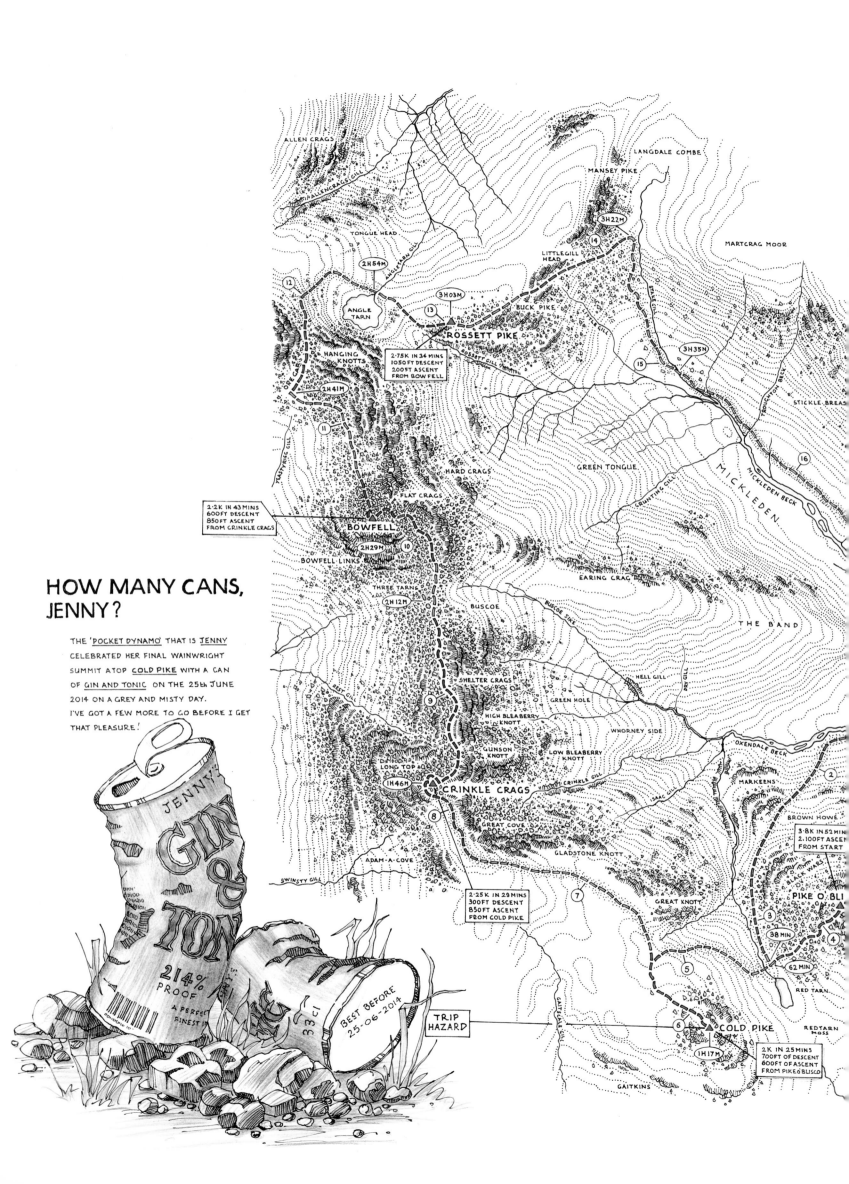

HOW MANY CANS, JENNY?

THE 'POCKET DYNAMO' THAT IS JENNY
CELEBRATED HER FINAL WAINWRIGHT
SUMMIT ATOP COLD PIKE WITH A CAN
OF GIN AND TONIC ON THE 25th JUNE
2014 ON A GREY AND MISTY DAY.
I'VE GOT A FEW MORE TO GO BEFORE I GET
THAT PLEASURE!

ALLEN CRAGS

LANGDALE COMBE

MANSEY PIKE

TONGUE HEAD

MARTCRAG MOOR

LITTLEGILL HEAD

3H22M
14

2H54M

12

3H03M
13

BUCK PIKE

ROSSETT PIKE

3H35N
15

HANGING KNOTTS

2·75K IN 34 MINS
1050FT DESCENT
200FT ASCENT
FROM BOW FELL

STICKLE-BREA

2H41M

11

GREEN TONGUE

16

HARD CRAGS

MICKLEDEN

FLAT CRAGS

2·2K IN 43 MINS
600FT DESCENT
850FT ASCENT
FROM CRINKLE CRAGS

BOWFELL

2H29M
10

BOWFELL LINKS

EARING CRAG

THREE TARNS

2H 12M

BUSCOE

BUSCOE SIKE

THE BAND

SHELTER CRAGS

GREEN HOLE

HELL GILL

PIG GILL

9

HIGH BLEABERRY KNOTT

WHORNEY SIDE

GUNSON KNOTT

LOW BLEABERRY KNOTT

OXENDALE BECK

LONG TOP

CRINKLE GILL

MARKEENS

2

1H46M

CRINKLE CRAGS

BROWN HOWE

8

ISAC GILL

3·8K IN 52 MIN
2,100FT ASCEN
FROM START

GREAT COVE

BLACK WARS

ADAM-A-COVE

GLADSTONE KNOTT

PIKE O' BLI

SWINSTY GILL

7

GREAT KNOTT

3

38 MIN

4

62 MIN

2·25K IN 29 MINS
300FT DESCENT
850FT ASCENT
FROM COLD PIKE

5

RED TARN

GAITHAM GILL

REDTARN MOSS

TRIP
HAZARD

6

COLD PIKE

1H17M

2K IN 25MINS
700FT OF DESCENT
600FT OF ASCENT
FROM PIKE O BLISCO

GAITKINS

JENNY'S

GIN & TON

214% PROOF

A PERFECT
FINEST I

33 CL

BEST BEFORE
25-06-2014

the DISTANCE
18k
the TIME
3hrs 55mins
the ASCENT
4,600ft

IT'S HOT, SO I PACK TWO WATER BOTTLES AND HEAD OFF DOWN THE LANE TOWARDS STOOL END FARM. I CHECK THE TIME, THEN JOIN THE RED TARN PATH, BUSY WITH WALKERS HEADING MY WAY. I CRACK ON AT A REASONABLE PACE, SCURRYING UP AND OVER THE TERRAIN AND THEN BACK INTO RUNNING PROPER AS THE PATH LEVELS OFF SLIGHTLY NEAR THE PIKE O'BLISCO - COLD PIKE INTERSECTION. I TURN LEFT FOR PIKE O'BLISCO AND CHASE DOWN A FEW MORE WALKERS PICKING THEIR WAY THROUGH THE ROCKY OUTCROPS.

MY HEAD'S DOWN AND MY BROW'S DRIPPING AS I REACH THE ROCKY PERCH OF THE SUMMIT. HAVE A QUICK LOOK AROUND; CHECK THE TIME AND TAKE A WELL-EARNED DRINK. MY LEGS ARE FEELING GOOD AS I HEAD BACK DOWN. AT RED TARN I CHECK THE TIME, THEN CONTINUE STRAIGHT ACROSS ON A CLEAR PATH TO CRINKLE CRAGS. MAN-MADE ROCK STEPS LEAD TO A FAINT GRASS TRACK ACROSS TO COLD PIKE.

COLD PIKE

THERE ARE THREE OR FOUR CAIRNS ON THE SUMMIT OF COLD PIKE, ALL WITH GREAT VIEWS. I GRAB A BITE TO EAT AND RUMMAGE AROUND FOR ANY CANS OF GIN AND TONIC LEFT OVER FROM JENNY'S CELEBRATIONS - NO CHANCE!

I GAZE OVER TO CRINKLE CRAGS, MY NEXT PORT OF CALL. THE PATH LOOKS GOOD, SO OFF I GO, RETRACING MY STEPS DOWN TO THE MAIN PATH AND ONTO THE FOOT OF THE FIRST CRINKLE.

I'VE BEEN RUNNING ON GOOD PATHS FOR THE MOST PART SO FAR. NOW THE FUN BEGINS... WITH NO MORE GENTLE GRADIENTS, NO CLEAR PATH, AND NO GRASS - JUST ROCKS, ROCKS AND MORE ROCKS; GREAT IF YOU'RE WALKING, BUT NOT IF YOU'RE RUNNING. I TAKE THE EASY WAY AROUND THE BAD STEP AND I'M SOON ON THE TOP OF THE SECOND AND HIGHEST CRINKLE, LONG TOP.

CRINKLE CRAGS - LONG TOP. BOWFELL IN THE DISTANCE

I TAKE A SUMMIT DRINK. THAT'S ONE BOTTLE DOWN ALREADY AND I'VE ONLY BEEN GOING ONE HOUR FORTY FIVE. NEXT COMES THE RIDGE TRAVERSE TO THREE TARNS. IT TAKES TOTAL CONCENTRATION TO NEGOTIATE THE CHAOTIC PILES OF STONES AND ROCKS STREWN ACROSS THE LANDSCAPE. FOLLOWING THE 'PATH' OVER THE UPS AND DOWNS, THE TWISTS AND TURNS, PROVES CHALLENGING BUT FUN, AND I'M PLEASED TO ARRIVE AT THREE TARNS IN ONE PIECE.

BOWFELL SUMMIT, MINUS HUMAN REMAINS!

THERE ARE PLENTY OF WALKERS HERE, HEADING FROM THE BAND UP BOWFELL LIKE ME. I SCRAMBLE UP TO THE LARGE SUMMIT CAIRN WITH THEM. THE TOP STONE IS COVERED IN SOMEONE'S ASHES, WHICH ARE NOW STUCK TO MY SWEATY PALM... NICE. I MOVE AWAY, WIPE MY HAND, CHECK THE TIME AND ADMIRE THE VIEWS ACROSS TO THE SCAFELLS, WHICH ARE SILHOUETTED AGAINST A BRIGHT BLUE CLOUD-FREE SKY; A PERFECT MOMENT ON THE FELLS.

YUK!

ENOUGH OF THIS. I'VE GOT A RUN TO FINISH, THOUGH I DO ENVY ALL THE WALKERS SAT ENJOYING THIS PERFECT MOMENT AS I RUN FROM THE SUMMIT ALL THE WAY TO ORE GAP ON A GOOD PATH AVOIDING MOST OF THE ROCKY TERRAIN.

I DROP DOWN TO ANGLE TARN AND JOIN THE ESK HAUSE PATH. PAST THE TARN I HEAD UP SOME STONE STEPS ONTO A GRASS PATH TO MY FINAL SUMMIT, ROSSETT PIKE.

I DRINK MY LAST DROP OF WATER AND TRY TO LOCATE A PATH FROM THE SUMMIT OVER TO STAKE PASS. FIND A VERY INDISTINCT TRACK AND GO WITH IT, EVENTUALLY REACHING THE STAKE PASS PATH AFTER A TRICKY KILOMETRE. I PICK UP THE PACE ON THE DESCENT TO THE BRIDGE. I'VE NOW BEEN GOING OVER THREE-AND-A-HALF HOURS IN SCORCHING SUNSHINE AND I'M STARTING TO WILT A LITTLE AS I HIT THE HOME STRAIGHT BACK TO THE PUB.

IT TAKES ME TWENTY NEVERENDING MINUTES TO REACH THE PUB, WHERE I BUY TWO PINTS OF SODA AND LIME, SIT OUTSIDE IN THE SHADE AND NOTICE THE SUMMIT OF BOWFELL WEARING A PURE WHITE CLOUD LIKE A FEATHER BOA. BEAUTIFUL! A GREAT DAY ON THE FELLS.

RUNNING TOTAL	
DISTANCE	550·6K
ASCENT	102,840FT
TIME	91HRS 15MINS
SUMMITS	143

the NORTH WESTERN fells

An early morning jaunt...

takes me over RANNERDALE KNOTTS & WHITELESS PIKE

EARLY TO BED AND EARLY TO RISE... I'M OUT OF THE CARAVAN AND ON THE ROAD BY SIX FIFTEEN AND OVER WHINLATTER TO CRUMMOCK WATER FOR MY FIRST FELL OF THE DAY, RANNERDALE KNOTTS.

THERE'S NOT A SOUL IN SIGHT AS I SET OFF FROM THE CAR. IT'S STRAIGHT UP FROM THE START ON A PRETTY STEEP INCLINE WITH NO RESPITE AND LOTS OF HANDS-ON-KNEES REQUIRED. BY THE TIME I REACH THE SUMMIT I'M PUFFING LIKE AN OLD MAN - OH I AM ONE!

A DELIGHTFUL RIDGE PATH HAS ME RUNNING EAST FOLLOWING LONG BANK JUST AS THE SUN POKES ITS HEAD UP FROM BEHIND ROBINSON. THE GOING'S EASY TO THE COL AT THE FOOT OF WHITELESS PIKE AND THE MAIN PATH FROM BUTTERMERE.

IT'S UPHILL NOW ON A GRASS PATH THROUGH ENCROACHING BRACKEN TOWARDS WHITELESS BREAST - NOT NEARLY AS STEEP AS IT LOOKED FROM AFAR - AND I'M ABLE TO RUN VIRTUALLY NON-STOP ALL THE WAY TO THE SUMMIT. IT'S NOT MUCH OF A SUMMIT OR A CAIRN, THOUGH, SO I CHECK THE TIME AND RETRACE MY FOOTSTEPS BACK TO THE COL.

THE DESCENT IS GREAT ALL THE WAY DOWN RANNERDALE TO SQUAT BECK ON A GRASS PATH SHARED ONLY WITH GRAZING SHEEP. I FEEL I COULD RUN FOR HOURS, BUT WITHIN MINUTES I'M BACK AT THE CAR, JOB DONE.

I ENJOYED THAT. IT'S ONLY TWENTY PAST EIGHT AND IT'S LIKE I'M THE ONLY PERSON ALIVE.

THAT'S TWO MORE SUMMITS IN THE BAG, WHICH NOW LEAVES ONLY ONE MORE NORTH WESTERN FELL TO DO, SO IT'S INTO THE CAR AND OVER HONISTER TO GRANGE FOR MY NEXT SUMMIT, CASTLE CRAG.

RUNNING TOTAL	
DISTANCE	557·85 K
TIME	92 HRS 31 MINS
ASCENT	104,900 FT
SUMMITS	145

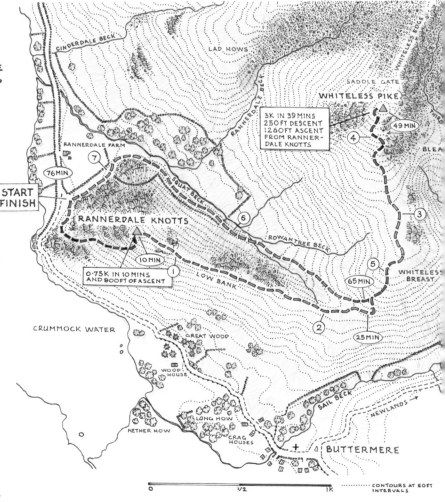

last of the **NORTH WESTERN** fells

It's all trees and slate -

on a banana-powered quickie up Castle Crag's scree...

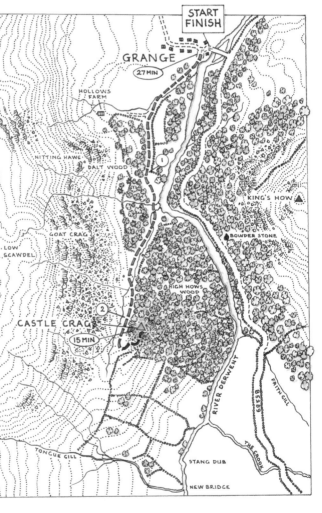

I MANAGE TO EAT A BANANA ON THE WAY OVER FROM BUTTERMERE AND ARRIVE IN GRANGE RECHARGED AND READY FOR ACTION. THERE'S STILL NOT A SOUL IN SIGHT, SO I GET TO CHOOSE MY SPOT TO PARK THE CAR FOR A CHANGE.

IT'S NINE O'CLOCK AS I SET OFF THROUGH THE VILLAGE TOWARDS HOLLOWS FARM BEFORE TURNING LEFT ONTO THE OLD QUARRY ROAD TO RIGGHEAD QUARRY AND HONISTER. THERE ARE TWO LONELY TENTS IN A FIELD ON MY LEFT, BUT ON MY RIGHT NO SIGN OF LIFE IN THE DALT WOOD YURTS. LEGS FEELING GOOD. **MUST BE THE BANANA!**

AS I REACH THE RIVER THE PATH DETERIORATES INTO A RIVER OF STONES, SOME OF WHICH HAVE BEEN PUT TO USE BY SOMEONE WHO HAS BUILT VARIOUS ARTISTIC CAIRNS IN THE SHALLOWS OF THE DERWENT... NICE ONE.

I'M STILL RUNNING AT A GOOD PACE AS THE PATH CLIMBS TOWARDS THE TURNOFF FOR CASTLE CRAG. OFF I GO, UP AND ACROSS THE SPOILS OF SLATE BEFORE REACHING THE PLEASANT TOP COMPLETE WITH A PLAQUE DECORATED WITH LITTLE WOODEN CROSSES. MAKES ME THINK HOW LUCKY AM I. NOTE THE TIME AND DESCEND BACK ACROSS THE SLATE, DOWN TO THE MAIN RIGGHEAD PATH AND ON HARD BACK TO GRANGE. THERE'S NO CAKE FOR ME TODAY - AT ONLY NINE THIRTY-ISH IT'S TOO EARLY. BUT I DO SEE MY FIRST WALKERS OF THE DAY AS I DRIVE BACK TO THE CARAVAN... AND MY PORRIDGE.

ANOTHER BOOK BITES THE DUST!

RUNNING TOTAL	
DISTANCE	562·85k
TIME	92 HRS 58 MINS
ASCENT	105,600 FT
SUMMITS	146

the DISTANCE **5**k - the TIME **27** mins - the ASCENT **700** ft

the **WESTERN** and **SOUTHERN** fells

What is this life if
we have no time to stand

...& WHERE BETTER TO STAND
THE SUMMIT OF

Next stop please...

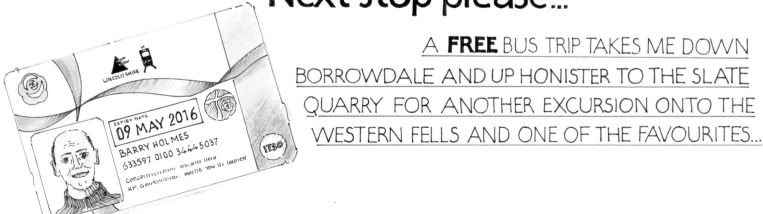

A **FREE** BUS TRIP TAKES ME DOWN
BORROWDALE AND UP HONISTER TO THE SLATE
QUARRY FOR ANOTHER EXCURSION ONTO THE
WESTERN FELLS AND ONE OF THE FAVOURITES...

ull of care,
nd stare...
William Henry Davies

ND STARE THAN

Gable

Barry Holmes:
too tired to stand
and stare?

I START THE RUN CROSSING THE QUARRY YARD, THEN HEAD UP
THE FENCE CLIMBING THE STEEP END OF GREY KNOTTS. THERE'S NO TROUBLE
ROUTE FINDING TODAY – I JUST FOLLOW THE FENCE – BUT IT'S STILL STIFF
GOING FROM THE START ON A MAN-MADE PATH WITH ONLY A FEW
PATCHES OF BOG AND ROCK OUTCROPS TO NEGOTIATE.

THERE'S NOT A CLOUD IN THE SKY AS I ARRIVE AT THE ROCKY SUMMIT.
IT'S BEEN A GLORIOUS WEEK FOR WEATHER SO FAR, WITH SHARP FROSTS
OVERNIGHT AND NON-STOP SUNSHINE DURING THE DAY. TODAY IS
NO EXCEPTION.

THE VIEWS AHEAD ARE IMPRESSIVE, WITH GREAT GABLE
CLOSER THAN I IMAGINED, BASE BROWN TOO. BUT FIRST IT'S ONTO
BRANDRETH OVER EASY TERRAIN. I'M SOON ON THE 'SUMMIT',
TRYING TO DECIDE WHICH ONE OF THE NUMEROUS CAIRNS IS
THE TRUE SUMMIT. I VISIT ALL OF THEM AS I CAN'T DECIDE, BEFORE
HEADING OFF TOWARDS GREEN GABLE.

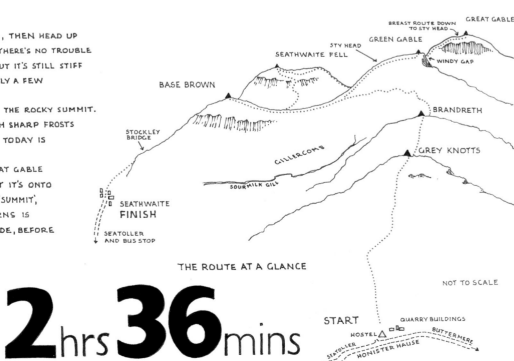

THE ROUTE AT A GLANCE

NOT TO SCALE

2hrs 36mins
INCLUDES TIME TO STAND AND STARE

IT'S A CLEAR PATH OVER EASY GROUND UNTIL A LEFT TURN AROUND THE HEAD OF GILLERCOMB TAKES ME OVER DIFFICULT ROCKS AND BOULDERS FOR A WHILE UNTIL I REACH THE MAIN PATH COMING UP FROM GILLERCOMB TO GREEN GABLE. I PICK UP SPEED NOW AS I HEAD DOWNHILL TOWARDS BASE BROWN, AND WITH ONLY A SLIGHT INCLINE TO THE SUMMIT IT'S EASY GOING ALL THE WAY TO THE CAIRN.

I RETRACE MY FOOTSTEPS TOWARDS GREEN GABLE AND CONTINUE RUNNING AS THE PATH STEEPENS, LEGS FEELING GOOD AS I PUSH ON PAST A FEW WALKERS. GREEN GABLE IS SOON CONQUERED, THEN IT'S DOWN TO WINDY GAP AND THE CLIMB TO GREAT GABLE.

all by myself

IT'S NOT LONG BEFORE HANDS ON KNEES ARE NEEDED - YOU KNOW WHAT IT'S LIKE! A CAREFUL JOG THEN TAKES ME TO THE SUMMIT CAIRN, WHICH I HAVE ALL TO MYSELF. THE VIEWS ARE MAGNIFICENT IN EVERY DIRECTION AS I TREAT MYSELF TO A MAGICAL MOMENT OR TWO AND AN ENERGY BAR BEFORE DRAGGING MYSELF AWAY FOR THE DESCENT DOWN THE BREAST ROUTE TO STY HEAD. IT'S A LONG DESCENT ON AN ENGINEERED PATH THAT REQUIRES ONE HUNDRED PER CENT CONCENTRATION TO AVOID USE OF THE STRETCHER AT THE BOTTOM OF THE PATH.'

from one book to another

THERE ARE A FEW MORE FOLK ABOUT AS I REACH THE STRETCHER BOX SAFE AND SOUND. THEY'RE ALL GOING IN DIFFERENT DIRECTIONS. MINE IS STRAIGHT ON TOWARDS SPRINKLING TARN AS I CROSS FROM ONE BOOK TO ANOTHER FOR THE FIRST TIME. SEATHWAITE FELL'S MY NEXT OBJECTIVE. IT'S ONE I'VE NEVER VISITED BEFORE SO I HOPE THERE'S A PATH. THERE IS - OF SORTS; A FAINT TRACK ON LONG GRASS GIVING GOOD RUNNING, AND A PLEASANT CHANGE FOR THE FEET AFTER THE ROCKS AND STONES OF GREAT GABLE.

I CONTINUE AS THE PATH MEANDERS AROUND HILLOCKS AND TARNS AND IT'S NOT LONG BEFORE I SPOT THE CAIRN ON THE NORTH 'SUMMIT'- CLEARLY NOT THE HIGHEST POINT OF THE FELL. I KEEP MY EYES PEELED FOR A PATH DOWN TO STOCKLEY BRIDGE, BUT THERE'S NOT A SIGN OF ONE ANYWHERE. NOW AT THE SUMMIT, I CHECK THE TIME AND GRAB A BAR - THANKS JANICE! - THEN SPOT A THIN TROD HEADING WEST. THE GRADIENT STEEPENS AND THE PATH BECOMES INDISTINCT AS PROGRESS SLOWS TO A STEADY DESCENT ALL THE WAY TO THE MAIN PATH.

BACK ONTO A GOOD PATH AND I RUN OVER STOCKLEY BRIDGE THEN CONTINUE FULL STEAM AHEAD TO SEATHWAITE AND THE END OF MY RUN.

IT HAS BEEN A LOT EASIER AND SHORTER IN TIME THAN I THOUGHT IT WAS GOING TO BE - THOROUGHLY ENJOYABLE - AND WITH THE SUN STILL SHINING I STROLL BACK TO SEATOLLER AND THE NUMBER SEVENTY EIGHT BUS BACK TO KESWICK WITH A SMILE ON MY FACE.

NOT REQUIRED TODAY
THANK GOODNESS

START
HONISTER HAUSE
BUS STOP

1·25K IN 20 MINS WITH 1,150FT OF ASCENT FROM BUS STOP

GREY KNOTTS
①
20 MIN

1K IN 7 MINS WITH 100FT OF ASCENT FROM GREY KNOTTS

②
27 MIN
BRANDRETH

49 MIN
BASE BROWN

2·25K IN 22 MINS WITH 550FT OF ASCENT FROM BRANDRETH

1·5K IN 19 MINS WITH 620FT OF ASCENT FROM BASE BROWN

③
④
⑤
BLACKMOOR POLS

GREEN GABLE
⑥
1H 8 MIN

0·5K IN 13 MINS WITH 500FT OF ASCENT FROM GREEN GABLE

GREAT GABLE
1H 21 MIN

⑦

1·25K IN 22 MINS WITH 1,350FT OF DESCENT FROM GREAT GABLE

STY HEAD
1H 43 M
⑧

FINISH
2H 36 M

2·9K IN 34 MINS WITH 1,500 FT OF DESCENT FROM SEATHWAITE FELL

⑫

⑪

2H 17 M
⑩

SEATHWAITE FELL
2H 2 M

2K IN 19 MINS WITH 470FT OF ASCENT FROM STY HEAD

⑨

SPRINKLING TARN

RUNNING TOTAL

DISTANCE	575·60 K
TIME	95 HRS 34 MINS
ASCENT	108,990 FT
SUMMITS	152

NEW YEARS EVE
1999

SAW THE NEW MILLENNIUM IN, TOGETHER WITH JANICE AND MY BROTHER PETER, CAMPED NEXT TO SPRINKLING TARN IN AN OLD VANGO FORCE TEN TENT WITH NO SLEEPING BAGS OR DOWN JACKETS, IN FREEZING CONDITIONS. ONE ROCKET WAS LET OFF AT THE MIDNIGHT HOUR.
A NIGHT NEVER TO BE FORGOTTEN!

the DISTANCE 12·75k   the ASCENT 3,390ft

the **FAR EASTERN** fells

My first and probably last ascent
of <u>WANSFELL</u>

WANSFELL SUMMIT - BORING

IT'S A LATE AFTERNOON RUN FOR A CHANGE.
IT'S ALSO SCORCHING, EVEN THOUGH THE CAR
WAS FROZEN OVER THIS MORNING, THANK YOU
HIGH PRESSURE.

NO PRESSURE ON ME TODAY, THOUGH, AS IT'S PENRITH
PARK RUN TOMORROW SO TODAY A SHORT RUN WILL DO
NICELY THANK YOU. I PARK THE CAR AT THE PUB THEN HEAD
BACK UP THE ROAD AND THROUGH THE WOODEN GATE AT THE
START OF NANNY LANE. THE LANE CONTINUES ON LOOSE
STONES BETWEEN WALLS FOR SOME DISTANCE UNTIL THE
STONES ARE REPLACED BY GRASS AND MUD AT A GENTLER
GRADIENT.

I'M STILL RUNNING AS I CLIMB A LADDER STILE ONTO
THE OPEN FELL TO JOIN A FLATTENED COTTON GRASS PATH
SNAKING ITS WAY AROUND NUMEROUS HILLOCKS EN ROUTE
TO THE SUMMIT.

THE SMALL CAIRN ON THE GRASS MOUND DOESN'T
MAKE FOR A VERY INTERESTING SUMMIT, AND I DON'T
HANG ABOUT; I'M DRIPPING IN SWEAT AND IT'S BECOMING
HOTTER BY THE MINUTE. I HEAD ALL THE WAY BACK
THE SAME WAY TO THE LOOSE STONES, WHERE I MOVE
ONTO A NARROW GRASS VERGE TO MAINTAIN A GOOD
PACE ALL THE WAY BACK TO THE CAR.

I'M HAPPY WITH MY TIME - TWENTY ONE MINUTES
UP AND TWELVE MINUTES DOWN. I FEEL LIKE I'M GETTING
MY FITNESS BACK. SHAME IT'S COMING TO THE
END OF MY FELL RUNNING SEASON.
PENRITH PARK RUN HERE I COME...

RUNNING TOTAL	
DISTANCE	580·60K
TIME	96 HRS 7 MINS
ASCENT	110,090 FT
SUMMITS	153

the DISTANCE **5**k - the TIME **33** mins - the ASCENT **1,100** ft

last of the **NORTHERN** fells

My first and definitely last ascent
of <u>BINSEY</u>

Sorry Binsey, but it's fifteen minutes of nothing much

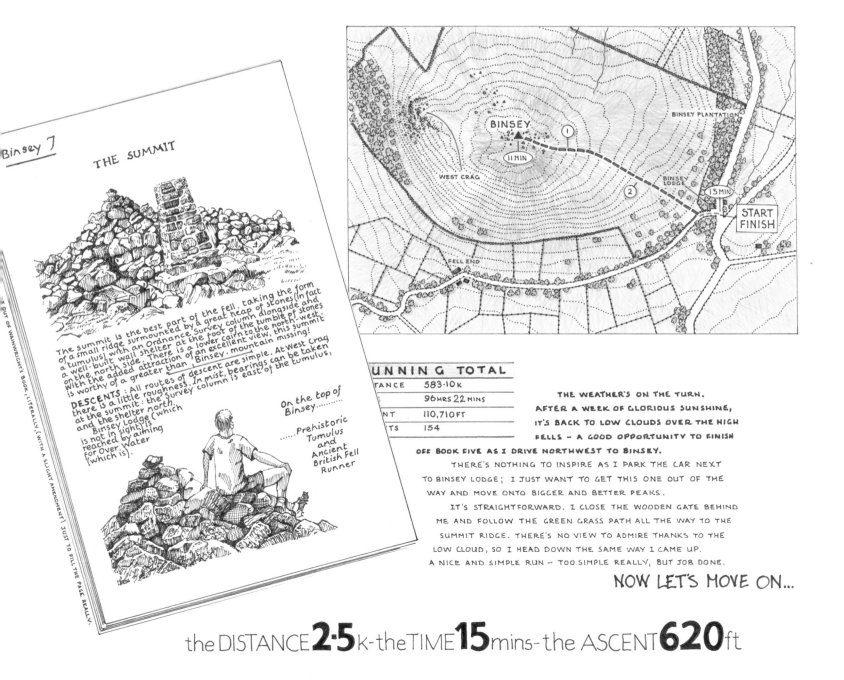

Binsey 7

THE SUMMIT

The summit is the best part of the fell, taking the form of a small ridge surmounted by a great heap of stones (in fact a tumulus) with an Ordnance Survey column alongside and a well-built wall shelter at the foot of the tumble of stones on the north side. There is a lower cairn to the north-west, with the added attraction of an excellent view, this summit is worthy of a greater than 'Binsey' mountain missing!

DESCENTS : All routes of descent are simple. At West Crag there is a little roughness. In mist, bearings can be taken at the summit : the Survey column is east of the tumulus, and the shelter north.
Binsey Lodge (which is not in sight) is reached by aiming for Over Water (which is).

On the top of Binsey........

......Prehistoric Tumulus and Ancient British Fell Runner

OUT OF WAINWRIGHT'S BOOK, LITERALLY (WITH A SLIGHT AMENDMENT) JUST TO FILL THE PAGE REALLY.

UNNING TOTAL	
TANCE	583·10k
	96HRS 22 MINS
NT	110,710FT
TS	154

THE WEATHER'S ON THE TURN. AFTER A WEEK OF GLORIOUS SUNSHINE, IT'S BACK TO LOW CLOUDS OVER THE HIGH FELLS — A GOOD OPPORTUNITY TO FINISH OFF BOOK FIVE AS I DRIVE NORTHWEST TO BINSEY.

THERE'S NOTHING TO INSPIRE AS I PARK THE CAR NEXT TO BINSEY LODGE; I JUST WANT TO GET THIS ONE OUT OF THE WAY AND MOVE ONTO BIGGER AND BETTER PEAKS.

IT'S STRAIGHTFORWARD. I CLOSE THE WOODEN GATE BEHIND ME AND FOLLOW THE GREEN GRASS PATH ALL THE WAY TO THE SUMMIT RIDGE. THERE'S NO VIEW TO ADMIRE THANKS TO THE LOW CLOUD, SO I HEAD DOWN THE SAME WAY I CAME UP. A NICE AND SIMPLE RUN — TOO SIMPLE REALLY, BUT JOB DONE.

NOW LET'S MOVE ON...

the **CENTRAL** fells

A godsend!

as dense hill fog drifts in

over <u>ULLSCARF</u> and <u>GREAT CRAG</u>

ON THE NUMBER 78 BUS AGAIN I DISEMBARK AT ROSTHWAITE ALONG WITH A TROOP OF RAMBLERS ALSO HEADING FOR THE FELLS.

BIG GREY CLOUDS GATHER OVER THE SCAFELLS AS I CHASE BLUE SKY EAST TO GREENUP EDGE. I'VE NEVER WALKED OVER ULLSCARF BEFORE AND UNDERSTAND IT'S QUITE FEATURELESS, SO I'M GLAD FOR THE CLEAR VISIBILITY AS I HEAD OFF ON A GOOD PATH ALONGSIDE STONETHWAITE BECK TOWARDS GREENUP EDGE.

THERE'S EASY RUNNING ALL THE WAY TO SMITHYMIRE ISLAND, WHEN THE PATH REDUCES IN WIDTH AND STARTS TO INCREASE IN GRADIENT. BUT I'M STILL RUNNING - MUST BE GETTING FITTER - UNTIL I REACH THE WATERFALL ON GREENUP GILL AND ROCK STAIRCASE ALONGSIDE LINING CRAG, WHEN HANDS-ON-KNEES MAKE AN APPEARANCE.

PHEW!

I TAKE A QUICK LOOK BACK DOWN THE VALLEY AND OVER TO THE HIGH TOPS OF BORROWDALE, NOW SHROUDED IN DARK GREY CLOUD. THEN I SET OFF FROM THE TOP OF LINING CRAG ACROSS NO-MAN'S-LAND - TOUGH GRASS AND BOGS - TOWARDS ULLSCARF, WHEN FROM OVER THE RIDGE THICK HILL FOG BLOWS IN FROM FAR EASEDALE.

TIME TO CHECK MY POSITION ON THE MAP AS ALL AROUND ME IS ENGULFED IN THE THICKEST OF HILL FOG

...IT'S SOD'S LAW... JUST WHEN I NEED GOOD VISIBILITY! I CONTINUE AHEAD, BUT IT'S DIFFICULT TO MAINTAIN A STRAIGHT COURSE OVER THE BOGS AND ROCK OUTCROPS. AS LUCK WOULD HAVE IT I SPOT A METAL POST THROUGH THE GLOOM... THEN ANOTHER... AND ANOTHER AS A PATH STARTS TO FORM ALONGSIDE ME THAT LEADS ON TO THE SUMMIT CAIRN - COMPLETE WITH METAL POST.

I CONTINUE STRAIGHT ON FOLLOWING THE POSTS, AND WHILE I KNOW I NEED TO HEAD OFF LEFT, THERE'S NO CLEAR PATH YET, JUST A FEW GRASSY TRACKS LEADING OFF INTO THE GLOOM. THEN THE FOG DISAPPEARS AS QUICKLY AS IT CAME...

HALLELUJAH!

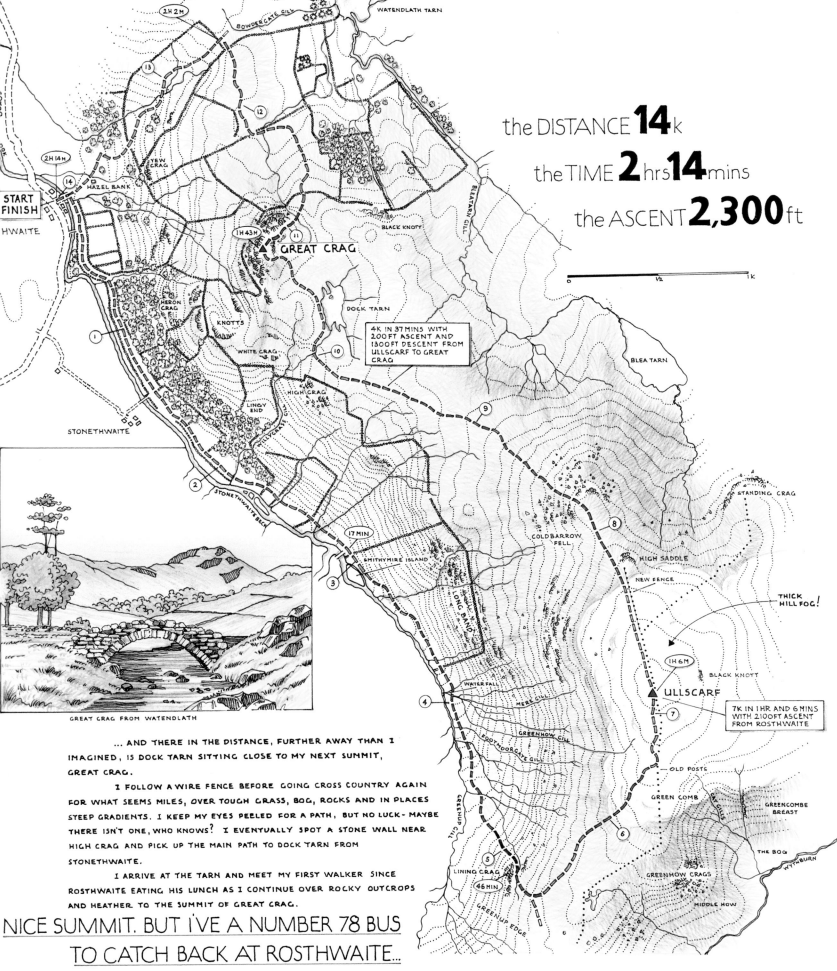

the DISTANCE **14**k

the TIME **2**hrs**14**mins

the ASCENT **2,300**ft

4K IN 37 MINS WITH 200FT ASCENT AND 1300FT DESCENT FROM ULLSCARF TO GREAT CRAG

7K IN 1HR AND 6 MINS WITH 2100FT ASCENT FROM ROSTHWAITE

THICK HILL FOG!

GREAT CRAG FROM WATENDLATH

... AND THERE IN THE DISTANCE, FURTHER AWAY THAN I IMAGINED, IS DOCK TARN SITTING CLOSE TO MY NEXT SUMMIT, GREAT CRAG.

I FOLLOW A WIRE FENCE BEFORE GOING CROSS COUNTRY AGAIN FOR WHAT SEEMS MILES, OVER TOUGH GRASS, BOG, ROCKS AND IN PLACES STEEP GRADIENTS. I KEEP MY EYES PEELED FOR A PATH, BUT NO LUCK - MAYBE THERE ISN'T ONE, WHO KNOWS? I EVENTUALLY SPOT A STONE WALL NEAR HIGH CRAG AND PICK UP THE MAIN PATH TO DOCK TARN FROM STONETHWAITE.

I ARRIVE AT THE TARN AND MEET MY FIRST WALKER SINCE ROSTHWAITE EATING HIS LUNCH AS I CONTINUE OVER ROCKY OUTCROPS AND HEATHER TO THE SUMMIT OF GREAT CRAG.

NICE SUMMIT. BUT I'VE A NUMBER 78 BUS TO CATCH BACK AT ROSTHWAITE...

I GRAB A CHOC BAR AND DESCEND ON ROCKS AND ROCK STEPS TOWARDS WATENDLATH. I'VE BEEN RUNNING NON-STOP NOW SINCE LINING CRAG AND MY LEGS STILL FEEL GOOD AS I LEAVE THE MAIN PATH AND HEAD OVER TO PUDDINGSTONE BANK AND ROSTHWAITE. IT'S SLOW GOING OVER BOG TO PUDDINGSTONE BANK AND I START TO REALISE I'M NOT GOING TO MAKE THE BUS... AND AT THIS TIME OF YEAR THEY ONLY RUN ONCE EVERY HOUR SO A LONG WAIT LOOKS TO BE ON THE CARDS!

THE MAIN WATENDLATH TO ROSTHWAITE PATH IS EASY GOING ALL THE WAY DOWN TO THE BUS STOP, BUT I STILL ARRIVE FIVE MINUTES LATE. SO IT'S ON WITH A WARM TOP AND OUT WITH MY THUMB. THE THIRD CAR TO COME ALONG STOPS AND OFFERS ME A LIFT.

GET LUCKY THE YOUNG MAN, MANAGER OF THE ROYAL OAK IN ROSTHWAITE — AND A FELL RUNNER - DELIVERS ME SAFE AND SOUND BACK TO KESWICK. CHEERS MATE.

RUNNING TOTAL

DISTANCE	597·10 K
TIME	98 HRS 36 MINS
ASCENT	113,010 FT
SUMMITS	156

the **FAR EASTERN** fells

Come so far, still so far to go...

Not today, though, as we stretch our legs over THE TONGUE

IT'S 2016. I'VE TICKED OFF 153 SUMMITS SO FAR, LEAVING 61 TO GO. THAT MEANS I NEED TO GET MY FINGER OUT IF I'M TO FINISH THE CHALLENGE ON MY 66th BIRTHDAY.

JANICE TAGS ALONG TODAY JUST FOR FUN... IT'S A STEEP DOWNHILL START ON A TARMAC SURFACE ALONG ING LANE BEFORE THE ROAD LEVELS OFF OVER ING BRIDGE. THEN IT'S EASY RUNNING ALONGSIDE FARMLAND AND GREEN PASTURES TO HAGG BRIDGE. OVER THE BRIDGE AND WE FINALLY HEAD OFF ROAD TOWARDS THE HAGG GILL PATH.

JANICE IS DOING WELL AS WE CONTINUE ALONG THE SIDE OF THE GILL TO THE FAR END OF THE RIDGE AND THEN UP THE FIRST INCLINE OF THE DAY ON A GRASS PATH.

I WAIT FOR JANICE AT THE TOP BEFORE WE SET OFF ALONG THE DELIGHTFUL RIDGE PATH COMPLETE WITH LITTLE DIPS AND MOUNDS TO TEST OUR LEGS AND LUNGS. IT'S NOT LONG BEFORE WE REACH THE SUMMIT (WAIT FOR JANICE - NOT LONG) AND ADMIRE THE VIEWS.

THE DESCENT IS NOT JANICE'S FAVOURITE BIT!! ROCK OUTCROPS SLOW US DOWN AND A VERY BOGGY BIT JUST BEFORE RE-JOINING THE HAGG GILL PATH MEAN WE RUN THE LAST COUPLE OF KILOMETRES BACK TO THE CAR WITH WET FEET.

RUNNING TOTAL	
DISTANCE	606.3 K
TIME	99 HRS 45 MINS
ASCENT	113,900 FT
SUMMITS	158

56 STILL TO GO

CORRECTION:- THE SUMMIT RUNNING TOTAL HAS BEEN -1 IN TOTAL SINCE RUN No. 41. BUT BACK ON TRACK.

DISTANCE **9·2** k

TIME **1** hr **9** mins

ASCENT **890** ft

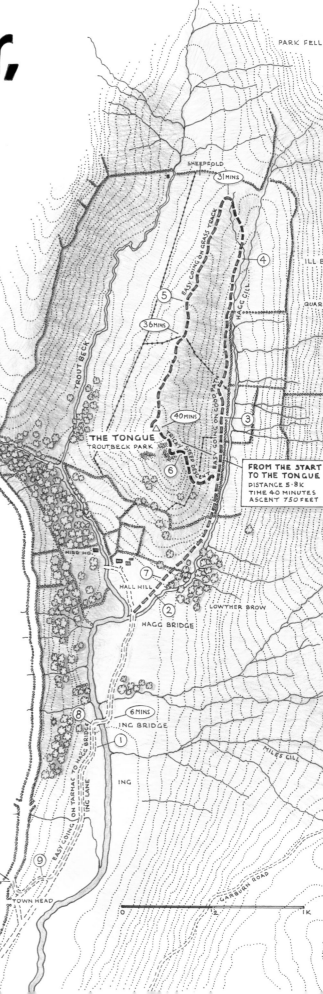

PARK FELL

SHEEPFOLD
31 MINS

EASY GOING ON GRASS TRACK

ILL B

HAGG GILL

QUAR

4

5

36 MINS

40 MINS

3

THE TONGUE
TROUTBECK PARK

FROM THE START
TO THE TONGUE
DISTANCE 5·8 K
TIME 40 MINUTES
ASCENT 750 FEET

TROUT BECK

WOUNDALE BECK

6

HAGG HO

7

HALL HILL

LOWTHER BROW

2

HAGG BRIDGE

8

6 MINS
ING BRIDGE

1

ING LANE

ING

MILES GILL

EASY GOING ON TARMAC TO HAGG BRIDGE

START FINISH

9

69 MINS

GARBURN ROAD

TOWN HEAD

TROUTBECK

MISTAKES,
I've maid a few

...AS YOU MAY HAVE NOTICED ALREADY!

SO WHY ARE THEY THERE? WELL, WITHOUT GOING INTO TECHNICALITIES, IT'S
VIRTUALLY IMPOSSIBLE TO MAKE A CORRECTION TO FULL COLOUR ARTWORK WITHOUT
IT STANDING OUT LIKE A SORE THUMB, SO MOST MISTAKES HAVE BEEN LEFT IN THE
ARTWORK IN THE HOPE THEY MAY BE RECTIFIED IN THE PRODUCTION PROCESS FURTHER
DOWN THE LINE - IF THIS BOOK EVER GOES TO PRINT!

IF I'D ONLY PRODUCED IT IN BLACK AND WHITE, AS WAINWRIGHT DID,
THEN ANY MISTAKES COULD HAVE BEEN RECTIFIED QUITE SIMPLY AND
NO ONE WOULD HAVE BEEN THE WISER...

WHICH GOT ME THINKING... IF HE HAD PRODUCED HIS GUIDES
IN FULL COLOUR, WHAT WOULD THEY LOOK LIKE? SO I'VE DRAWN A FEW...
(A RAINY DAY IN THE CARAVAN).

CUTE AREN'T THEY?

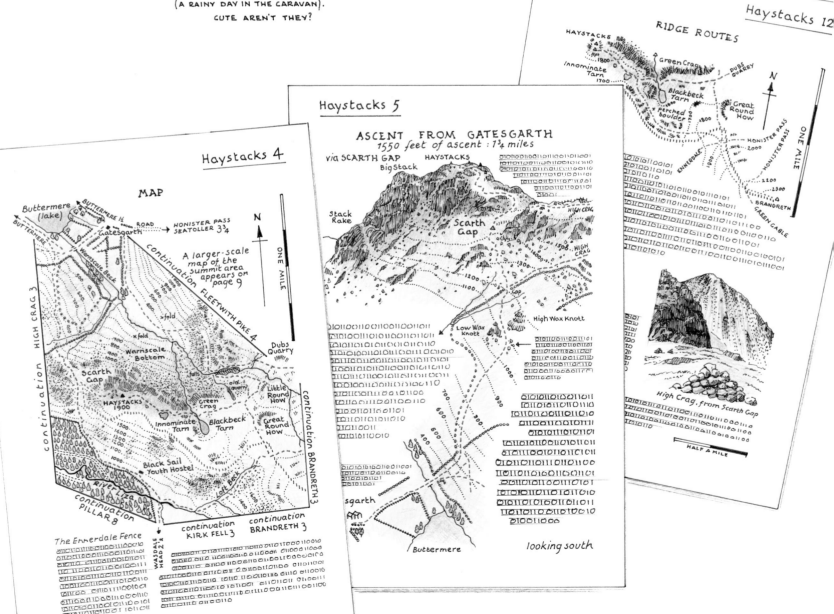

the SOUTHERN fells

Easy on the eyes but hard on the feet

ROSTHWAITE FELL, GLARAMARA, ALLEN CRAGS and ESK PIKE

easy going at first

IT'S GLORIOUS WEATHER; CLEAR BLUE SKY AND NO WIND AS I LEAVE THE BUS STOP AT SEATOLLER AND HEAD UP THE ROAD TO MOUNTAIN VIEW. THROUGH A GATE IN THE HEDGE, ACROSS A FIELD, OVER A BRIDGE AND I'M ON THE OPEN FELL. A THIN PATH THEN HEADS TO COMB GILL. IT'S EASY GOING UNTIL I REACH A FAINT TRACK FOR TARN AT LEAVES, WHEN HANDS-ON-KNEES MAKE AN APPEARANCE. BY THE TIME I REACH THE SUMMIT PLATEAU I'M WET THROUGH WITH SWEAT.

ROSTHWAITE FELL: EASY ON THE EYE

I NIP UP THROUGH THE ROCKS TO THE PLEASANT LITTLE SUMMIT OF BESSYBOOT. I'VE NEVER BEEN THIS WAY BEFORE, SO I TAKE A MINUTE TO CHECK THE LIE OF THE LAND AND SEE IF THERE'S A PATH LEADING OVER TO GLARAMARA. THERE IS, BUT IT LOOKS LIKE THE NEXT FEW KILOMETRES COULD BE INTERESTING...

a long hard slog

I'M NOT WRONG! THE INTER-MITTENT TRAIL IS RUNNABLE ALL THE WAY TO COMBE DOOR WITH LITTLE HEIGHT GAIN AS IT THREADS ITS WAY ALONG THE LANGSTRATH SIDE OF THE FELL. THE SUMMIT OF MY NEXT FELL, GLARAMARA, COMES INTO VIEW WAY UP ON THE RIGHT. IT LOOKS LIKE IT'S GOING TO BE A LONG, HARD SLOG TO THE TOP...

IT IS! I PLOD ON TO THE BOULDER SLOPES BEFORE A FINAL PUSH TO THE SUMMIT. MY LEGS AND FACE ARE NOW BURNING, SO I REFRESH AND REFUEL... AND INWARDLY CONGRATULATE MYSELF FOR ARRIVING AT GLARAMARA AFTER FORTY-FIVE MINUTES OF EFFORT OVER TRICKY GROUND... NOT ONE FOR A MISTY DAY THAT'S FOR SURE!

last bit of hard graft

I'M BACK ON FAMILIAR GROUND NOW, BUT MY LEGS AND FEET ARE STILL BURNING AS I PICK OFF SUBSIDIARY SUMMITS BEFORE THE BIG CLIMB UP TO ALLEN CRAGS, WHERE I GLANCE OVER TO MY NEXT AND FINAL SUMMIT, ESK PIKE.

THE LAST BIT OF HARD GRAFT IS ABOUT TO COME UP, I TELL MYSELF, AS I HEAD UP TO ESK HAUSE BEFORE THE ASCENT TO ESK PIKE'S ROCKY SUMMIT. MY FEET ARE TENDER NOW AS I PARK MY BUM ON A ROCK AND TAKE TIME FOR A BITE TO EAT AND DIGEST THE VERY IMPRESSIVE VIEWS.

hate them!

I SHAKE THE LEGS OUT THEN RUN BACK DOWN TO THE SHELTER AND INTO THE SHADE, AT LAST, OF GREAT END BEFORE DESCENDING TO GRAINS GILL AND ALL THOSE MAN-MADE SLAB STEPS. HATE THEM! THEY'RE GOOD FOR ASCENDING – BUT NOT DESCENDING AT SPEED WITH TENDER FEET. I AVOID AS MANY AS POSSIBLE, AND AM GLAD TO REACH STOCKLEY BRIDGE AND THE FINAL SMOOTH FINISH TO SEATHWAITE.

MAN-MADE STEPS, HARD ON THE FEET!

DISTANCE **15·6**k TIME **3**hrs**11**mins ASCENT **3,600**ft

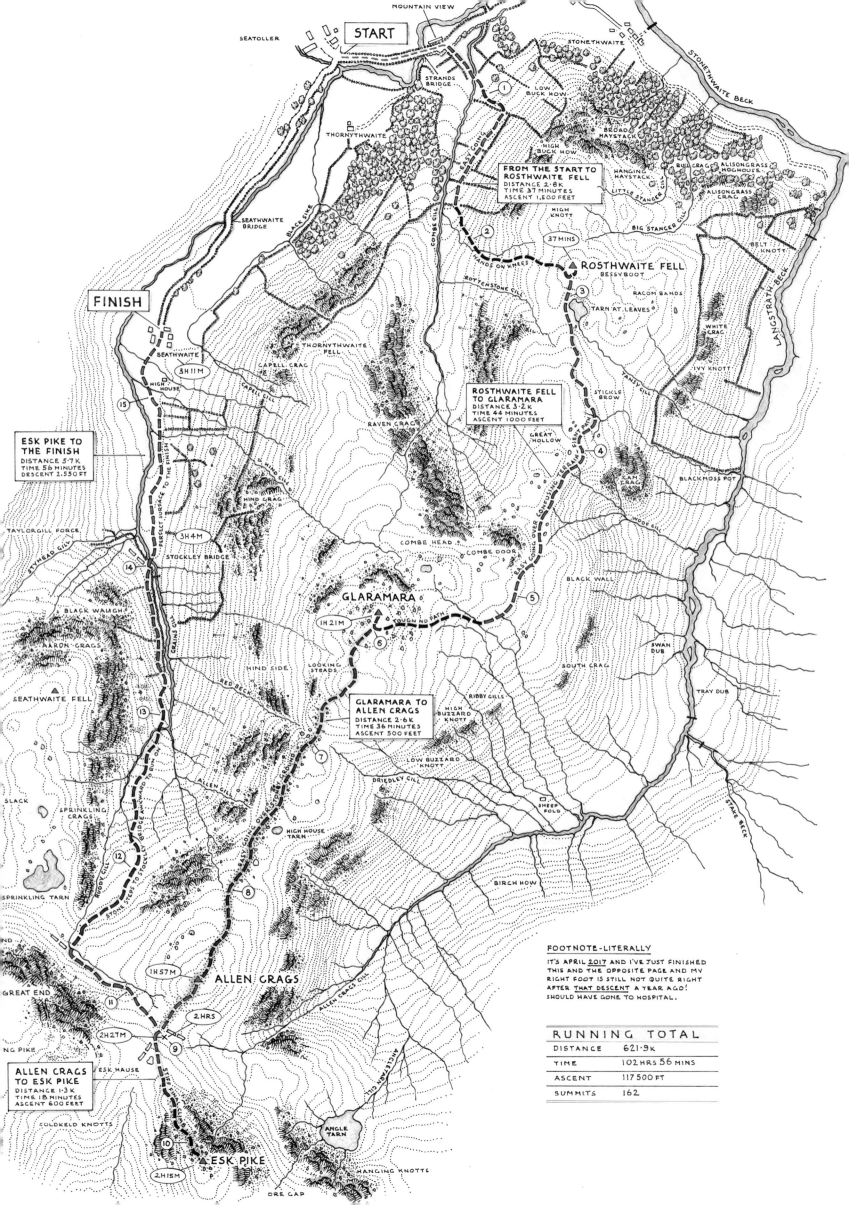

SEATOLLER

MOUNTAIN VIEW

START

STONETHWAITE

STRANDS BRIDGE

THORNYTHWAITE

LOW BUCK HOW

BROAD HAYSTACK

HIGH BUCK HOW

BULL CRAG ALISONGRASS HOGHOUSE

HANGING HAYSTACK

LITTLE STANGER GILL

ALISONGRASS CRAG

FROM THE START TO ROSTHWAITE FELL
DISTANCE 2·8K
TIME 37 MINUTES
ASCENT 1,500 FEET

HIGH KNOTT

BIG STANGER

BELT KNOTT

①

②

HANDS ON KNEES

37 MINS

ROSTHWAITE FELL
BESSYBOOT

ROTTENSTONE GILL

TARN AT LEAVES

RACOM BANDS

③

WHITE CRAG

SEATHWAITE BRIDGE

BLACK SIKE

FINISH

SEATHWAITE

3H11M

THORNYTHWAITE FELL

CAPELL CRAG

RAVEN CRAG

STICKLE BROW

IVY KNOTT

ROSTHWAITE FELL TO GLARAMARA
DISTANCE 3·2K
TIME 44 MINUTES
ASCENT 1000 FEET

GREAT HOLLOW

CAM CRAG

④

BLACKMOSS POT

ESK PIKE TO THE FINISH
DISTANCE 5·7K
TIME 56 MINUTES
DESCENT 2,550 FT

HIGH HOUSE

⑮

CAPELL GILL

HIND GILL

HIND CRAG

3H4M

COMBE HEAD

COMBE DOOR

BLACK WALL

⑤

TAYLORGILL FORCE

STYHEAD GILL

STOCKLEY BRIDGE

GLARAMARA

1H21M

⑥

SWAN DUB

TRAY DUB

⑭

BLACK WAUGH

HIND SIDE

LOOKING STEADS

RED BECK

SOUTH CRAG

AARON CRAGS

SEATHWAITE FELL

⑬

GLARAMARA TO ALLEN CRAGS
DISTANCE 2·6K
TIME 36 MINUTES
ASCENT 500 FEET

RIBBY GILLS

HIGH BUZZARD KNOTT

⑦

SLACK

SPRINKLING CRAGS

ALLEN GILL

HIGH HOUSE TARN

LOW BUZZARD KNOTT

DRIEDLEY GILL

⑫

⑧

SPRINKLING TARN

BIRCH HOW

GREAT END

1H57M

ALLEN CRAGS

SHEEP FOLD

STAKE BECK

⑪

2 HRS

NG PIKE

2H27M

⑨

ALLEN CRAGS TO ESK PIKE
DISTANCE 1·3K
TIME 18 MINUTES
ASCENT 600 FEET

ESK HAUSE

ALLEN CRAGS GILL

ALLENCRAGS GILL

FOOTNOTE-LITERALLY
IT'S APRIL 2017 AND I'VE JUST FINISHED
THIS AND THE OPPOSITE PAGE AND MY
RIGHT FOOT IS STILL NOT QUITE RIGHT
AFTER THAT DESCENT A YEAR AGO!
SHOULD HAVE GONE TO HOSPITAL.

COLDKELD KNOTTS

ANGLE TARN

⑩

ESK PIKE

2H15M

HANGING KNOTTS

ORE GAP

RUNNING TOTAL	
DISTANCE	621·9K
TIME	102 HRS 56 MINS
ASCENT	117500 FT
SUMMITS	162

the **WESTERN** fells

Just me, a fence and a pipit

as I fly over

GAVEL FELL, **BLAKE FELL** and

BURNBANK FELL

I'VE GOT THREE MORE 'VIRGIN' FELLS TODAY. AFTER THE LAST RUN MY FEET ARE READY FOR PLENTY OF GRASS - NOT ROCK AND STONES.

IT'S OVERCAST WITH A COOL BREEZE - PRETTY GOOD CONDITIONS FOR A RUN AS I SET OFF UP THE FARM ROAD TOWARDS **HIGH NOOK FARM**. IT'S A HIVE OF ACTIVITY AS I PASS THROUGH, WITH FATHER AND SON (A TODDLER AGED ABOUT 3 DRESSED IN OVERALLS - CUTE) SORTING SHEEP AND LAMBS OUT. WHAT A LIFE; HARD BUT SPECIAL.

I PRESS ON THROUGH THE FARM GATE TO THE OPEN FELL ON A CLEAR PATH TOWARDS **HIGH NOOK TARN** THEN VEER OFF, RIGHT, ON A PATH HEADING FOR SOME ZIGZAGS IN THE DISTANCE. IT'S **HANDS-ON-KNEES** UP THE ZIGZAGS UNTIL EASIER GROUND IS REACHED ABOVE HIGH NOOK BECK, THEN BACK TO EASY RUNNING ALL THE WAY TO THE FENCE, OVER THE STILE AND UP TO THE SUMMIT OF **GAVEL FELL**.

a new running companion

IT'S BEEN ALL GRASS AND HEATHER SO FAR, SO MY FEET ARE HAPPY AS I HEAD BACK TO THE STILE, WHERE I MEET A **PIPIT** PERCHED ON A FENCE POST. OFF HE FLIES TO THE NEXT POST... AND THE NEXT... AS HE LEADS ME UP THE STEEPISH SLOPE TO **BLAKE FELL**.

DOWNHILL I RUN, THROUGH AND AROUND A FEW **BOGGY PATCHES** REQUIRING DETOURS AWAY FROM THE FENCE - AND MY NEW RUNNING COMPANION, THE PIPIT. IT'S STILL EASY GOING ALL THE WAY TO THE 'SUMMIT' OF **BURNBANK FELL**, AND IT FEELS GOOD TO BE GETTING A STRETCH OF RUNNING IN.

TIME TO SAY FAREWELL TO THE PIPIT AS I CROSS THE FENCE AND START MY DESCENT TO LOWESWATER. IT'S EASY GOING AND GIVES ME A CHANCE TO ADMIRE THE VIEWS INSTEAD OF LOOKING DOWN AT THE PATH UNTIL THE FINAL STEEP SECTION DOWN TO THE **TERRACE PATH** ABOVE **HOLME WOOD**.

THE WIDE TERRACE PATH CUT INTO THE SIDE OF THE FELL IS A DELIGHT. I'M RELUCTANT TO LEAVE IT AS I HEAD THROUGH

A GATE INTO THE WOODS AND A TARMAC FARM ROAD AT **WATERGATE FARM** THAT LEADS BACK TO THE FINISH AT **MAGGIE'S BRIDGE**. PLENTY OF RUNNING FOR THE OLD LEGS TODAY, AND HARDLY ANY ROUGH GROUND, SO...

happy feet!

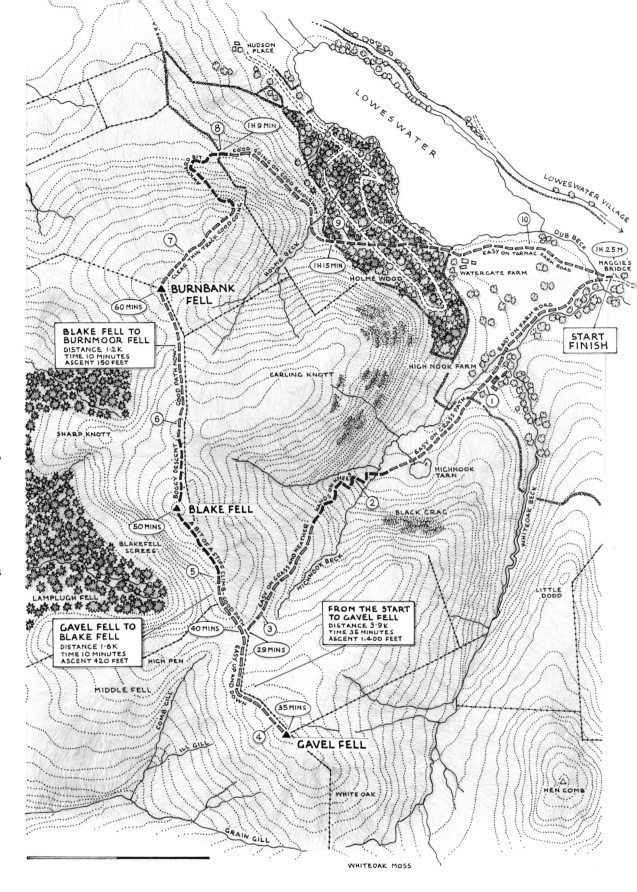

BLAKE FELL TO BURNMOOR FELL
DISTANCE 1·2 K
TIME 10 MINUTES
ASCENT 150 FEET

GAVEL FELL TO BLAKE FELL
DISTANCE 1·6 K
TIME 10 MINUTES
ASCENT 420 FEET

FROM THE START TO GAVEL FELL
DISTANCE 3·9 K
TIME 35 MINUTES
ASCENT 1,400 FEET

RUNNING TOTAL	
DISTANCE	632·4 K
TIME	104 HRS 21 MINS
ASCENT	119,470 FT
SUMMITS	165

10·5k 1h 25mins 1,970ft

the **FAR EASTERN** fells

An upside down
version of the
KENTMERE HORSESHOE
turns out to be

the
toughest

DISTANCE **24·7**k TIME **4**hrs **26**mins ASCENT **4,775**ft

MARDALE ILL BELL
TO HAWESWATER
DISTANCE 3K
TIME 40 MINUTES
DESCENT 1,700 FEET

START
FINISH

MARDALE HEAD

HAWESWATER

BLEA WATER

HIGH STREET

BLEA WATER CRAG

MARDALE ILL BELL

4H 26MIN

MARDALE BECK

24

4H 11MIN

SMALL WATER BECK

21

THRESHTHWAITE
MOUTH

23

SMALL
WATER

GATESGARTH BECK

1

HARTER FELL GULLY

THORNTHWAITE
CRAG

20

SMALL WATER
CRAG

22

BLACK JOHN
HOLE

BLEATHWAITE
CRAG

NAN BIELD PASS

3H 58MIN

3H 46MIN

2·0 MINS

PARK FELL HEAD

GAVEL
CRAG

FROSWICK TO
MARDALE ILL BELL
DISTANCE 3K
TIME 36 MINUTES
ASCENT 410 FEET

HARTER FELL

3

2

ADAM SEAT

WANDER SCAR

LINGMELL END

40 MINS

START TO
HARTER FELL
DISTANCE 3·5K
TIME 40 MINUTES
ASCENT 1,750 FEET

WREN GILL

GREENGROVE
FOLDS

4

19

RIVER KENT

LINGMELL GILL

DRYGROVE GILL

STEEL RIGG

3H 10MIN

FROSWICK

BAND KNOTTS

BROWN
HOWE

STEEL PIKE

ILL BELL TO
FROSWICK
DISTANCE 1·1K
TIME 16 MINUTES
ASCENT 285 FEET

LEADS
HOWE

KENTMERE
RESERVOIR

SMALLTHWAITE
KNOTT

5

RAVEN CRAG

OVER COVE

HARTER FELL TO
KENTMERE PIKE
DISTANCE 2K
TIME 14 MINUTES
ASCENT 150 FEET

KENTMERE PIKE

BROW CRAGS

18

54 MINS

ILL BELL

2H 54MIN

RAINSBORROW COVE

QUARRIES

WHETHER
FOLD

6

YOKE TO ILL BELL
DISTANCE 1K
TIME 11 MINUTES
ASCENT 300 FEET

HIGH MERE GREAVE

STEEL RIGG

KILLSTONE GILL

HAGG GILL

17

RESERVOIR COTTAGE

STAR CRAG

TONGUE SCAR

HALLOW BANK
QUARTER

KENTMERE PIKE TO
SHIPMAN KNOTTS
DISTANCE 1·9K
TIME 14 MINUTES
ASCENT 80 FEET

RAINSBORROW
CRAG

YOKE

2H 43MIN

KENTMERE CHURCH
TO YOKE
DISTANCE 4·9K
TIME 62 MINUTES
ASCENT 1,800 FEET

RIVER KENT

GOAT SCAR

7

RIVER SPRINT

SHIPMAN KNOTTS

16

SKEEL GILL

BRYANT'S GILL

CRAG QUARTER

11

1H 8MIN

one, so far...

OVEREND

8

ROWANTREE
KNOTTS

HALLOW
BANK

BROCKSTONES

WRAY
CRAG

15

CASTLE CRAG

PIKED HOWES

COWSTY KNOTTS

STILE END

BUCK
CRAG

EWE CRAGS

KENTMERE
VILLAGE

HIGH LANE

1H 21MIN

9

GARBURN PASS

10

GARBURN
NOOK

2H 13MIN

14

13

KENTMERE
HALL

THE
NOOK

12

1H 41MIN

NUNNERY BECK

SALLOWS

HALL GILL

GREEN QUARTER

SHIPMAN KNOTTS TO
KENTMERE CHURCH
DISTANCE 4·3K
TIME 33 MINUTES
DESCENT 1,400 FEET

LOWFIELD LANE

10

DIFFERENT STYLE
DIFFERENT SCALE

0   ½   1K

500-800 FEET   1700-2000 FEET

800-1100 FEET   2000-2300 FEET

1100-1400 FEET   2300-2600 FEET

1400-1700 FEET   2600-2900 FEET

what to do

I SET OFF TO HAWESWATER IN GOOD CONDITIONS - BLUE SKY AND HIGH CLOUD - BUT ON ARRIVAL AT THE LAKE HEAD CAR PARK THICK, LOW CLOUD HAS MOVED IN, CLOAKING ALL THE FELLS. THESE ARE NOT IDEAL CONDITIONS FOR RUNNING THE KENTMERE HORSESHOE. WHAT DO I DO? HANG BACK AND SEE IF IT CLEARS? CALL IT A DAY AND RETURN TO PENRUDDOCK? OR JUST GO FOR IT? I DECIDE ON THE LATTER AND SET OFF UP GATESCARTH PASS, RUNNING ALL THE WAY TO THE ZIGZAGS, WHERE I CAN'T SEE A THING.

eerie

I REACH THE TOP OF THE PASS WITH NO GREAT EFFORT, WHERE I BEAR RIGHT ONTO LITTLE HARTER FELL. IT'S STEEP GOING AT FIRST, ON A CLEAR PATH, EASING AS I REACH THE FENCE. I FOLLOW IT TO THE FIRST CAIRN AND THEN MY FIRST SUMMIT OF THE DAY, HARTER FELL. THE DENSE MIST GIVES THE WHOLE SUMMIT AN EERIE ATMOSPHERE AND I'M PLEASED I HAVE A FENCE TO ACCOMPANY ME ONTO KENTMERE PIKE. MY LEGS FEEL GOOD, THE GOING IS EASY AND THANKS TO THE FENCE ROUTE FINDING TO THE PIKE IS A DODDLE. AS THE FENCE CHANGES TO A WALL I ARRIVE AT THE SUMMIT CAIRN.

follow my nose

I STILL CAN'T SEE A THING AND THE TERRAIN IS NOT STRAIGHTFORWARD, BUT I FOLLOW MY NOSE AND EVENTUALLY PICK UP A FAINT TRACK THAT LEADS TO SHIPMAN KNOTTS.

A MORE DISTINCT BUT STEEP PATH DESCENDS TO THE KENTMERE - SADGILL PATH, WHERE I STEP OUT OF THE GLOOM AND SPOT KENTMERE VILLAGE WAY DOWN IN THE VALLEY BELOW.

ON THE MAIN PATH NOW I HEAD TOWARDS THE VILLAGE AT A GOOD PACE - SO GOOD IN FACT THAT I MISS THE FOOTPATH DOWN TO THE VILLAGE. I CONTINUE DOWN LOWFIELD LANE AND THEN DOUBLE BACK INTO KENTMERE.

last bite to eat

ONLY ONE HOUR FORTY- ONE TO GET TO KENTMERE CHURCH; I'M HAPPY WITH THAT IN THESE CONDITIONS. I EAT MY LAST BIT OF FOOD AND REALISE I SHOULD HAVE PACKED A LOT MORE!

nearly lost!

reassurance required

THERE'S NO SIGN OF THE CLOUD LIFTING AND NO SIGN OF ANY LANDMARKS EITHER, SO I CHECK THE MAP TO REASSURE MYSELF ABOUT THE NEXT SECTION TO SHIPMAN KNOTTS. I STICK WITH THE WALL 'TIL THE PATH WANDERS OFF INTO THE GLOOM, WHEN MORE MAP READING IS REQUIRED.

BACK INTO THE GLOOM NOW AS I START MY ASCENT OF GARBURN PASS AND THE LONG DRAG TO THE SUMMIT OF YOKE. MY LEGS ARE STARTING TO FEEL A LITTLE TIRED AND THERE'S STILL A LOT OF RUNNING TO GO.

ROUTE FINDING'S EASY ON THE CLEAR RIDGE PATH AS I PASS OVER YOKE, ILL BELL AND FROSWICK. I COULD REALLY DO WITH SOMETHING TO EAT AT THIS POINT TO RAISE MY SPIRITS AND ENERGY LEVELS AS THE CLOUD BECOMES EVEN THICKER, WHICH COULD MAKE THE NEXT SECTION VERY INTERESTING! MARDALE ILL BELL HERE I COME... I HOPE.

compass out

I DESCEND TO THE OLD METAL BOUNDARY POST IN REAL 'PEA SOUP' CONDITIONS. IT'S NOT LOOKING GOOD, SO OFF WITH THE RUCKSACK AND OUT WITH THE COMPASS. IT'S THE FIRST TIME IT'S BEEN NECESSARY ON MY FELL RUNS. I TAKE A BEARING, THEN FOLLOW THE ARROW INTO THE MURK... AND HIT THE PATH JUST BEFORE THE MARDALE ILL BELL SUMMIT... PHEW!

definitely lost!

gone

I CHECK THE TIME AND DECIDE TO HAVE A DRINK BEFORE HEADING DOWN TO NAN BIELD... NO WATER BOTTLE! IT OBVIOUSLY FELL OUT WHEN I TOOK MY RUCKSACK OFF TO RUMMAGE AROUND FOR THE COMPASS. SO I'VE NO FOOD NOW, AND NO DRINK, AND NO WATER BOTTLE - LET'S HOPE IT GOES TO A GOOD HOME.

THE WIND'S GETTING UP, SO I RUN DOWN TO NAN BIELD SHELTER PRONTO. MY LEGS ARE WRECKED AS I REACH THE SHELTER, SO I SPEND A COUPLE OF MINUTES WITH THREE BLOKES ALSO SHELTERING FROM THE WIND - AND THE FIRST PEOPLE I'VE COME ACROSS SINCE THE START OVER FOUR HOURS AGO.

AT LAST I CAN MAKE OUT SMALL WATER DOWN BELOW, SO OFF I GO WITH A TENTATIVE DESCENT ON A ROUGH PATH DOWN TO THE TARN. AS I REACH THE TARN I FORCE MY LEGS BACK INTO RUNNING MODE AND PUSH ON AS HARD AS MY WEARY LEGS ALLOW ALL THE WAY TO THE FINISH.

THAT WAS A TOUGH, TOUGH RUN FOR ME, NOT HELPED BY THE LACK OF FOOD AND DRINK, OR THE CHALLENGING WEATHER CONDITIONS, SO WELL DONE ME!

GLUG! GLUG! GLUG!

STOP OFF AT BAMPTON VILLAGE SHOP FOR CAN OF POP AND BOTTLE OF WATER - BLISS!!!

RUNNING TOTAL	
DISTANCE	657.1K
TIME	108 HRS 47 MINS
ASCENT	124,245 FT
SUMMITS	172

the SOUTHERN fells

It's down to BLACK CRAG for
pastures new
and cow pats galore!

I SPEND THE MORNING WATCHING THE WINDERMERE HALF AND FULL MARATHONS TO CHEER ON OUR FRIENDS IAN AND SHIELA. AFTER SEEING THEM OVER THE FINISH LINE IT'S TIME TO MOVE ON AND DO MY BIT... AND I DO MEAN BIT.

FROM A LAY-BY ON THE CONISTON ROAD I HEAD ONTO PARK FELL AND THE WIDE BRIDLEWAY TO ARNSIDE. IT'S PASTORAL AND PLEASANT AND VERY, VERY EASY GOING AS I PASS THROUGH A SMALL HERD OF COWS ENJOYING THE SPRING SUNSHINE, LIKE ME.

I HEAD TOWARDS THE SUMMIT CAIRN ON ONE OF MANY GRASS TRACKS. A STEEP FINAL SECTION REQUIRES HANDS ON KNEES TO REACH THE IMPRESSIVE CAIRN.

I NOTICE A SLIGHTLY BETTER ROUTE OFF THE SUMMIT DOWN TO THE BRIDLEWAY. I HAVE TO CROSS A FEW BOGGY PATCHES, BUT IT'S SO EASY GOING I'M NOT GOING TO COMPLAIN. BACK ON THE BRIDLEWAY... BACK PAST THE COWS... DOWN THE SLOPE TO FELL, AND INTO THE CAR. RUN DONE! IT'S BEEN EASY AND ENJOYABLE, AND MY LEGS ARE READY TO GO AGAIN SOON.

RUNNING TOTAL	
DISTANCE	661·85k
TIME	109 HRS 17 MINS
ASCENT	124,695 FT
SUMMITS	173

"Watch where you're putting your feet mate, we've all been very busy!**"**

DISTANCE **4·75**k TIME **30**mins ASCENT **450**ft

the WESTERN fells

It's run, run, run
all the way over
FELLBARROW and LOW FELL
and back to the finish

THACKTHWAITE TO FELLBARROW
DISTANCE 2·25k
TIME 15 MINUTES
1000 FEET OF ASCENT

LOW FELL SOUTH SUMMIT TO THACKTHWAITE
DISTANCE 3·25k
TIME 20 MINUTES
1250 FEET OF DESCENT

FELLBARROW TO LOW FELL SOUTH SUMMIT
DISTANCE 2·5k
TIME 22 MINUTES
400 FEET OF ASCENT

START FINISH

THACKTHWAITE

57 MINS

34 MINS

37 MINS

LOW FELL NORTH SUMMIT

LOW FELL SOUTH SUMMIT

HATTERINGILL HEAD
DODD WOOD
MEREGILL BECK
SMITHY FELL
FELL ROW
SOURFOOT FELL
WATCHING CRAG
THACKTHWAITE WOOD
WATCHING GILL
BECKHEAD MOSS
RAVEN CRAG
LATTER HEAD
LOWESWATER FELL
OAKBANK
RLING FELL
CRABTREE BECK
WHINNY RIDDING
RIVER COCKER
FOULSYKE
HIGH THRUSHBANK
HIGHCROSS
WATER
GODFERHEAD
LOWESWATER

A LOVELY DRIVE ALONG A SINGLE TRACK LANE TAKES ME TO THE CLUSTER OF COTTAGES CALLED THACKTHWAITE. I MANAGE TO PARK UP ON A WIDE VERGE FIFTY YARDS PAST THE WOODEN SIGNPOST POINTING THE WAY TO LOW FELL.

OFF I GO ON A PATH SQUEEZED BETWEEN COTTAGES AND TREES, RUNNING WITH WATER AND VERY STONY, BEFORE I ESCAPE INTO A FIELD OF GRAZING COWS. THERE'S A GENTLE GRADIENT FOR STARTERS ONTO THE OPEN FELL, WHERE I LEAVE THE OLD DROVE ROAD TO LOW FELL AND HEAD UPHILL - THE RUNNING BECOMING HARDER - TO A WALL ON ITS WAY UP FELLBARROW.

A LITTLE WALKING IS REQUIRED BEFORE I REACH THE RIDGE AND WIRE FENCE, WHICH I FOLLOW TO THE SUMMIT TRIG POINT. A CLEAR PATH NOW FOLLOWS THE FENCE TO LOW FELL, ALTERNATING FROM ONE SIDE TO ANOTHER VIA WOODEN STILES. IT'S EASY, EASY RUNNING OVER UNDULATING GRASSLAND.

SUDDENLY FROM NOWHERE A MARSH HARRIER GLIDES PAST ME NO MORE THAN FOUR FEET ABOVE THE GROUND - WOW!

THE NEXT WOW IS THE VIEW AHEAD AS I RETURN TO THE OLD DROVE ROAD AND CONTINUE TO THE TWIN SUMMITS OF LOW FELL - A BEAUTIFUL PANORAMIC VIEW OF CRUMMOCK WATER AND THE SURROUNDING FELLS. WITH IDEAL CONDITIONS UNDERFOOT THERE'S NO NEED TO STOP TO LOOK; I CAN CARRY ON RUNNING AND TAKE IT ALL IN WITHOUT FEAR OF FALLING OVER!

RUNNING TOTAL	
DISTANCE	669·85k
ASCENT	126,195 FT
TIME	110 HRS 14 MINS
SUMMITS	175

I VISIT BOTH SUMMITS, CHECK THE TIME, TURN MY BACK ON THE VIEWS AND START THE DESCENT TO THACKTHWAITE.

I'VE LOVED EVERY MINUTE OF TODAY'S RUN. IT'S A SHAME MY LEGS WERE A LITTLE TIRED AFTER A FOUR HOUR BIKE RIDE BECAUSE YOU COULD REALLY TRAVEL ON THIS RUN IF YOU SO DESIRED. STILL, VERY ENJOYABLE AND PLENTY OF RUNNING.

DISTANCE **8**k   TIME **57**mins   ASCENT **1,500**ft

last of the **CENTRAL** fells

No eagles in sight... but plenty of folk about on a hot Bank Holiday run...

over **EAGLE CRAG** and **SERGEANT'S CRAG**

IT'S BANK HOLIDAY MONDAY AND I HAVE A BUS TO CATCH. I ALIGHT AT ROSTHWAITE AND HEAD STRAIGHT ON TO THE GREENUP EDGE FOOTPATH TOWARDS LANGSTRATH DALE. IT'S VERY EASY GOING ALONGSIDE STONETHWAITE BECK AND ON THE FAR BANK THE CAMPSITE IS ALIVE WITH PEOPLE.

I CAN SMELL BACON AND EGGS SIZZLING AWAY ON ALL THOSE STOVES - I'VE HAD TO MAKE DO WITH A BOWL OF PORRIDGE!

I LEAVE THE GREENUP PATH AND CROSS THE BECK FOR LANGSTRATH DALE. THERE ARE PLENTY OF PEOPLE ABOUT ON THE BIG ROCK SLABS ENJOYING THE WARM SUNSHINE.

INITIAL SQUELCH GIVES WAY TO A GOOD PATH FOLLOWING THE BECK. A FEW WALKERS ARE ON THE OPPOSITE SIDE OF THE VALLEY - WITH MORE PEOPLE ENJOYING THE ROCK POOLS - FAR TOO COLD FOR ME!

PAST BLEA ROCK AND I PUSH ON TO THE BRIDGE AT THE FOOT OF STAKE PASS. I TOUCH THE BRIDGE AND CHECK THE TIME: FORTY SIX MINUTES. IT'S BEEN EASY GOING WITH LITTLE HEIGHT GAIN SO FAR, BUT THINGS ARE ABOUT TO CHANGE. I TURN BACK AND HEAD OFF-ROAD ACROSS THE OPEN FELL TO SERGEANT'S CRAG, CROSSING NUMEROUS STREAMS AND A CARPET OF BRACKEN LUCKILY ONLY JUST STARTING TO UNFOLD AND REACH FOR THE SKY.

I GAIN HEIGHT GRADUALLY, WITH A COUPLE OF HANDS-ON-KNEES SECTIONS THROWN IN FOR FUN, AND ARRIVE AT THE RIDGE NOT TOO SHORT OF THE SUMMIT. IT'S A NICE SUMMIT, WITH GOOD VIEWS ACROSS TO GLARAMARA AND AHEAD TO EAGLE CRAG, MY NEXT PORT OF CALL.

FROM SERGEANT'S CRAG A CLEAR PEAT PATH TAKES ME OVER TO A WALL, AND ONTO EAGLE CRAG. THE GOING IS EASY ALL THE WAY TO ITS SUMMIT, WHERE I CHECK THE TIME, THEN RETRACE MY STEPS BACK TO THE STILE OVER THE WALL AND THE START OF MY DESCENT TO GREENUP GILL. WITH NO CLEAR PATH I HEAD SOUTHEAST ACROSS OPEN FELL AND DROP DOWN OVER STEEP GROUND TO A RUIN NEXT TO THE GILL.

THE RUNNING'S BETTER BACK ON THE GREENUP PATH, WITH HOLIDAYMAKERS GALORE AT SMITHYMIRE ISLAND AS I PUSH ON TO ROSTHWAITE AND A BUS BACK TO KESWICK. THE TIMING IS PERFECT; AS I CROSS THE ROAD TO THE SHELTER AND STOP MY WATCH A BUS PULLS ROUND THE CORNER AND I GET TO STOP THAT TOO. I'M WELL PLEASED WITH THIS RUN; PLENTY OF RUNNING, NO STONE STEPS TO NEGOTIATE, AND...

RUNNING TOTAL	
DISTANCE	683·95K
TIME	112 HRS 22 MINS
ASCENT	127,845 FT
SUMMITS	177

OR

only 37 to go!

DISTANCE **14·1**k   TIME **2**hrs**8**mins   ASCENT **1,650**ft

the WESTERN fells

Far two remote-
CAW FELL and HAYCOCK

just too far
out of the way
to have been
bothered with
before, but no
excuses today

AFTER AN HOUR'S DRIVE FROM
PENRUDDOCK I PARK IN THE SHADE OF
THE TREES AT THE BOWNESS KNOTT CAR PARK.
I SET OFF DOWNHILL AT FIRST ON THE FOREST
ROAD TOWARDS THE HEAD OF THE LAKE.
    IT SOON LEVELS OFF, STICKING CLOSE
        TO THE LAKESHORE. IT'S
        SO EASY I'M ABLE TO
        LOOK ACROSS THE LAKE
        AND ADMIRE THE
        DISTANT VIEW OF
        CAW FELL AND
        HAYCOCK, TODAY'S
        OBJECTIVES AND TWO
        FELLS I'VE NEVER
        BOTHERED TO VISIT.

BUT NO EXCUSES TODAY-
THEY HAVE TO BE DONE !!

DISTANCE **14·9**k

TIME **2**hrs**13**mins

ASCENT **2,400**ft

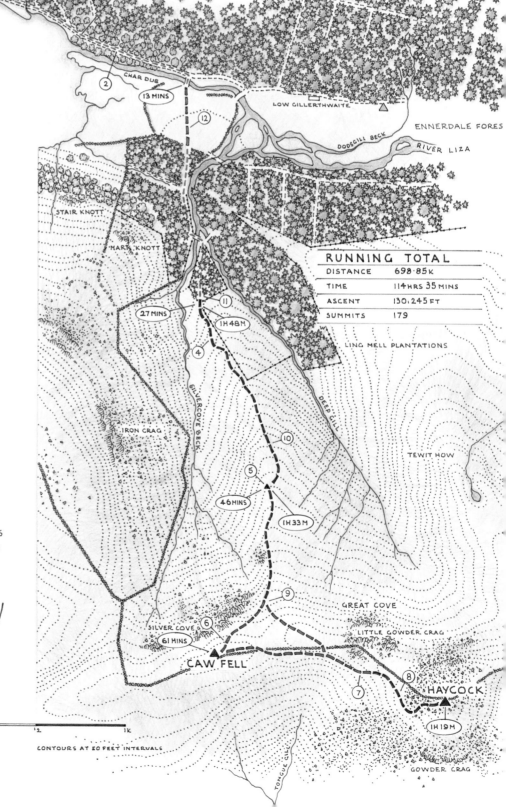

RUNNING TOTAL	
DISTANCE	698·85k
TIME	114HRS 35MINS
ASCENT	130,245FT
SUMMITS	179

CONTOURS AT 50 FEET INTERVALS

flat as a pancake

THE RUNNING'S FLAT FOR NEARLY THREE KILOMETRES TO CHAR DUB BRIDGE. I'M SWEATING PROFUSELY NOW AS THE TEMPERATURE SOARS - UNLIKE THE CONTOUR LINES - AND I WELCOME SHADE AS I ENTER THE PLANTATION ON THE FAR SIDE OF THE LAKE.

an abrupt halt

UP I GO, IN THE SHADE, ON A DELIGHTFUL ALPINE PATH TWISTING ITS WAY BETWEEN CONIFER, LARCH AND BIRCH. I CROSS OVER THE BECK AND UP TO A FENCE AND STILE. IT'S BEEN GOOD RUNNING SO FAR, BUT THAT'S ABOUT TO CHANGE; ONCE OVER THE STILE THE RUNNING COMES TO AN ABRUPT HALT. A DEEP TRENCH OF A PATH WORN INTO THE FELLSIDE IS FULL OF STONES AND PART HIDDEN BY OVERGROWN HEATHER. RUNNING IS IMPOSSIBLE, SO IT'S HANDS-ON-KNEES TIME AND WATCH WHERE I'M PUTTING MY FEET.

I CHECK TO SEE IF THERE'S ANY SIGN OF A PATH DOWN OVER TEWIT, BUT I CAN'T MAKE ONE OUT, SO I DECIDE TO RETRACE MY STEPS MORE OR LESS THE WAY I CAME ALL THE WAY BACK TO ENNERDALE. NOW WATERED AND FED I HEAD OFF THE SUMMIT AND BACK ROUND LITTLE GOWDER CRAG TO THE WALL.

HERE I SPOT A BREAK IN THE WALL THAT I DIDN'T SEE ON THE WAY UP. AS I APPROACH I NOTICE A BRIGHT YELLOW SIGN ON A STAKE. WHAT!? WHY WOULD ANYONE WITH MORE THAN ONE BRAIN CELL REMOVE LARGE AMOUNTS OF STONE FROM A WALL TWO THOUSAND FEET UP A MOUNTAIN? MAYBE THEY'VE ONLY GOT ON BRAIN CELL BETWEEN THEM. I ALSO ASK MYSELF WHY YOU WOULD PUT A SIGN UP WARNING THEM. WE ALL KNOW THERE'S NO CAMERA... OR DO WE!?

time for a drink

IT'S A RELIEF WHEN HEATHER GIVES WAY TO GRASS AND RUNNING IS RESUMED. I PASS A BIG CAIRN, AND THE FIRST AND ONLY WALKER OF THE DAY, AS THE PATH CONTINUES ITS STEADY CLIMB OF CAW FELL, THEN I VEER OFF RIGHT TO SURMOUNT THE SUMMIT. THERE'S NOT MUCH CORRR FACTOR, BUT IT'S A GOOD PLACE FOR A DRINK.

risk it

THERE'S NO SIGN SAYING I CAN'T GO THROUGH THE GAP, SO I RISK IT AND THROUGH I GO!

SMOOTH GRASS AND DOWNHILL MEANS GOOD RUNNING ALL THE WAY TO THE BIG CAIRN, THEN I'M BACK ONTO TREACHEROUS HEATHER AND STONES, WITH NO TUMBLES BUT PLENTY OF SCRATCHES ON THE SHINS AS I ESCAPE BACK OVER THE STILE.

WHAT! I don't believe it

NOW WITH GRASS UNDERFOOT I MAKE GOOD PROGRESS ON THE SOUTH SIDE OF THE WALL, ONLY LEAVING IT TO SUMMIT LITTLE GOWDER CRAG.

HERE THE PATH BECOMES ROUGH AND STONY ON THE FINAL SECTION. I SOON REACH THE SUMMIT OF HAYCOCK AND VISIT BOTH CAIRNS FOR GOOD VIEWS OVER SCOAT FELL AND PILLAR - BOTH STILL TO BE CONQUERED ON THIS CHALLENGE.

CCTV

IN OPERATION

IN THE FIGHT AGAINST THE REMOVAL OF STONES FROM THIS WALL

NOT WHAT YOU EXPECT 2000 FT UP A MOUNTAIN

back to the delightful path

IT'S PLAIN SAILING NOW I'M BACK ON THE ALPINE PATH DOWN TO THE FLOOR OF THE VALLEY. A LONG RUN TO THE FINISH AND I'M READY FOR A SIT DOWN ON THE WOODEN BENCH ACROSS THE ROAD FROM THE CAR PARK; TIME FOR A BITE TO EAT AND A DRINK AS I SOAK UP THE SUNSHINE AND BEAUTIFUL VIEWS.

the **SOUTHERN** fells

Great views

make it hard knott to enjoy this threesome

HARD KNOTT, HARTER FELL and GREEN CRAG

- except for the BOG!

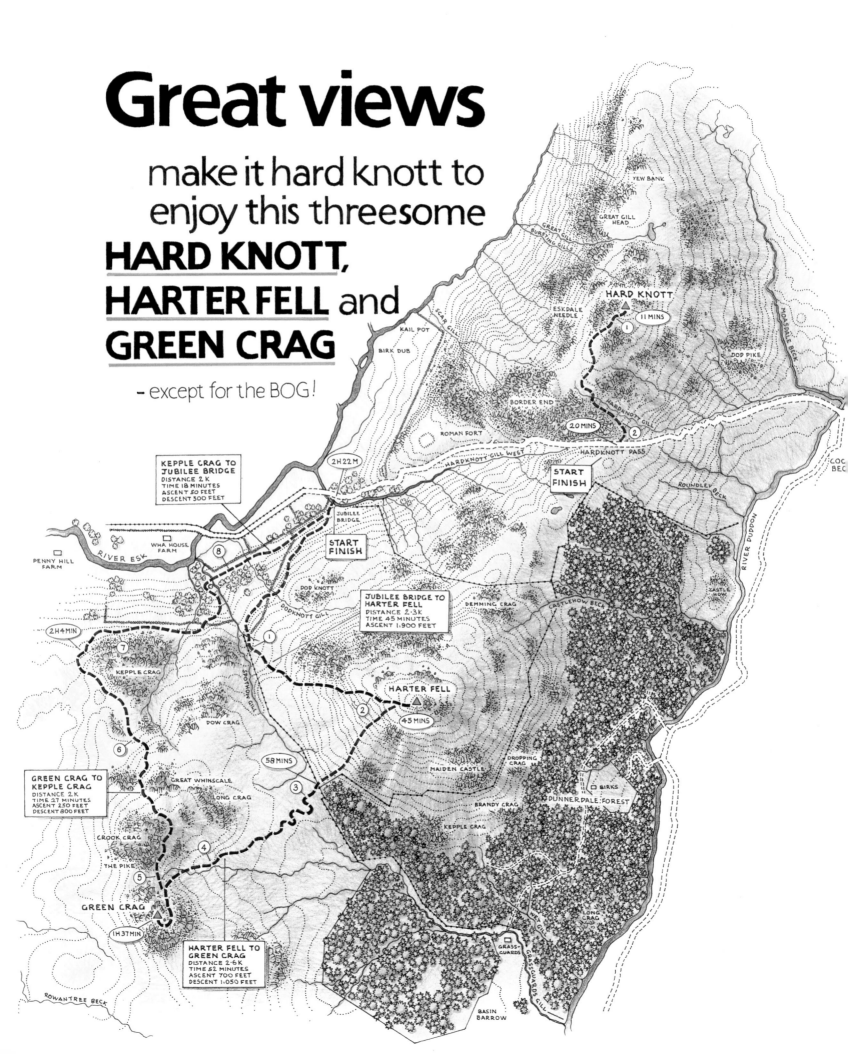

KEPPLE CRAG TO
JUBILEE BRIDGE
DISTANCE 2 K
TIME 18 MINUTES
ASCENT 50 FEET
DESCENT 500 FEET

JUBILEE BRIDGE TO
HARTER FELL
DISTANCE 2·3 K
TIME 45 MINUTES
ASCENT 1,900 FEET

GREEN CRAG TO
KEPPLE CRAG
DISTANCE 2 K
TIME 27 MINUTES
ASCENT 250 FEET
DESCENT 800 FEET

HARTER FELL TO
GREEN CRAG
DISTANCE 2·6 K
TIME 52 MINUTES
ASCENT 700 FEET
DESCENT 1·050 FEET

Hard Knott

IT'S AN EARLY MORNING START FOR THE DRIVE DOWN TO HARD KNOTT PASS VIA AMBLESIDE AND WRYNOSE PASS. A HOT, HOT DAY'S FORECAST, WITH A TEMPERATURE OF 26°C. OVER THE TOP OF WRYNOSE CARS ARE ALREADY PARKED ROADSIDE AT THE THREE SHIRES STONE. I DRIVE ON DOWN TO COCKLEY BECK, THEN ASCEND HARD KNOTT PASS IN FIRST AND SECOND GEAR - A BIT LIKE FELL RUNNING IN A CAR! - ALL THE WAY TO THE TOP.

THERE'S JUST ONE CAR PARKED. I HAVE A QUICK CHAT TO THE GUY. HE'S FROM PONTEFRACT, AND HE'S ALSO DOING THE WAINWRIGHTS - HEADING OVER HARD KNOTT AND CONTINUING TO THE HEAD OF ESKDALE AND DOWN TO WASDALE FOR THE NIGHT.

NOW FOR THE RUN. I SET OFF PAST THE BIG CAIRN ON A GRASS PATH THAT CONTINUES ALL THE WAY TO HARD KNOTT SUMMIT, FLUCTUATING BETWEEN WET AND DRY, AND GRASS AND RUSHES/REEDS. I ADMIRE THE VIEWS NORTH UP ESKDALE AND ACROSS TO THE SCAFELLS, THEN RETURN TO THE CAR PASSING THE GUY FROM WEST YORKSHIRE ON THE WAY.

IT'S BEEN A SHORT AND SIMPLE RUN - NO PROBLEM WITH ROUTE-FINDING AND NO BIG DEAL FOR THE LEGS; AN IDEAL WARM UP FOR MY NEXT OUTING AS I HEAD DOWN, DOWN, DOWN TO JUBILEE BRIDGE AND START MY NEXT RUN.

DISTANCE **2**k

TIME **20**mins

ASCENT **550**ft

RUNNING TOTAL	
DISTANCE	700·85 K
TIME	114 HRS 55 MINS
ASCENT	130,795 FT
SUMMITS	180

Harter Fell and Green Crag

I COULD HAVE CONTINUED MY RUN FROM HARD KNOTT PASS SUMMIT AND RUN UP HARTER FELL VIA THE BACK. BUT HAVING NEVER WALKED IT BEFORE I FELT I SHOULD ASCEND BY A MORE TRADITIONAL ROUTE. SO HERE GOES...

OFF I GO FROM UNDER THE SHADE OF THE JUBILEE BRIDGE CAR PARK TREES AND OVER THE BRIDGE, THROUGH A COUPLE OF WOODEN GATES AND OUT ONTO THE OPEN FELL ON A CLEAR PATH. MY LEGS FEEL GOOD AFTER THE WARM UP RUN, AND IT'S PLEASANT GOING ON THE GRASS AND STONE AS I CATCH UP AND PASS TWO GROUPS OF WALKERS - MUST BE A POPULAR WALK.

I SOON LEAVE THE MAIN PATH BEHIND FOR A MUDDY SIDE TRACK CUTTING THROUGH BRACKEN AND STARTING TO CLIMB AT A STEEPER GRADIENT.

SWEAT'S DRIPPING OFF ME AS I GAIN HEIGHT WITH A COMBINATION OF HANDS-ON-KNEES AND A SHUFFLY SORT OF RUN UNTIL I JOIN THE MAIN PATH AT A SMALL CAIRN. THERE'S STILL A FAIR WAY TO GO AS THE GROUND STEEPENS AND ROCKS MAKE AN APPEARANCE. I KEEP PLODDING ON UNTIL I REACH THE TOP AND HEAD FIRST TO THE FAR RIGHT OUTCROP, THEN ROUND THE BACK TO GAIN THE TRUE SUMMIT

I ADMIRE THE VIEWS AND CHECK THE TIME, THEN DOWN I GO, THIS TIME TO THE THIRD 'SUMMIT' - THE ONE WITH THE TRIG POINT; THREE GOOD SUMMITS FOR THE PRICE OF ONE! THE VIEWS ARE BEAUTIFUL, AND MY ATTENTION IS DRAWN TO MY NEXT OBJECTIVE: GREEN CRAG OVER ON THE HORIZON. THE DISTANT RIDGE, INCLUDING CROOK CRAG, LOOKS PRETTY GOOD, BUT HOW DO I GET THERE?

BELOW ME LIES A VAST FEATURELESS PLATEAU WITH SMALL PONDS, STREAMS, PEAT HAGS, RUSHES, REEDS, HEATHER AND BOG! THERE'S NO PATHS MARKED ON THE MAP AND NONE VISIBLE FROM MY VIEWPOINT. I WILL JUST HAVE TO SEE WHAT AWAITS ME ONCE I'M DOWN THERE.

A STRAIGHTFORWARD DESCENT TO THE ESKDALE - DUDDON PATH TAKES ME TO A WIRE FENCE SEPARATING FELL FROM SWAMP. TO MY DELIGHT THERE'S ALSO A STILE. AND WHERE THERE'S A STILE THERE'S A PATH...

MY SPIRITS ARE RAISED - BUT NOT FOR LONG. THE PATH IS SWALLOWED BY THE BOG WITHIN MINUTES. FROM THERE IT'S UNBELIEVABLY SLOW GOING JUMPING THE PEAT HAGS AND THE BOGS AND CROSSING LITTLE BRIDGES MADE FROM CLUMPS OF HEATHER, ALL OF WHICH ARE NEXT TO USELESS.

IT TAKES ME OVER THIRTY MINUTES TO GO JUST ONE KILOMETRE, SO I'M RELIEVED TO REACH TERRA FIRMA AS THE GROUND STARTS TO INCLINE TOWARDS GREEN CRAG. THERE'S GRASS UNDERFOOT NOW AND I'M BACK TO RUNNING TO THE TINY SUMMIT CAIRN. IT'S A PLEASANT LITTLE SUMMIT WITH GOOD VIEWS TO BOOT.

I TAKE ANOTHER DRINK THEN HEAD DOWN AND ALONG A CLEAR PATH TO THE PIKE, CROOK CRAG AND KEPPLE CRAG TO PICK UP THE OLD PEAT ROAD FROM PENNY HILL. IT'S GOOD RUNNING NOW, SO GOOD I NEARLY MISS THE TURNOFF BACK TO JUBILEE BRIDGE, BUT SPOT A TINY SIGN ON A THICK STAKE POINTING THE WAY.

I KEEP RUNNING AS THE PATH FOLLOWS A WALL DOWN TO SPOTHOW GILL. OVER THE STREAM I GO, AND THEN SHARP LEFT THROUGH A GATE ONTO A GRASS PATH LEADING DOWN TO PENNY HILL FARM AND JUBILEE BRIDGE.

A FUNNY SIGN HERE PROCLAIMS: 1,200 YARDS TO JUBILEE BRIDGE. WHATEVER HAPPENED TO THE GOOD OLD 3/4 MILE?

I'VE BEEN RUNNING NON-STOP NOW FROM GREEN CRAG'S SUMMIT. MY LEGS STILL FEEL GOOD, BUT THE HEAT IS RELENTLESS, AND I'M GLAD TO REACH THE CAR, ANOTHER BOTTLE OF WATER - AND SHADE.

A VERY ENJOYABLE RUN, EVEN WITH THE HEAT - AND THAT BOG.

RUNNING TOTAL	
DISTANCE	709·75 K
TIME	117 HRS 17 MINS
ASCENT	133,695 FT
SUMMITS	182

DISTANCE **8·9**k TIME **2**hrs **22**mins ASCENT **2,900**ft

the **WESTERN** fells

Slow, slow, quick, quick, slow

just about sums up this run over

STARLING DODD

and GREAT BORNE

WE HEAD DOWN TO BUTTERMERE ON AN OVERCAST MORNING AND PARK THE CAR BY THE CHURCH.

I HAVE COMPANY TODAY, BUT ONLY FOR THE FIRST KILOMETRE. JANICE AND I SET OFF DOWN TO SCALE BRIDGE ON A GOOD FLAT LANE, WHERE ON ARRIVAL WE GO OUR SEPERATE WAYS; JANICE TO THE LEFT FOR A RUN AROUND BUTTERMERE, WHILE I HEAD RIGHT TO CRUMMOCK WATER AND THE PATH TO SCALE FORCE.

slow

THE GRADIENTS ARE GENTLE, BUT THE PATH WET AND STONY MOST OF THE WAY. I MAKE IT TO THE BRIDGE OVER SCALE BECK WET-THROUGH.

I CROSS THE BRIDGE - BIG MISTAKE! - AND FOLLOW A PATH UPSTREAM THROUGH BRACKEN, HEATHER, BILBERRIES AND ROCKS. IT'S NOT GOOD, BUT I'M COMMITED TO IT UNTIL I FIND A SAFE POINT FURTHER UP THE FELL WHERE I CROSS TO THE MAIN PATH ON THE OPPOSITE BANK.

slow

AS THE MAIN PATH HEADS OFF TOWARDS RED PIKE I RETURN TO THE BECK BANK AND BACK TO HEATHER, BILBERRIES, ROCKS, BOG AND NOW BEAUTIFUL BRIGHT GREEN CLUMPS OF MINIATURE FERNS. BUT IT'S STILL SLOW GOING. I HEAD ACROSS OPEN FELLSIDE AS THE BECK PETERS OUT TO A SHEEPFOLD, WHERE I CHECK THE TIME BEFORE CONTINUING ONWARDS AND UPWARDS TO STARLING DODD. THERE ARE STILL LOTS OF ROCKS TO NEGOTIATE UNTIL I REACH THE PATH FROM RED PIKE.

quick

IT'S EASY GOING NOW TO THE SUMMIT CAIRN, WHICH LOOKS JUST LIKE THE ONE ILLUSTRATED IN THE GUIDEBOOK. FROM THE CAIRN GREAT BORNE LOOKS A FAIR WAY OFF, ACROSS A HEATHER- AND PEAT-COVERED DEPRESSION. ON ARRIVAL IT TURNS OUT TO BE QUITE A GOOD SURFACE UNDERFOOT, ALLOWING QUICK RUNNING · AT LAST · ALL THE WAY TO THE FINAL SLOPE OF GREAT BORNE.

quick

GRASS AND PROTRUDING STONES PAVE THE WAY TO THE WIDE SUMMIT. I PASS THE WIND SHELTER, TAP THE TRIG POINT AND CHECK OUT THE VIEW OVER TO THE COAST. I CAN SEE FOR MILES, BUT INLAND THE CLOUD IS STARTING TO DROP; PILLAR IS ALREADY SHROUDED IN GREY MIST AND THE HIGH STILE

RIDGE LOOKS TO BE NEXT. IT'S TIME TO GET A MOVE ON AND HEAD BACK OVER THE DEPRESSION TO STARLING DODD.

slow

I GIVE STARLING DODD'S SUMMIT A MISS AND CONTOUR ROUND THE FINAL SLOPE OVER MORE HEATHER AND ROCKS, WHERE I TAKE A TUMBLE IN AN ANKLE-SNAPPING HOLE. ALTHOUGH I MANAGE TO ARREST MY FALL WITH MY HAND, IT'S BACK TO SLOW GOING ALL THE WAY TO THE SHEEPFOLD AND ALONGSIDE THE RE-APPEARING STREAM TO RENEW MY ACQUAINTANCE WITH THE MINIATURE FERNS.

THE GOING'S SLOW DOWN, DOWN, DOWN ONTO THE RED PIKE PATH, WITH ROCK STEPS AND OVERHANGING BRANCHES TO CONTEND WITH. IT'S A RELIEF FOR THE

LEGS AS I REACH SCALE FORCE BRIDGE AND THE PATH TO BUTTERMERE, WHERE I PICK UP THE PACE, AT LAST, FOR THE FINAL KILOMETRE BACK TO BUTTERMERE, JANICE AND A DELICIOUS SLICE OF CAKE IN A CAFE.

JANICE ENJOYED HER CIRCUM-NAVIGATION OF BUTTERMERE AND I ENJOYED MY RUN BETWEEN THE TWO SUMMITS, BUT THE REST WAS EITHER TOO WET, TOO ROCKY, TOO STEEP - OR A COMBINATION OF ALL THREE.

I SHOULDN'T COMPLAIN TOO MUCH THOUGH. AFTER ALL, IT WAS A FELL RUN - AND NOT A PARK RUN!

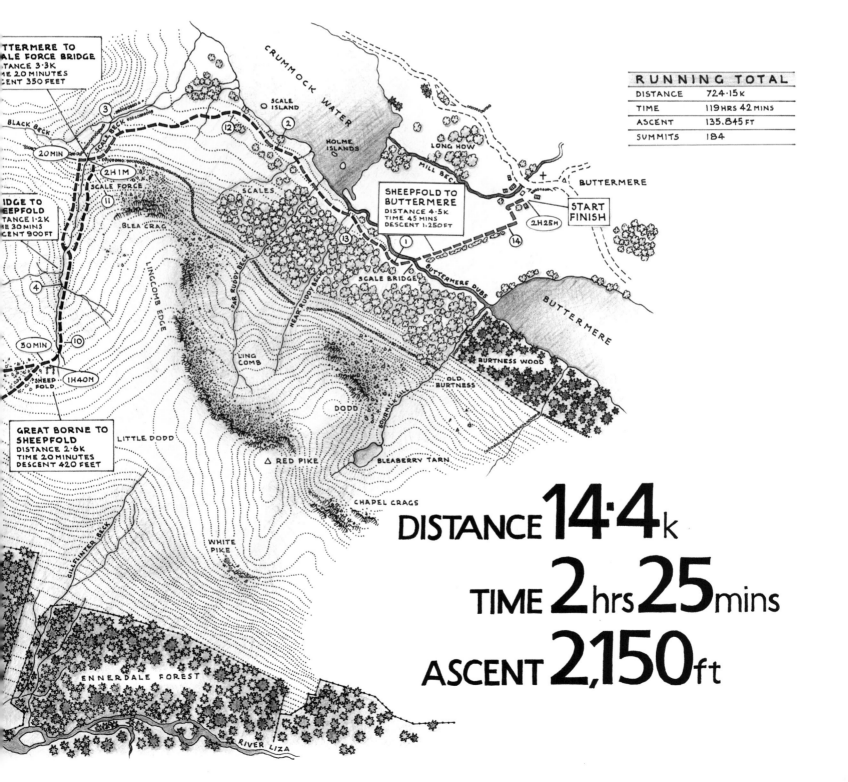

RUNNING TOTAL	
DISTANCE	724·15 K
TIME	119 HRS 42 MINS
ASCENT	135,845 FT
SUMMITS	184

DISTANCE **14·4**k

TIME **2**hrs **25**mins

ASCENT **2,150**ft

the SOUTHERN fells

A GREAT RUN OVER
Great Carrs, Grey Friar,
Swirl How SPOILT ONLY BY
AN AWFUL DESCENT OFF
Wetherlam

I CHOOSE FELL FOOT IN LITTLE LANGDALE FOR THE START AND FINISH OF TODAY'S RUN. I START ALONG A LANE TOWARDS BRIDGE END. AS IT TURNS INTO A BRIDLEPATH TO HIGH TILBERTHWAITE I TURN SHARP RIGHT ONTO A CLEAR TRACK IN THE DIRECTION OF GREENBURN TARN.

IT'S BEEN EASY RUNNING SO FAR; LEGS FEELING GOOD AND EAGER TO CARRY ON. I CONTINUE DOWN OVER A SUBSTANTIAL WOODEN BRIDGE AND ONTO THE START OF WET SIDE EDGE. AS HEIGHT IS GAINED AND I REACH THE RIDGE A GREAT VIEW OF THE LANGDALE PIKES BURSTS ONTO THE SCENE.

I PUSH ON, LEGS STILL GOOD, BUT LUNGS HAVING TO PUT EXTRA EFFORT IN NOW AS THE PATH STEEPENS PAST HELL GILL PIKE TO GREAT CARRS' SUMMIT. THE BEST RUNNING OF THE DAY LOOKS TO BE JUST AHEAD AS I TURN DOWNHILL ON SHORT GRASS TO FAIRFIELD THEN UP THE OTHER SIDE TOWARDS GREY FRIAR. THERE ARE NO PROBLEMS HERE EITHER AS I REACH THE INTERESTING SUMMIT, WITH LOTS OF ROCK OUTCROPS AND PROTRUDING STONES EMBEDDED IN SHORT GRASS. I TIPTOE OVER TO THE MAIN CAIRN AND ADMIRE THE VIEW OVER THE SCAFELLS.

BACK DOWN TO FAIRFIELD AND I HEAD OVER TO SWIRL HOW ON A GRASSY PATH THAT'S IDEAL FOR RUNNING TO ARRIVE AT THE STONY SUMMIT, AGAIN WITH A LOVELY CAIRN ATOP. THERE ARE A FEW PEOPLE ABOUT NOW AS I START THE TRICKY DESCENT OF THE PRISON BAND: FULL CONCENTRATION REQUIRED ALL THE WAY TO SWIRL HAUSE. PHEW!

GREAT CARRS
TO GREY FRIAR
DISTANCE 1·4 K
TIME 12 MINUTES
ASCENT 275 FEET

GREEN HOW

1H 14M

SHEEP CRAG

GREAT BLAKE R

SEATHWAITE
TARN

WETHERLAM

WETHERLAM LOOKED A FAIR WAY FROM THE SUMMIT OF SWIRL HOW SO I'D BETTER GET A MOVE ON. A BETTER PATH THAN EXPECTED, WITH GENTLE GRADIENTS, TAKES ME ROUND BLACK SAILS AND ONTO THE BROAD SUMMIT OF WETHERLAM. IT'S TIME NOW FOR A DRINK AND A BITE TO EAT. THE CLOCK'S STILL TICKING THOUGH, SO I CHECK MY WATCH: TWO HOURS TO THIS POINT FROM THE START WAY DOWN BELOW. I FEEL PRETTY HAPPY WITH THAT - BUT THE GOOD GOING IS ABOUT TO CHANGE!

BIRK FELL HAUSE - SPELT HAWES ON O.S. MAPS - IS MY NEXT OBJECTIVE, SO DOWN WETHERLAM EDGE I GO ON A TERRIBLE PATH, BADLY ERODED AND FULL OF LOOSE STONES AND BIG ROCK STEPS. IT'S A LABOURIOUS SCRAMBLE ALL THE WAY DOWN TO THE HAUSE, WHERE I CHECK FOR THE PATH DOWN TO GREENBURN BECK AS SHOWN ON THE O.S. MAP - AND THERE'S NO SIGN OF IT ANYWHERE!

RUNNING TOTAL	
DISTANCE	738·85 K
TIME	122 HRS 45 MINS
ASCENT	139,270 FT
SUMMITS	188

I HAVE NO CHOICE BUT TO DROP STRAIGHT DOWN INTO THICK, CHEST-HIGH BRACKEN WITH FLASHBACKS TO THE HORROR OF STONE ARTHUR.

IT'S HORRENDOUS GOING; STEEP, AND UNDERFOOT ROCKS, ROCKS AND MORE ROCKS. WITH THICK BRACKEN MAKING IT IMPOSSIBLE TO SEE THE GROUND AND DEEP HOLES IN FRONT PROGRESS IS PAINFULLY SLOW.

I CATCH UP WITH A COUPLE OF WALKERS IN THE SAME PREDICAMENT AS ME, SEARCHING FOR A BREAK IN THE BRACKEN, AND TOGETHER WE EVENTUALLY FIND ONE AND HEAD DOWN TO THE DERELICT MINE BUILDINGS.

FORTY FIVE MINUTES TO DESCEND TWO AND A HALF KILOMETRES ..! AND IT WAS ALL GOING SO WELL! ONCE ON THE MAIN PATH, THOUGH, IT'S BACK TO RUNNING, NOW ON WEARY LEGS, ALL THE WAY TO THE CAR.

I ENJOYED THIS RUN A LOT. IT'S JUST A SHAME THERE WAS NO PATH OFF BIRK FELL HAUSE. IF I'D HAVE KNOWN, I COULD HAVE CHOSEN A BETTER ENDING. I'LL BLAME IT ON YOU O.S...

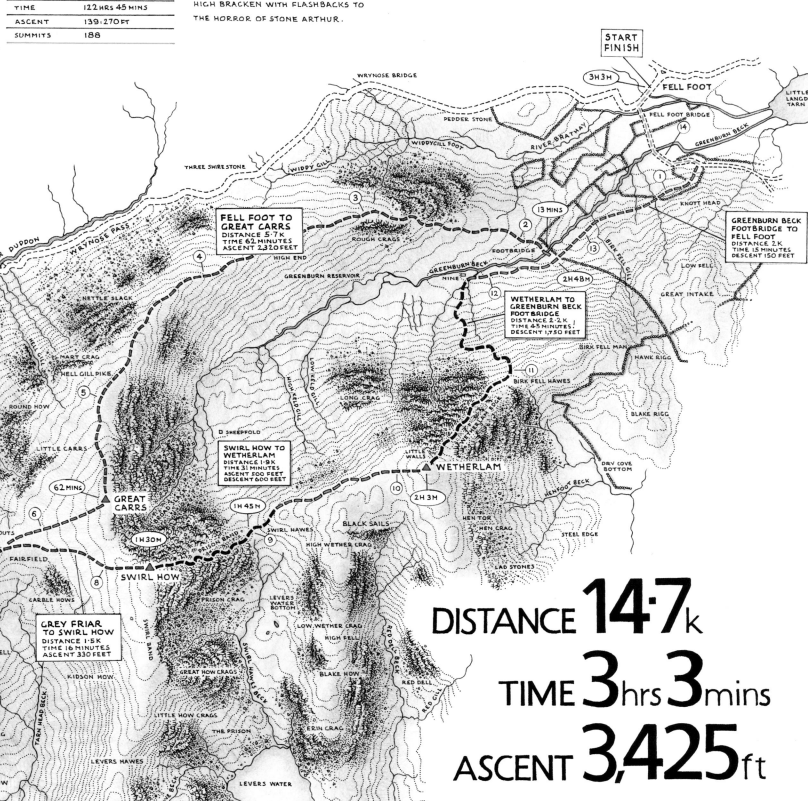

DISTANCE **14·7**k

TIME **3**hrs **3**mins

ASCENT **3,425**ft

the **WESTERN** fells

OH CRIKEY,
where have all the trees

as I lumber over <u>GRIKE</u>, <u>CRAG FELL</u> and <u>LANK RIGG</u>

I DRIVE WEST TO KINNISIDE STONE CIRCLE, HAVE A QUICK LEG STRETCH, GET MY BEARINGS, THEN HEAD OFF ON THE COLD FELL TARMAC ROAD BEFORE CROSSING ONTO THE OLD MINE ROAD AS IT CLIMBS GENTLY OVER BLAKELEY MOSS.

THIS IS ALL NEW GROUND FOR ME, SO I MUST PAY CLOSE ATTENTION TO THE MAP AND NOT GO ASTRAY, ALTHOUGH THE CHOSEN ROUTE SEEMS STRAIGHT-FORWARD ENOUGH ON PAPER. THE GOING IS EASY UNTIL I REACH A GATE, WHERE I'M EXPECTING TO BE RUNNING ALONGSIDE A HUGE PLANTATION ON THE LOWER SLOPES OF GRIKE. BUT NO; ALL LIFE HAS BEEN EXTERMINATED. IT MUST HAVE BEEN SOME TIME AGO, TOO, SO WHY IS IT REPRESENTED ON O.S. MAPS?

ANYWAY, BACK TO THE RUN. AS THE MINE ROAD CONTINUES ON ITS GENTLE WAY I CROSS A FENCE VIA A STILE ONTO THE OPEN FELL, AND PUSH ON, NOW AT A STEEPER GRADIENT, TO THE SUMMIT OF GRIKE. CRAG FELL IS CLEARLY IN VIEW ACROSS A DEPRESSION, SO I CONTINUE RUNNING STRAIGHT AHEAD ON A CLEAR, IF SQUELCHY, PATH TO A FENCE BEFORE THE EASY ASCENT TO CRAG FELL'S SUMMIT, WHICH IS NOT TOO IMPRESSIVE FROM THIS SIDE.

A NARROW PATH DESCENDS SOUTH TOWARDS WHOAP. I CROSS THE MINE ROAD AND PASS THROUGH WHAT WAS ONCE A FOREST, WITH THOUSANDS OF STUMPS STANDING IN ROWS LIKE GRAVESTONES ON THE FELLSIDE, THEN CLIMB TO THE BROAD SUMMIT OF WHOAP. ONCE ON TOP IT'S DOWN TO RED GILL AND THE START OF THE FINAL CLIMB OF THE DAY, HANDS ON KNEES REQUIRED TO REACH THE SUMMIT AND ITS TRIG POINT.

I RETRACE MY STEPS TO RED GILL BEFORE DESCENDING BESIDE WHOAP BECK FOR THE LONG RUN BACK TO THE CAR. IT'S A CLEAR, RUNNABLE PATH, WET IN PLACES, THAT KEEPS ME ON MY TOES ALL THE WAY TO THE COLD FELL ROAD, WHERE I STEP BACK ONTO TARMAC AND PICK UP THE PACE TO MY CAR.

NOT TOO EXCITING THIS RUN, THAT'S FOR SURE, BUT PLENTY OF GOOD PATHS, AND MORE ENJOYABLE THAN I EXPECTED.

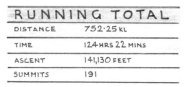

RUNNING TOTAL	
DISTANCE	752·25 KL
TIME	124 HRS 22 MINS
ASCENT	141,130 FEET
SUMMITS	191

LANK RIGG ORDNANCE SURVEY COLUMN

GRIKEY!!!
gone?

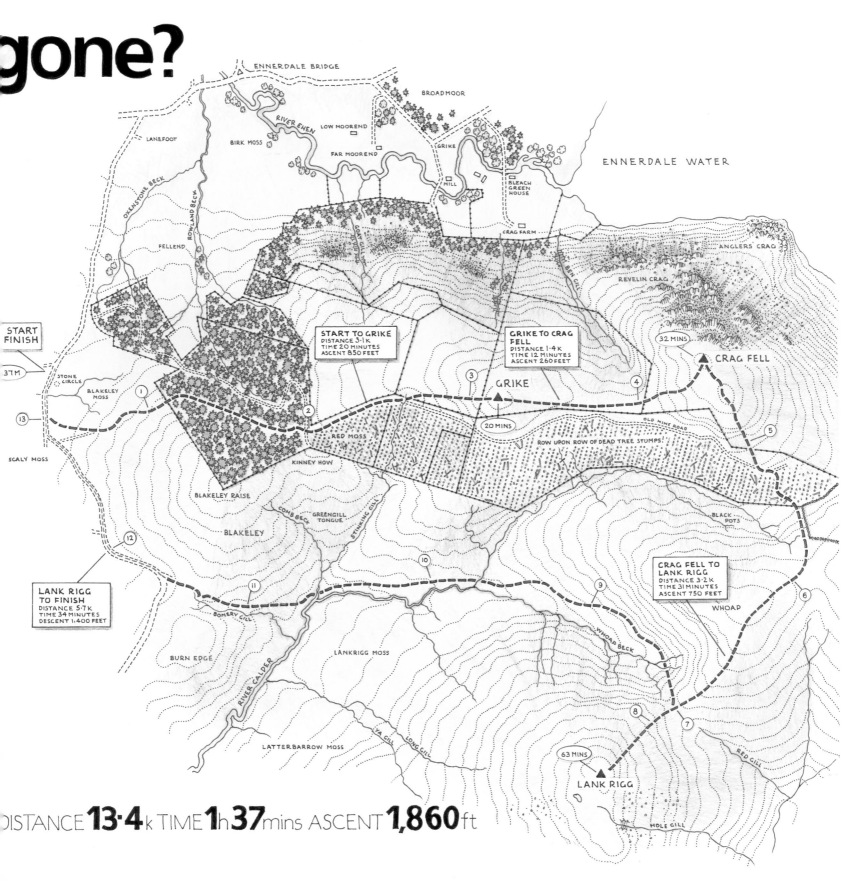

ENNERDALE BRIDGE

BROADMOOR

RIVER EHEN

LOW MOOREND

LANEFOOT

BIRK MOSS

FAR MOOREND

GRIKE

ENNERDALE WATER

MILL

BLEACH GREEN HOUSE

CRAG FARM

ANGLERS CRAG

FELLEND

REVELIN CRAG

START FINISH

37M

START TO GRIKE
DISTANCE 3·1K
TIME 20 MINUTES
ASCENT 850 FEET

GRIKE TO CRAG FELL
DISTANCE 1·4K
TIME 12 MINUTES
ASCENT 260 FEET

32 MINS

CRAG FELL

STONE CIRCLE

BLAKELEY MOSS

①

③

GRIKE

④

13

②

20 MINS

OLD MINE ROAD

⑤

SCALY MOSS

RED MOSS

ROW UPON ROW OF DEAD TREE STUMPS

KINNEY HOW

BLAKELEY RAISE

COMB BECK

GREENGILL TONGUE

BLACK POTS

BLAKELEY

⑫

STINKING GILL

⑩

CRAG FELL TO LANK RIGG
DISTANCE 3·2K
TIME 31 MINUTES
ASCENT 750 FEET

⑥

LANK RIGG TO FINISH
DISTANCE 5·7K
TIME 34 MINUTES
DESCENT 1,400 FEET

⑪

BOMERY GILL

⑨

WHOAP

BURN EDGE

LANKRIGG MOSS

WHOAP BECK

RIVER CALDER

⑧

⑦

RED GILL

YA GILL

LONG GILL

LATTERBARROW MOSS

63 MINS

LANK RIGG

DISTANCE **13·4**k TIME **1**h**37**mins ASCENT **1,860**ft

HOLE GILL

the **SOUTHERN** fells

I just love contour lines, even the tight ones

on **SCAFELL** and **SLIGHT SIDE**

Talking of tight, I only just manage to squeeze into the Brackenclose car park. Busy, busy, busy with walkers milling around ready for the off...

... OFF I HEAD ALONG WITH EVERYONE ELSE, THEN AS I TURN ONTO THE OLD CORPSE ROAD TO BURNMOOR TARN I LEAVE THEM ALL BEHIND; EVERY SINGLE ONE OF THEM TURNS TOWARDS LINGMELL GILL AND SCAFELL PIKE.

PEACE AND QUIET PREVAILS AS I CLIMB GENTLY AWAY, KEEPING AN EYE OPEN FOR A PATH UP TO GREEN HOW. I CROSS A LOVELY STONE BRIDGE,

THEN PASS A COUPLE OF RUINS, BUT THERE'S NO SIGN OF A PATH. IS THERE ONE?, I ASK MYSELF. UNSURE, I LEAVE THE CORPSE ROAD AND HEAD OFF ALONGSIDE GROOVE GILL.

I KEEP CHECKING AHEAD FOR ANY SIGN OF THE PATH, BUT NO LUCK, SO IT'S HEAD DOWN AND HANDS ON KNEES INTO THE BLAZING SUN UNTIL I'M DRIPPING IN SWEAT. IT'S A RELENTLESS TRUDGE ON TOUGH GRASS AND REEDS; HEAD DOWN, HEAD UP, CHECK FOR A PATH; HEAD DOWN, HEAD UP, CHECK FOR A PATH... EVENTUALLY THE GRADIENT EASES, AND THERE IN THE DISTANCE I SPOT 'THE' PATH... BUT WITH BURNING SUN BEATING DOWN IT'S STILL TOUGH GOING.

TIME FOR A DRINK AND MY FIRST EVER SACHET OF ENERGY GEL. AS THE GRADIENT INCREASES THE PATH CHANGES CHARACTER, BECOMING A RIVER OF STONES AND ROCKS AS IT SNAKES ITS WAY UP THE FINAL THOUSAND FEET TO THE ROCKY SUMMIT OF SCAFELL.

is it supposed to taste of something??

I EXPERIENCE A GREAT FEELING OF SOLITUDE AS I SIT FOR A MOMENT ON ENGLAND'S SECOND HIGHEST SUMMIT AND GAZE OVER TO THE CROWDED SUMMIT OF SCAFELL PIKE. IT'S SO CLEAR I CAN PICK OUT INDIVIDUAL PEOPLE SILHOUETTED AGAINST THE BRIGHT BLUE SKY. THERE ARE NOT MANY DAYS LIKE THIS IN THE LAKES!

WITH MY LEGS FEELING GOOD I HEAD SOUTH FOR SLIGHT SIDE, A VIRGIN FELL FOR ME. I DESCEND CAUTIOUSLY FOR STARTERS, BUT AM SOON RUNNING ON A NARROW GRASS TRACK THREADING THROUGH PATCHES OF ROCK AND ROCKY OUTCROPS.

THE GOING'S EASY NOW, IN COOLER CONDITIONS AS A SLIGHT BREEZE BLOWS IN. I'M SOON ON THE LITTLE ROCKY SUMMIT OF SLIGHT SIDE ENJOYING ANOTHER DRINK WHILE WORKING OUT MY LINE OF DESCENT TO BURNMOOR TARN WAY DOWN IN THE DISTANCE.

IT'S STEADY GOING OVER GRASS AND ROCK OUTCROPS AT FIRST AS I MAKE A BEELINE FOR BROAD TONGUE. REEDS AND COTTON GRASS MAKE AN APPEARANCE FURTHER DOWN, AND AS I HEAD TOWARDS

HARDRIGG GILL BRACKEN MAKES ITS OBLIGATORY APPEARANCE. IT'S HERE THAT I TAKE A NASTY LITTLE TUMBLE - THOUGH I'VE HAD WORSE AND LIVED TO TELL THE TALE.

EVENTUALLY I REACH THE GILL AND CROSS OVER TO A PROPER PATH LEADING TO BURNMOOR TARN. THIS PROPER PATH TURNS OUT TO BE NO BETTER THAN WHAT I'VE JUST BEEN RUNNING ON. IT'S BOGGY AND WET, AND DISAPPEARS INTO POOLS OF WATER AT A WHIM. I REACH TERRA FIRMA AT THE SIDE OF THE TARN AND JOIN THE OLD CORPSE ROAD FOR THE RUN BACK TO WASDALE.

THE RUNNING'S GOOD NOW ON GENTLE GRADIENTS - SLIGHTLY UPHILL BEFORE A LONG DESCENT TO THE FINISH. IT'S ONLY NOW THAT I PASS THE FIRST WALKERS SINCE I STARTED OUT. I'M NEARLY BACK AT THE LOVELY STONE BRIDGE WHEN OUT OF MY EYE CORNER I SPOT A TINY, TINY CAIRN. COULD THIS BE THE START OF THE PATH I UNSUCCESSFULLY LOOKED FOR EARLIER?

RUNNING TOTAL	
DISTANCE	763·95 K
TIME	126 HRS 46 MINS
ASCENT	144,180 FT
SUMMITS	193

BACK TO THE CAR PARK AND SOME WELCOME SHADE!

THAT WAS TOUGH GOING. NOT MUCH FAST RUNNING, WITH DIFFICULT CONDITIONS UNDERFOOT AND STEEP ASCENTS AND DESCENTS. ENJOYABLE THOUGH.

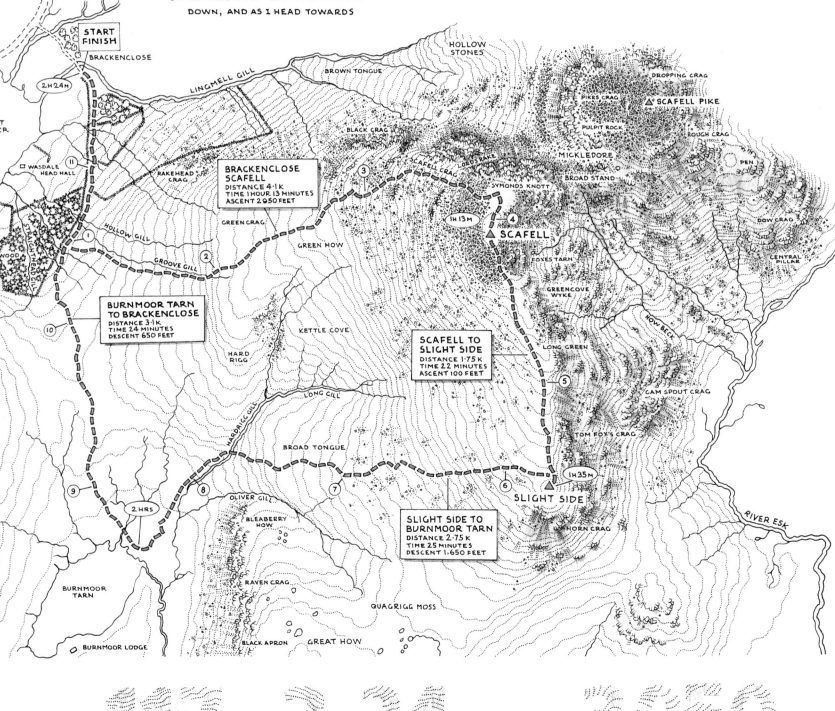

BRACKENCLOSE
SCAFELL
DISTANCE 4·1 K
TIME 1 HOUR 13 MINUTES
ASCENT 2,950 FEET

BURNMOOR TARN
TO BRACKENCLOSE
DISTANCE 3·1 K
TIME 24 MINUTES
DESCENT 650 FEET

SCAFELL TO
SLIGHT SIDE
DISTANCE 1·75 K
TIME 22 MINUTES
ASCENT 100 FEET

SLIGHT SIDE TO
BURNMOOR TARN
DISTANCE 2·75 K
TIME 25 MINUTES
DESCENT 1,650 FEET

DISTANCE 11·2 k TIME 2 24 hrs mins ASCENT

the WESTERN fells

No sign of Joss
as I tramp over his back garden
BUCKBARROW, SEATALLAN
and MIDDLE FELL

PILLAR OF STONES, BUCKBARROW

AFTER HEAVY OVERNIGHT RAIN A BEAUTIFUL SUNNY MORNING SENDS ME ON MY WAY UP A DELIGHTFUL PATH ALONGSIDE A STONE WALL OVERHUNG WITH LARCH BRANCHES. OVER A FEW NOBBLES AND I'M ONTO THE SUMMIT OF BUCKBARROW.

THERE ARE NO PROBLEMS RUNNING AS I CONTINUE TO THE CAIRN ON GLADE HOW. WITH NO SIGN OF A CLEAR PATH IN ANY DIRECTION, I HEAD OFF OVER TUSSOCKY OLD GRASS TOWARDS MY NEXT SUMMIT, SEATALLAN. THE NEXT COUPLE OF KILOMETRES TO THE BROAD FLAT SUMMIT ARE RUN CROSS COUNTRY. I TAP THE O.S. COLLUMN AND CONTINUE OVER TO THE NEARBY PILE OF STONES.

WITH TWO SUMMITS DOWN AND ONE TO GO I COMMENCE THE VERY SLIPPERY DESCENT TO SHOOTING HOW ON SATURATED SHORT GRASS, MAKING THE MOST OF THE MUD STEPS WORN INTO THE FELLSIDE. MY LEGS ARE FEELING GOOD AS I VEER BACK ONTO ROUGH GRASS AND ROCKS TOWARDS MIDDLE FELL, MY LAST SUMMIT OF THE DAY.

THE PATH BECOMES WETTER AND WETTER THE CLOSER I GET TO GREENDALE TARN UNTIL I'M UP TO MY SHINS IN WATER, SPLASHING MY WAY OVER A WIDE BED OF REEDS AT THE FOOT OF MIDDLE FELL.

DRY GROUND RE-APPEARS AS I START THE ASCENT. IT'S BETTER GOING NOW, ON A GOOD PATH, AND I MANAGE

A PILE OF STONES - MIDDLE FELL SUMMIT

TO ENJOY THE GREAT VIEWS OVER YEWBARROW AND BEYOND. FROM THE SUMMIT CAIRN WASTWATER IS IN FULL VIEW, BUT THE SCREES ARE STILL IN EARLY MORNING SHADE SO NOT QUITE AT THEIR BEST.

I'VE NOT SEEN A SOUL ALL DAY AS I DESCEND THROUGH BRACKEN AND ON SLIPPERY GRASS DOWN TO THE ROAD PACKED WITH CARS AND PEOPLE... BUT NO SIGN OF MR. NAYLOR!

SHOOTING HOW

WINSCALE HOWS

(4)

43 MINS

SEATALLAN ▲

56 MINS

ROUGH CRAG

(5)
BIG BAD BOG

BUCKBARROW TO SEATALLAN
DISTANCE 2·5 K
TIME 28 MINUTES
ASCENT 850 FEET

(3)

CARLING STONE

GREENDALE TARN

SEATALLAN TO MIDDLE FELL
DISTANCE 2·4 K
TIME 23 MINUTES
DESCENT 750 FEET
ASCENT 400 FEET

(6)

▲ MIDDLE FELL

66 MINS

NETHER BECK

(2)

△ CAT BIELDS

BROWN HOW

IRON CRAG

NETHERBECK BRIDGE

GOAT CRAG

TONGUES GILLS

(7)

MIDDLE FELL TO GREENDALE
DISTANCE 2 K
TIME 18 MINUTES
DESCENT 1,650 FEET

GOAT GILL

19 MINS

△ GLADE HOW

15 MINS

HARROW HEAD TO BUCKBARROW
DISTANCE 1·2 K
TIME 15 MINUTES
ASCENT 1,100 FEET

(1)

▲ BUCKBARROW

WATER CRAG

BULL CRAG

HAUSEGREEN CRAG

GREENUP

PIKE CRAG

RUNNING TOTAL	
DISTANCE	773·55 K
TIME	128 HRS 19 MINS
ASCENT	146,530 FT
SUMMITS	196

LONG CRAG

1H 24 M

GREENDALE

(8)

WAST WATER

DISTANCE **9·6** k TIME **1** hr **33** mins ASCENT **2,350** ft

the **FAR EASTERN** fells

SELSIDE and BRANSTREE
Never heard of 'em

ANOTHER OUT-OF-THE-WAY DRIVE INTO UNKNOWN TERRITORY TAKES ME DOWN TO SWINDALE HEAD (NO PARKING SPACE), WHERE I END UP PARKING IN SOMEONE'S GARDEN. IT'S EARLY MORNING. A HOT DAY'S FORECAST FOR THE WHOLE COUNTRY - BUT NOT SWINDALE, OH NO!

I SET OFF UPHILL ON THE OLD MARDALE CORPSE ROAD. IT'S A STEEP, WET CLIMB BEFORE DRYING OUT AND EASING OFF SLIGHTLY AS THE RUNNING GATHERS PACE.

I CONTINUE ON THE CORPSE ROAD AND SCAN THE FELLSIDE FOR A PATH UP TO SELSIDE'S SUMMIT. NO LUCK; THICK HILL FOG IS NOW MOVING IN AND OBLITERATING ALL.

I TURN OFF OVER ROUGH GROUND AND HEAD TOWARDS THE SUMMIT. IT'S SLOW GOING, BUT I EVENTUALLY REACH A PATH THAT LEADS TO THE UNTIDY SUMMIT CAIRN. I CAN'T SEE A THING NOW, SO I'M RELIEVED TO HAVE A FENCE AS COMPANY ALL THE WAY PAST THE LARGE CAIRN ON ARTLECRAG PIKE TO MY NEXT SUMMIT OF THE DAY, BRANSTREE.

WHICH WAY NOW? TO MOSEDALE VIA THE WALL DOWN SELSIDE BROW? OR RETRACE MY STEPS BACK TO AND OVER SELSIDE? I CHOOSE THE LATTER AS I STILL CAN'T SEE A THING AND HAVE NO IDEA WHAT THE PATHS - IF ANY - ARE LIKE UNDERFOOT ON THE MOSEDALE ROUTE.

BACK THE WAY I CAME IT IS THEN, EASY GOING ALL THE WAY TO SELSIDE, WHERE I MEET A LADY FELL RUNNER AND LEAN BORDER COLLIE OUT FOR A RUN. I SAY HI AND RUN ON. THE PATH TAKES ME DOWN TO A WOODEN STAKE ABOUT SIX FOOT TALL NEXT TO THE CORPSE ROAD. HOW ON EARTH I DIDN'T SEE IT I DON'T KNOW!

BACK ON THE CORPSE ROAD IT'S GOOD GOING RIGHT UP TO THE FINAL WET DESCENT. I REACH THE CAR WITH WET FEET, THEN HEAD BACK TO THE CARAVAN FOR SOME OF THAT PROMISED SUNSHINE.

HOW COULD YOU MISS SOMETHING THIS OBVIOUS!!!?

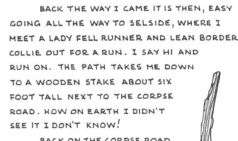

SELSIDE TO SWINDALE HEAD
DISTANCE 2·8K
TIME 17 MINUTES
DESCENT 1,200 FEET

START FINISH

1H 14M

SWINDALE HEAD

SELSIDE TO BRANSTREE
DISTANCE 1·8K
TIME 16 MINUTES
ASCENT 450 FEET

SWINDALE HEAD TO SELSIDE
DISTANCE 3K
TIME 27 MINUTES
ASCENT 1,200 FEET

BRANSTREE TO SELSIDE
DISTANCE 1·8K
TIME 14 MINUTES
ASCENT 200 FEET

57 MIN

27 MIN ▲ SELSIDE

43 MIN ▲ BRANSTREE

RUNNING TOTAL	
DISTANCE	782·95K
TIME	129 HRS 33 MINS
ASCENT	148 380 FT
SUMMITS	198

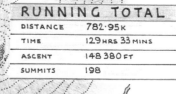

the DISTANCE **9·4**k theTIME **1h 14** mins the ASCENT **1,850** ft

the SOUTHERN fells

An early morning drive to
Lingmoor Fell
and then on to Holme Fell

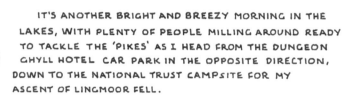

IT'S ANOTHER BRIGHT AND BREEZY MORNING IN THE LAKES, WITH PLENTY OF PEOPLE MILLING AROUND READY TO TACKLE THE 'PIKES' AS I HEAD FROM THE DUNGEON GHYLL HOTEL CAR PARK IN THE OPPOSITE DIRECTION, DOWN TO THE NATIONAL TRUST CAMPSITE FOR MY ASCENT OF LINGMOOR FELL.

THROUGH THE BUSY CAMPSITE AND I JOIN THE ZIGZAG PATH AT THE FOOT OF SIDE PIKE TO THE CATTLEGRID ON THE ROAD TO BLEA TARN HOUSE. MY LEGS FEEL GOOD AND STRONG AND I HAVE A FEELING I'M GOING TO ENJOY THE NEXT HOUR OR TWO AS I STRETCH THE LEGS OUT DOWN TO BLEA TARN HOUSE BEFORE THE HARD WORK BEGINS ON THE PATH UP TO BROWN HOW. IT'S A DELIGHTFUL PATH, THROUGH BRACKEN AT FIRST, BUT TOUGH GOING AS IT CLIMBS STEEPLY IN PLACES, REQUIRING HANDS ON KNEES NOW AND AGAIN.

two sights for sore eyes!

I REACH A CLUMP OF TREES AS THE GRADIENT RELENTS AND DIP UNDER A ROWAN LADEN WITH THOUSANDS OF THE BRIGHTEST BERRIES. IN THE DISTANCE IS A MOST BEAUTIFUL VIEW OF THE LANGDALE PIKES. STUNNING! A SIGHT FOR SORE EYES INDEED.

full concentration required

IT'S NOT FAR TO THE SUMMIT AS I CONTINUE TO RUN ON GRASS. AT THE CAIRN ALL THAT CHANGES, WITH HEATHER, PEAT AND ROCKS NOW DOMINATING. I CHECK THE TIME THEN HEAD HOMEWARD ON A CLEAR PATH WORN DEEP INTO THE PEAT.

WHAT A PATH TO WALK ON, WITH TWISTS AND TURNS, ROCKY STEPS TO NEGOTIATE, NUMEROUS UPS AND DOWNS, AND, TO CAP IT ALL, BEAUTIFUL VIEWS TO TAKE IN. FULL CONCENTRATION'S REQUIRED WHILE RUNNING THOUGH, ALL THE WAY TO THE FAR END OF THE RIDGE BEFORE I DESCEND TO THE FOOT OF SIDE PIKE.

I'M GIVING SIDE PIKE A MISS. IT'S NOT REALLY FELL RUNNING TERRITORY, AND IS BETTER LEFT ALONE ON THIS OCCASION.

i'll be back

I HEAD BACK ONTO GRASS AND INTO BRACKEN AS I DROP DOWN TO TARMAC AND THE CATTLE GRID, WHERE I GIVE THE ZIGZAGS A MISS AND STICK WITH THE WALL — EASY GOING ALL THE WAY BACK TO DUNGEON GHYLL. I PASS LOADS OF WALKERS HEADING OFF TO THE FELLS. LUCKY LOT! I'LL BE BACK TO WALK LINGMOOR FELL, AND TAKE IN SIDE PIKE AND THOSE LOVELY VIEWS.

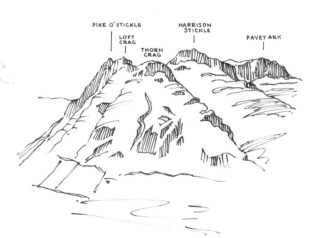

RUNNING TOTAL	
DISTANCE	789·45 K
TIME	130 HRS 34 MINS
ASCENT	149,630 FT
SUMMITS	199

200 HERE I COME

DISTANCE **6·5** k TIME **61** mins ASCENT **1,250** ft

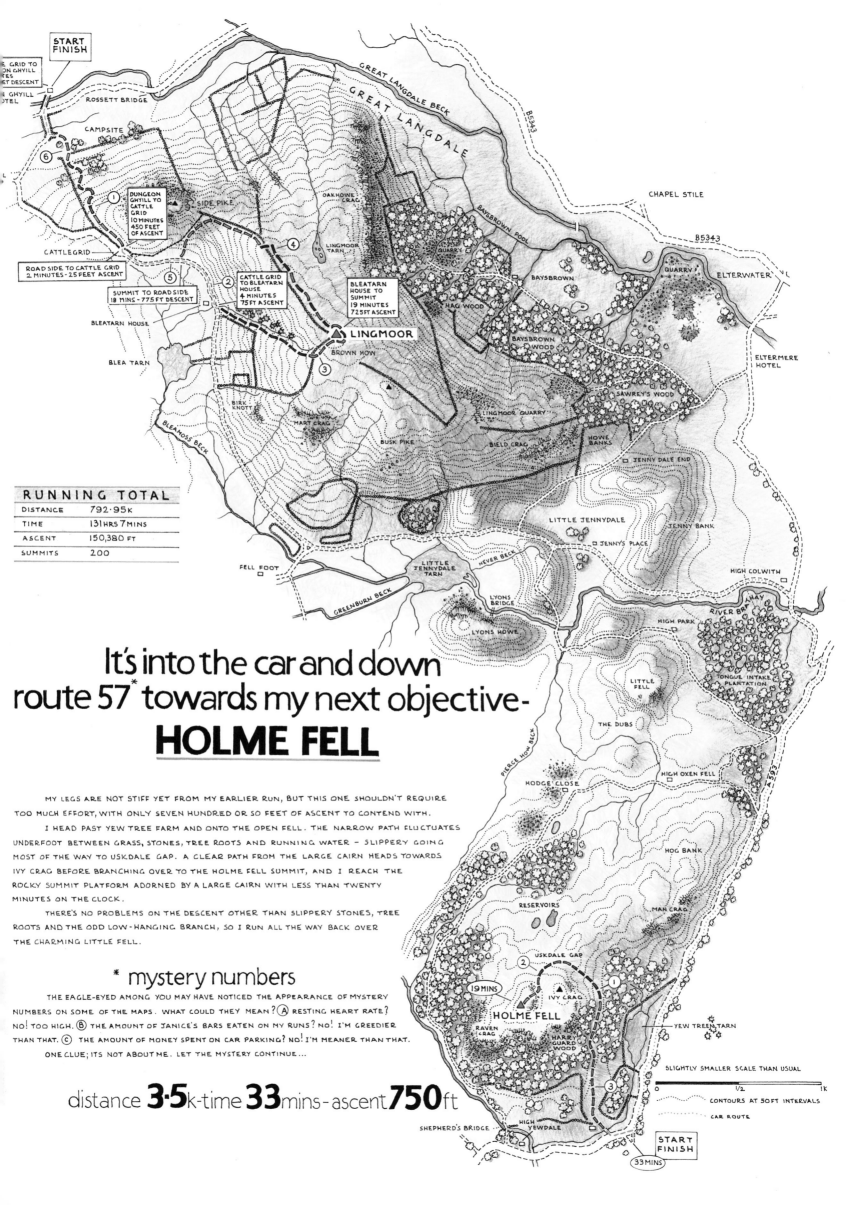

START FINISH

GREAT LANGDALE BECK

GREAT LANGDALE

ROSSETT BRIDGE

CAMPSITE

CHAPEL STILE

B5343

B5343

DUNGEON GHYLL TO CATTLE GRID 10 MINUTES 450 FEET OF ASCENT

SIDE PIKE

OAKHOWE CRAG

QUARRY

QUARRY

ELTERWATER

CATTLEGRID

LINGMOOR TARN

BAYSBROWN POOL

BAYSBROWN

ROAD SIDE TO CATTLE GRID 2 MINUTES - 25 FEET ASCENT

SUMMIT TO ROAD SIDE 18 MINS - 775 FT DESCENT

CATTLE GRID TO BLEATARN HOUSE 4 MINUTES 75 FT ASCENT

BLEATARN HOUSE TO SUMMIT 19 MINUTES 725 FT ASCENT

HAG WOOD

BAYSBROWN WOOD

BLEATARN HOUSE

LINGMOOR

ELTERMERE HOTEL

BLEA TARN

BROWN HOW

SAWREY'S WOOD

BIRK KNOTT

LINGMOOR QUARRY

BLEAMOSS BECK

MART CRAG

BUSK PIKE

BIELD CRAG

HOWE BANKS

JENNY DALE END

RUNNING TOTAL

DISTANCE	792·95k
TIME	131 HRS 7 MINS
ASCENT	150,380 FT
SUMMITS	200

LITTLE JENNYDALE

TENNY BANK

JENNY'S PLACE

FELL FOOT

LITTLE JENNYDALE TARN

NEVER BECK

HIGH COLWITH

GREENBURN BECK

LYONS BRIDGE

LYONS HOWE

RIVER BRATHAY

HIGH PARK

TONGUE INTAKE PLANTATION

A593

It's into the car and down
route 57* towards my next objective-
HOLME FELL

LITTLE FELL

THE DUBS

PIERCE HOW BECK

HODGE CLOSE

HIGH OXEN FELL

MY LEGS ARE NOT STIFF YET FROM MY EARLIER RUN, BUT THIS ONE SHOULDN'T REQUIRE TOO MUCH EFFORT, WITH ONLY SEVEN HUNDRED OR SO FEET OF ASCENT TO CONTEND WITH.

I HEAD PAST YEW TREE FARM AND ONTO THE OPEN FELL. THE NARROW PATH FLUCTUATES UNDERFOOT BETWEEN GRASS, STONES, TREE ROOTS AND RUNNING WATER – SLIPPERY GOING MOST OF THE WAY TO USKDALE GAP. A CLEAR PATH FROM THE LARGE CAIRN HEADS TOWARDS IVY CRAG BEFORE BRANCHING OVER TO THE HOLME FELL SUMMIT, AND I REACH THE ROCKY SUMMIT PLATFORM ADORNED BY A LARGE CAIRN WITH LESS THAN TWENTY MINUTES ON THE CLOCK.

THERE'S NO PROBLEMS ON THE DESCENT OTHER THAN SLIPPERY STONES, TREE ROOTS AND THE ODD LOW-HANGING BRANCH, SO I RUN ALL THE WAY BACK OVER THE CHARMING LITTLE FELL.

HOG BANK

RESERVOIRS

MAN CRAG

USKDALE GAP

19 MINS

IVY CRAG

* mystery numbers

THE EAGLE-EYED AMONG YOU MAY HAVE NOTICED THE APPEARANCE OF MYSTERY NUMBERS ON SOME OF THE MAPS. WHAT COULD THEY MEAN? Ⓐ RESTING HEART RATE? NO! TOO HIGH. Ⓑ THE AMOUNT OF JANICE'S BARS EATEN ON MY RUNS? NO! I'M GREEDIER THAN THAT. Ⓒ THE AMOUNT OF MONEY SPENT ON CAR PARKING? NO! I'M MEANER THAN THAT. ONE CLUE; ITS NOT ABOUT ME. LET THE MYSTERY CONTINUE...

HOLME FELL

RAVEN CRAG

YEW TREE TARN

HARRY GUARD WOOD

SLIGHTLY SMALLER SCALE THAN USUAL

distance **3·5**k-time **33**mins-ascent**750**ft

SHEPHERD'S BRIDGE

HIGH YEWDALE

START FINISH

33 MINS

1/2   1k

CONTOURS AT 50 FT INTERVALS

CAR ROUTE

last of the **FAR EASTERN** fells

TARN CRAG and GREY CRAG

Surprisingly much better than expected

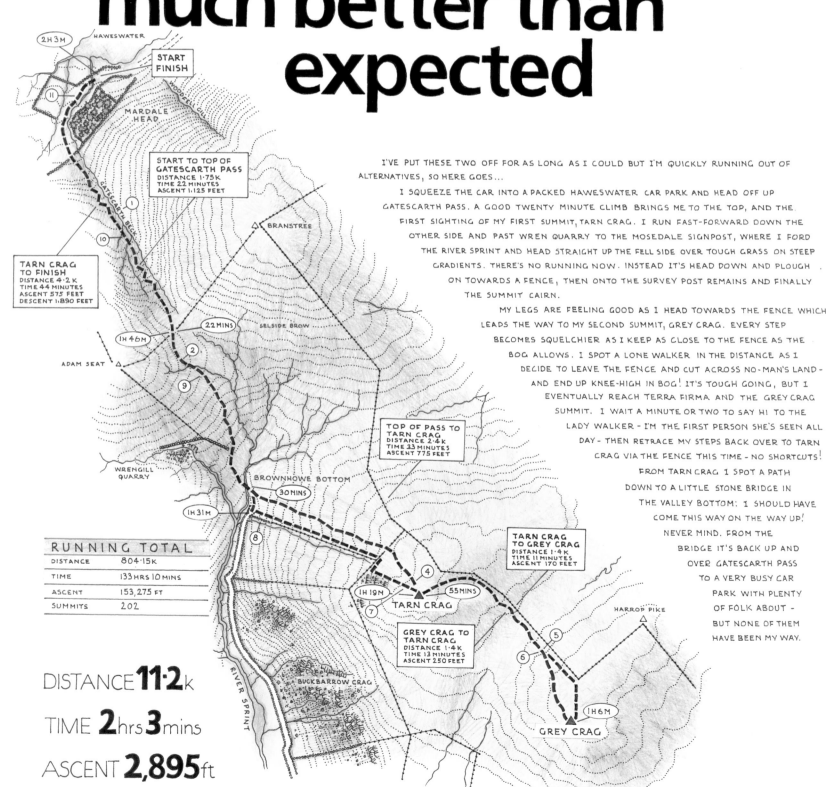

START TO TOP OF GATESCARTH PASS
DISTANCE 1·75K
TIME 22 MINUTES
ASCENT 1,125 FEET

TARN CRAG TO FINISH
DISTANCE 4·2 K
TIME 44 MINUTES
ASCENT 575 FEET
DESCENT 1,890 FEET

TOP OF PASS TO TARN CRAG
DISTANCE 2·4 K
TIME 33 MINUTES
ASCENT 775 FEET

TARN CRAG TO GREY CRAG
DISTANCE 1·4K
TIME 11 MINUTES
ASCENT 170 FEET

GREY CRAG TO TARN CRAG
DISTANCE 1·4K
TIME 13 MINUTES
ASCENT 250 FEET

RUNNING TOTAL	
DISTANCE	804·15K
TIME	133 HRS 10 MINS
ASCENT	153,275 FT
SUMMITS	202

DISTANCE **11·2**k

TIME **2**hrs **3**mins

ASCENT **2,895**ft

I'VE PUT THESE TWO OFF FOR AS LONG AS I COULD BUT I'M QUICKLY RUNNING OUT OF ALTERNATIVES, SO HERE GOES...

I SQUEEZE THE CAR INTO A PACKED HAWESWATER CAR PARK AND HEAD OFF UP GATESCARTH PASS. A GOOD TWENTY MINUTE CLIMB BRINGS ME TO THE TOP, AND THE FIRST SIGHTING OF MY FIRST SUMMIT, TARN CRAG. I RUN FAST-FORWARD DOWN THE OTHER SIDE AND PAST WREN QUARRY TO THE MOSEDALE SIGNPOST, WHERE I FORD THE RIVER SPRINT AND HEAD STRAIGHT UP THE FELL SIDE OVER TOUGH GRASS ON STEEP GRADIENTS. THERE'S NO RUNNING NOW. INSTEAD IT'S HEAD DOWN AND PLOUGH ON TOWARDS A FENCE, THEN ONTO THE SURVEY POST REMAINS AND FINALLY THE SUMMIT CAIRN.

MY LEGS ARE FEELING GOOD AS I HEAD TOWARDS THE FENCE WHICH LEADS THE WAY TO MY SECOND SUMMIT, GREY CRAG. EVERY STEP BECOMES SQUELCHIER AS I KEEP AS CLOSE TO THE FENCE AS THE BOG ALLOWS. I SPOT A LONE WALKER IN THE DISTANCE AS I DECIDE TO LEAVE THE FENCE AND CUT ACROSS NO-MAN'S LAND - AND END UP KNEE-HIGH IN BOG! IT'S TOUGH GOING, BUT I EVENTUALLY REACH TERRA FIRMA AND THE GREY CRAG SUMMIT. I WAIT A MINUTE OR TWO TO SAY HI TO THE LADY WALKER - I'M THE FIRST PERSON SHE'S SEEN ALL DAY - THEN RETRACE MY STEPS BACK OVER TO TARN CRAG VIA THE FENCE THIS TIME - NO SHORTCUTS!

FROM TARN CRAG I SPOT A PATH DOWN TO A LITTLE STONE BRIDGE IN THE VALLEY BOTTOM: I SHOULD HAVE COME THIS WAY ON THE WAY UP! NEVER MIND. FROM THE BRIDGE IT'S BACK UP AND OVER GATESCARTH PASS TO A VERY BUSY CAR PARK WITH PLENTY OF FOLK ABOUT - BUT NONE OF THEM HAVE BEEN MY WAY.

the **WESTERN** fells

A funny thing happened on the way to Overbeck Bridge...

Mr Naylor I presume?

It's destination Wasdale on a bright and sunny morning. As I negotiate the sheep enjoying the warmth on the tarmac ahead of me I spot a guy with a dog crossing the road. His face looks familiar. Could it really be who I think it is...

YES IT COULD. AND YES IT IS.

as I introduce myself to a true legend...

ILLUSTRATION BASED ON A PHOTOGRAPH BY VAL CORBETT

WHACK! WORST TUMBLE YET

PILLAR

SCOAT FELL TO STEEPLE
DISTANCE 0·4K
TIME 5 MINS
ASCENT 70FT
DESCENT 140FT

BLACK CRAG TO SCOAT FELL
DISTANCE 0·8 KILOMETRE
TIME 8 MINUTES
ASCENT 300 FEET

STEEPLE
2H21M

SCOAT FELL
2H16M
2H8M

PILLAR TO BLACK CRAG
DISTANCE 0·8KILOMETRES
TIME 13 MINUTES
ASCENT 50 FEET
DESCENT 1200 FEET

BLACK SAIL PASS TO PILLAR
DISTANCE 2·4 KILOMETRES
TIME 33 MINUTES
ASCENT 1120 FEET

1H 55M

BLACK SAIL PASS
1H 22M

KIRK FELL TO BLACK SAIL PASS
DISTANCE 1 KILOMETRE
TIME 17 MINUTES
DESCENT 830 FEET

STEEPLE TO RED PIKE
DISTANCE 1·6 KILOMETRES
TIME 18 MINUTES
ASCENT 350 FEET

RED PIKE
2H39M

KIRK FELL
1H 5M

FOOT OF KIRK FELL TO SUMMIT
DISTANCE 1·7 KILOMETRES
TIME 46 MINUTES
ASCENT 2330 FEET

RED PIKE TO DORE HEAD
DISTANCE 1·9 KILOMETRES
TIME 23 MINUTES
DESCENT 1200 FEET

3H 2M

3H15M
YEWBARROW NORTH SUMMIT

DORE HEAD TO YEWBARROW
DISTANCE 1·4 K
TIME 20 MINS
ASCENT 650 FT

19 MINS

WASDALE HEAD

3H22M
YEWBARROW

YEWBARROW TO OVERBECK BRIDGE
DISTANCE 2·2 KILOMETRES
TIME 32 MINUTES
DESCENT 1900 FEET

3H 54M

OVERBECK BRIDGE TO FOOT OF KIRK FELL
DISTANCE 3·3 KILOMETRES
TIME 19 MINUTES
ASCENT 20 FEET

START FINISH

WAST WATER

DISTANCE 16·75k
TIME 3hrs 54mins
ASCENT 4,870ft

down to the last 10!!!

I HEAD BACK TO THE CAR AND CONTINUE TO OVERBECK CAR PARK, WHERE I CHAT TO A COUPLE PARKED NEXT TO ME. THEY'RE GETTING READY FOR A DAY ON THE FELLS AND ALSO DOING THE WAINWRIGHTS. THEY ONLY HAVE FIVE REMAINING, ONE OF WHICH IS YEWBARROW. I, ON THE OTHER HAND, HAVE TWICE AS MANY, SO I BETTER GET GOING...

AFTER THE LONG DRIVE DOWN I GET TO LOOSEN THE OLD LEGS ON A GOOD LONG STRETCH OF TARMAC BEFORE TAKING THE FOOTPATH ALONGSIDE MOSEDALE BECK INTO WASDALE HEAD. I PASS THE PUB, THEN HEAD OVER THE BRIDGE ONTO THE FOOT OF KIRK FELL.

SOMEONE ONCE SAID THERE'S NO EASY WAY OUT OF WASDALE, AND THIS MUST BE ONE OF THE TOUGHEST: OVER TWO THOUSAND FEET OF ASCENT WITH NO RESPITE. SO IT'S HEAD DOWN, HANDS ON KNEES AND ONE STEP AT A TIME UP THE LITTLE MUD STEPS WORN INTO THE GRASS UNTIL I REACH THE SCREE. HERE THE PATH TWISTS ITS WAY OVER LOOSE STONES, EVENTUALLY REACHING FIRMER GROUND AND A CLEAR PATH TO THE BROAD SUMMIT. IT'S TOUGH GOING - BUT THERAPEUTIC IN A MASOCHISTIC SORT OF WAY!

easier than it looked

THERE'S A CHANCE FOR THE LEGS TO RECOVER AS I FOLLOW THE FENCE ON ITS WAY TO BLACK SAIL PASS - EASY GOING AT FIRST, BUT BECOMING TRICKY OVER KIRK FELL CRAG. MY LEGS ARE FEELING GOOD AS I START THE LONG DRAG OVER LOOKING STEAD TO PILLAR. IT TURNS OUT TO BE A LOT EASIER THAN IT APPEARED FROM THE TOP OF KIRK FELL, AND I'M SOON ADMIRING THE VIEWS FROM PILLAR'S SUMMIT. I SPOT THREE WALKERS IN THE DISTANCE STARTING THE DESCENT TO WIND GAP, SO OFF I GO TO JOIN THEM.

WHACK! SUDDENLY I'M PROSTRATE ON THE GROUND, LYING THERE TRYING MY BEST JUST TO BREATH, ALL THE WIND KNOCKED OUT OF ME BY THE FORCE OF A FALL I NEVER SAW COMING.

I ROLL ONTO MY BACK AND SUCK AIR INTO MY BODY. THEN I TRY TO SIT UP.

AHH! MY SHOULDER'S KILLING ME. IS IT BROKEN? I SHUFFLE ONTO A ROCK AND CHECK MY COLLAR BONE. IT'S TOO PAINFUL TO MOVE JUST YET. I LOOK DOWN AT MY SHINS: I'VE MANAGED TO PEEL THE TOP LAYER OF SKIN OFF THE FRONT OF MY RIGHT SHIN. BACK TO MY SHOULDER. DEEP BREATHS ARE REQUIRED TO MOVE MY ARM. IT'S NOT BROKEN! BUT IT IS REALLY PAINFUL. LUCKY IT WAS MY COLLAR BONE AND NOT MY HEAD OR I'D HAVE BEEN IN BIG TROUBLE!

there and back

THE FALL'S SHAKEN ME UP A BIT, SO I MAKE A CAREFUL DESCENT TO WIND GAP, THEN UP THROUGH ROCKS TO BLACK CRAG'S SUMMIT. IT'S EASY GOING NOW TO SCOAT FELL, WHERE I TAP THE CAIRN ON THE WALL THEN FOLLOW THE OTHER CAIRNS TO STEEPLE - THERE AND BACK IN TEN MINUTES, GREAT VIEWS ALL THE WAY.

vertical scrambling

I HEAD ONTO RED PIKE OVER GRASS AND PROTRUDING STONES, DOWNHILL BEFORE A GENTLE INCLINE TO THE SUMMIT, WITH BEAUTIFUL VIEWS OVER TO KIRK FELL, GABLE AND BEYOND. ON THE LONG, STEADY DESCENT TO DORE HEAD YEWBARROW GROWS IN STATURE THE CLOSER I GET TO STIRRUP EDGE.

FROM THE FOOT OF STIRRUP EDGE A CLEAR PATH TAKES ME UP THE INITIAL SLOPE, WHERE HANDS-ON-KNEES AND ROCKS COME INTO PLAY AS A ROUTE PUSHES ITS WAY BETWEEN ROCKS AND CRAGS. IT'S A LOT EASIER THAN IT LOOKED FROM THE BOTTOM - THOUGH I WOULDN'T FANCY COMING DOWN IN A HURRY.

head over heels

IT'S STRAIGHT BACK INTO RUNNING ON THE GRASSY SUMMIT RIDGE, AND I'M SOON AT THE TRUE SUMMIT AND ON MY WAY TOWARDS BELL RIB FOR THE FINAL DESCENT OF THE DAY. IN MY WISDOM I DECIDE TO DROP OFF THE RIDGE PATH EARLY TO AVOID BELL RIB. THE GOING'S SLOW DOWN A STEEP GULLY FULL OF ROCKS AND SCREE...

... THEN I HAVE ONE MORE TUMBLE. THIS TIME IT'S HEAD OVER HEELS, BUT ON GOOD OLD GRASS, AND THE MOMENTUM CARRIES ME BACK ONTO MY FEET AND BACK TO RUNNING.

I SOON REACH THE OVER BECK PATH TO DORE HEAD, WHERE I TURN LEFT AND PASS BELOW DROPPING CRAG. ON REACHING THE WALL DOWN TO OVER BECK I CATCH UP WITH LIZ AND DAVE FROM THE CAR PARK WHO ARE MOST IMPRESSED TO SEE ME AS THEY HAVE ONLY BEEN UP YEWBARROW.

all's well that ends well

WELL, IT'S BEEN AN EVENTFUL RUN, GOOD RUNNING IN PLACES WITH A FEW TOUGH ASCENTS AND DESCENTS AND GREAT VIEWS THROWN IN FOR GOOD MEASURE.

AS I CHANGE MY T-SHIRT I CHECK OUT MY COLLAR BONE. A LUMP THE SIZE OF A GOLF BALL HAS APPEARED, SO I HOPE IT'S GOING TO BE OK.

...AND I'VE GOT ANOTHER SCAR ON MY SHIN TO ADD TO THE COLLECTION.

ONLY 6 TO GO, YIPPEE!

YEWBARROW

RUNNING TOTAL	
DISTANCE	820·9K
TIME	137 HRS 4 MINS
ASCENT	158,145 FT
SUMMITS	208

the **SOUTHERN** fells

Wasdale - home to the deepest lake, the highest mountain and now the largest scale map in the book!

Oh, and **WHIN RIGG** & **ILLGILL HEAD** too

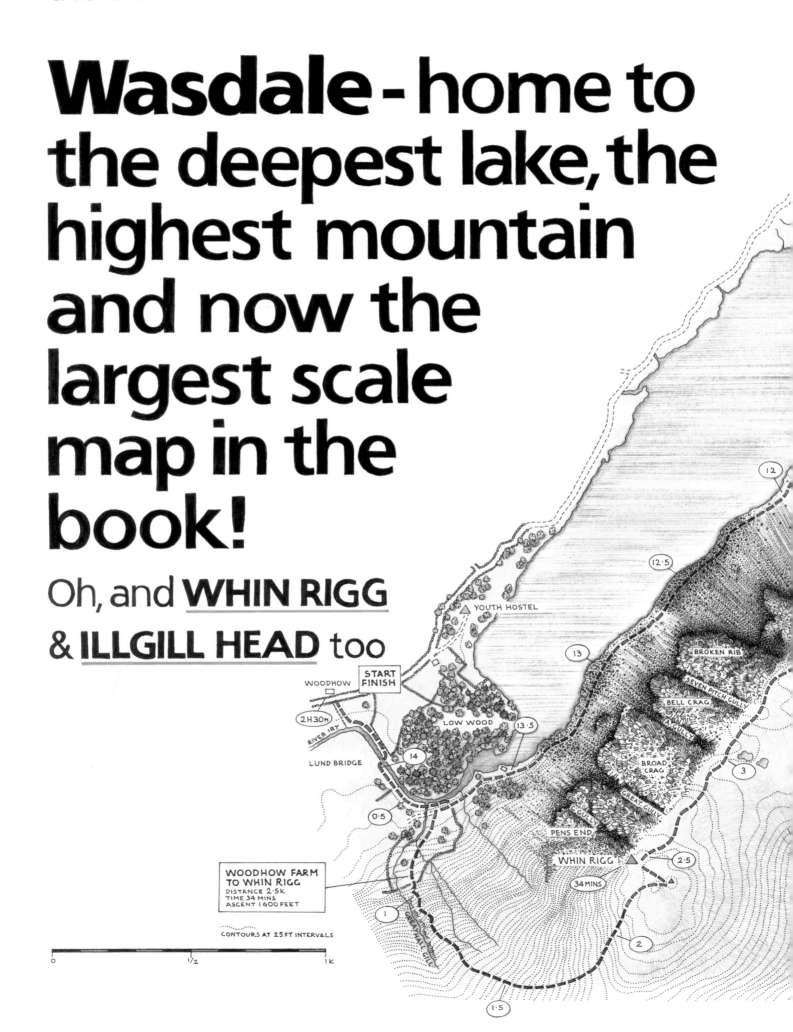

YOUTH HOSTEL

BROKEN RIB

SEVEN PITCH GULLY

BELL CRAG

START FINISH

WOODHOW

2H30M

RIVER IRT

LUND BRIDGE

LOW WOOD

BROAD CRAG

PENS END

WHIN RIGG

34 MINS

WOODHOW FARM
TO WHIN RIGG
DISTANCE 2·5K
TIME 34 MINS
ASCENT 1600 FEET

CONTOURS AT 25FT INTERVALS

0   ½   1k

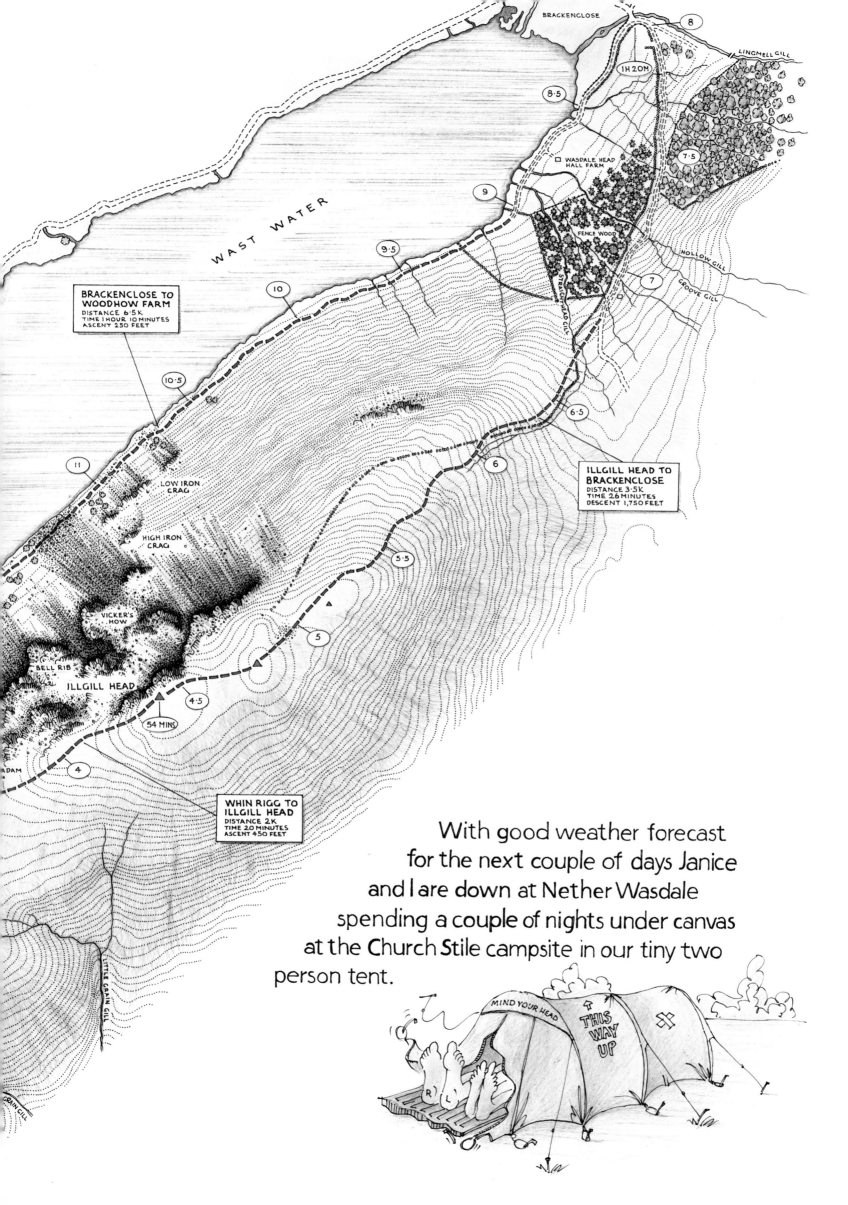

BRACKENCLOSE

LINGMELL GILL

8

1H 20M

8.5

7.5

□ WASDALE HEAD
HALL FARM

9

HOLLOW GILL

FENCE WOOD

7

GROOVE GILL

9.5

STRAIGHT HEAD GILL

W A S T   W A T E R

10

6.5

BRACKENCLOSE TO
WOODHOW FARM
DISTANCE 6·5K
TIME 1 HOUR 10 MINUTES
ASCENT 230 FEET

10.5

6

ILLGILL HEAD TO
BRACKENCLOSE
DISTANCE 3·5K
TIME 26 MINUTES
DESCENT 1,750 FEET

11

LOW IRON
CRAG

HIGH IRON
CRAG

5.5

VICKER'S
HOW

5

BELL RIB

ILLGILL HEAD

4.5

54 MINS

DAM

4

WHIN RIGG TO
ILLGILL HEAD
DISTANCE 2K
TIME 20 MINUTES
ASCENT 450 FEET

LITTLE GRAIN GILL

GRAIN GILL

With good weather forecast
for the next couple of days Janice
and I are down at Nether Wasdale
spending a couple of nights under canvas
at the Church Stile campsite in our tiny two
person tent.

MIND YOUR HEAD

THIS
WAY
UP

R L

A hot and stuffy night brings a hot and humid start to the day as I prepare for my fell run...

I HAVE A SPRIGHTLY WALK WITH JANICE DOWN TO WOODHOW FARM, THE START OF MY RUN, BEFORE WE GO OUR SEPERATE WAYS, JANICE ON A LAKESIDE STROLL WHILE I HEAD OFF TOWARDS WHIN RIGG. THE RUNNING'S EASY FOR STARTERS, OVER A BRIDGE AND THEN UNDER OVERHANGING BRANCHES BEFORE HEADING ONTO THE OPEN FELL TOWARDS GREATHALL GILL ON A GOOD PATH WITH TIGHT ZIGZAGS. IT'S STEEP BUT SHORT, THROUGH BRACKEN AT FIRST, THEN OVER TOUGH GRASS, AND I'M SOON UP TO THE GRASS RIDGE AND THE TWIN CAIRNED SUMMIT OF WHIN RIGG. I GIVE JANICE A WAVE JUST IN CASE SHE'S WATCHING.

IT'S STILL HOT AND HUMID — EVEN AT THIS ALTITUDE — BUT MY LEGS FEEL GOOD TO GO, AND I'M REALLY LOOKING FORWARD TO THE NEXT BIT OF RUNNING. THE FAINT TRACK HUGGING THE CLIFF EDGE IS A DELIGHT, WITH UNSURPASSED VIEWS DOWN THE VARIOUS GULLIES AS THEY PLUNGE TO THE SHORE OF WAST WATER.

IT'S EASY GOING, SO THERE ARE PLENTY OF OPPORTUNITIES TO KEEP SNEAKING A QUICK LOOK AND GIVE A WAVE OR TWO IN CASE JANICE CAN SPOT ME WAY UP ON THE SKYLINE.

THE SUMMIT OF ILLGILL HEAD ARRIVES FAR TOO EARLY — I'M ALMOST TEMPTED TO TURN ROUND AND DO IT ALL AGAIN! INSTEAD I HAVE A QUICK DRINK AT THE SUMMIT BEFORE THE LONG DESCENT TO BRACKENCLOSE. IT'S PLAIN SAILING, WITH NO STEEP GRADIENTS AS I VEER LEFT ON A THIN TRACK AND THEN FOLLOW A WALL DOWN TO THE OLD CORPSE ROAD.

IT'S TAKEN JUST ONE HOUR AND TWENTY MINUTES SO FAR FROM THE START DOWN TO BRACKENCLOSE. I'M HAPPY WITH THAT, BUT NOT SO OPTIMISTIC ABOUT THE NEXT FIVE KILOMETRES AS I HEAD TO WASDALE HEAD HALL AND THE LAKESIDE PATH BACK TO LOW WOOD ALONG THE SCREES.

RUNNING TOTAL	
DISTANCE	835·4 K
TIME	139 HRS 34 MINS
ASCENT	160,195 FT
SUMMITS	210

MY ROUTE IS THROUGH FIELDS OF COWS TO START WITH ON A FARM ROAD, BEFORE IT REDUCES IN WIDTH AND A PATH STARTS UNDULATING ABOVE THE SHORELINE. A MORE CAUTIOUS PACE IS NEEDED NOW, AND IT'S NOT LONG BEFORE THE FIRST PATCH OF SCREE MAKES AN APPEARANCE. THE SCREE CALLS FOR STOP-START RUNNING, WITH EACH PATCH OF SCREE SLIGHTLY WORSE THAN THE LAST!

THE LAST ONE IS THE BIGGEST AND BY FAR THE WORST. HUGE ROCKS AND NO CLEAR ROUTE MAKE IT FEEL MORE LIKE HORIZONTAL SCRAMBLING THAN RUNNING. THE SLOW GOING GIVES ME A CHANCE TO STOP AND VIEW THE IMPRESSIVE GULLIES AND ROCK ARCHITECTURE WITHOUT LOSING TIME.

BY THE TIME I'VE CLEARED THE LAST OF THE BOULDERS MY LEGS ARE READY FOR THE FINAL RUN OF THE DAY: I PASS THE POWER HOUSE, DIP UNDER THE TREES, CROSS LUND BRIDGE AND REACH THE OLD METAL GATE AT WOODHOW FARM.

time to refuel

I WALK BACK TO THE CAMPSITE FOR A WELL-EARNED SHOWER AND LATER A MEAL AT THE LOCAL PUB, THE STRANDS, CONSISTING OF STEAK AND ALE PIE, CHIPS AND PEAS FOLLOWED BY A BAILEYS BREAD AND BUTTER PUDDING AND A FEW PINTS OF BLACKCURRANT AND SODA TO REFUEL THE BODY READY FOR ANOTHER RUN IN THE MORNING...

no chance!

...STRONG WINDS AND HEAVY RAIN HIT THE TENT THROUGHOUT THE NIGHT AND CONTINUE INTO THE MORNING, SO IT'S PORRIDGE AND COFFEE IN A STEAMY CAR BEFORE PACKING UP A WET TENT AND HEADING BACK TO A WARM AND DRY CARAVAN.

SO MUCH FOR THE GOOD WEATHER FORECAST!

HORIZONTAL SCRAMBLING

DISTANCE 14·5 k TIME 2 hrs 30 mins ASCENT 2,050 ft

Last of the **western** fells and Mellbreak's poor neighbour...
it's Hen Comb
and grass, grass, grass!

I HEAD TO THE RED PHONE BOX AT LOWESWATER, NOW A HOME FOR A
DEFIBRILLATOR! LET'S HOPE IT'S NOT REQUIRED AT THE END OF THIS RUN! IT WONT BE
THROUGH EXCITEMENT, IF IT IS, THAT'S FOR SURE. I'D HOPED TO RUN THIS ONE THE SAME

TIME AS MELLBREAK BUT HAD TO ABORT DUE TO INJURY.

I SET OFF DOWN THE LANE PAST THE PUB, THEN HEAD
OVER THE STEPPING STONES ACROSS MOSEDALE BECK
AND ONTO A PATH LEADING TO THE OLD MINE WORKINGS.
THERE'S HARDLY ANY PATH; IT'S A GOOD JOB ALL THE
BRACKEN HAS DIED BACK OR THERE WOULD BE NO CHANCE
OF FOLLOWING IT. HEIGHT IS GAINED SLOWLY, WITH GOOD
RUNNING UNTIL THE PATH DRIES UP AND I HEAD UP TO-
WARDS THE RIDGE. IT'S TOUGH GOING NOW AS I
CROSS A FENCE AND THEN MAKE THE FINAL STIFF
PULL TO THE GRASS SUMMIT.

A TINY CAIRN ON A ROCK PLINTH
MARKS THE SUMMIT. IT RECEIVES A
QUICK TAP FROM ME - I DON'T HANG
ABOUT DUE TO THE GALE FORCE WIND
THAT'S WHIPPED UP - THEN IT'S
DOWN ALONG A SPONGY RIDGE
PATH WITH THE WIND ON MY BACK.
TOGETHER WITH GOOD CONDITIONS
UNDERFOOT IT'S THE BEST BIT OF
RUNNING SO FAR. WHEN THE PATH FORKS AT LITTLE DODD I BEAR RIGHT
TOWARDS THE STONE WALL, WHICH LEADS ME DOWN TO MOSEDALE BECK
AND THE STEPPING STONES. DOWN THE LANE PAST THE PUB - THE
DRINK WILL HAVE TO WAIT A LITTLE LONGER - PAST THE CHURCH - THAT
WILL HAVE TO WAIT A LOT LONGER! - AND I'M BACK TO LOWESWATER.

PLEASED TO SAY DEFIBRILLATOR NOT REQUIRED!

HEN COMB: A GOOD EXERCISE FOR THE LEGS - BUT A POOR
NEIGHBOUR FOR MELLBREAK.

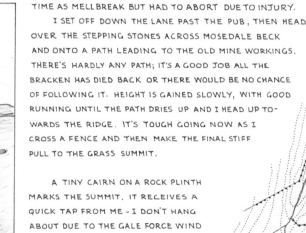

RUNNING TOTAL	
DISTANCE	842·4K
TIME	140HRS 37MINS
ASCENT	161,495FT
SUMMITS	211

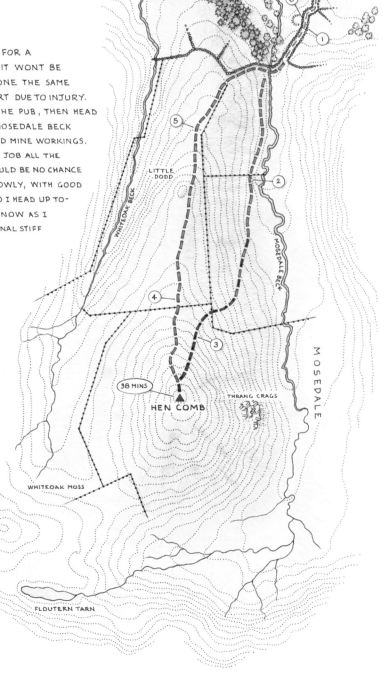

the DISTANCE **7**k theTIME **63**mins theASCENT **1,300**ft

OCTOBER 15th 2016

the **SOUTHERN** fells

THE
GREAT
END
ING!!!

via

LINGMELL and SCAFELL PIKE

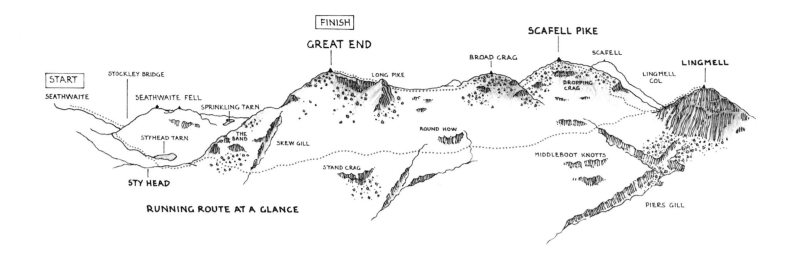

RUNNING ROUTE AT A GLANCE

I HAVE A PLAN

It's my 66th birthday today and therefore it's exactly 6 years since my Blencathra run and the spark for my challenge to run the Wainwrights...

CONSIDERING I'VE HAD **NO PLAN** EVERYTHING, SO FAR, HAS GONE TO PLAN, SO LET'S HOPE MY LUCK CONTINUES, BECAUSE TODAY

I DO HAVE A PLAN
AND THIS IS IT...

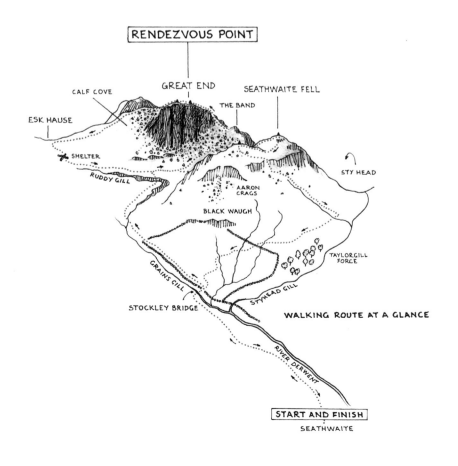

WALKING ROUTE AT A GLANCE

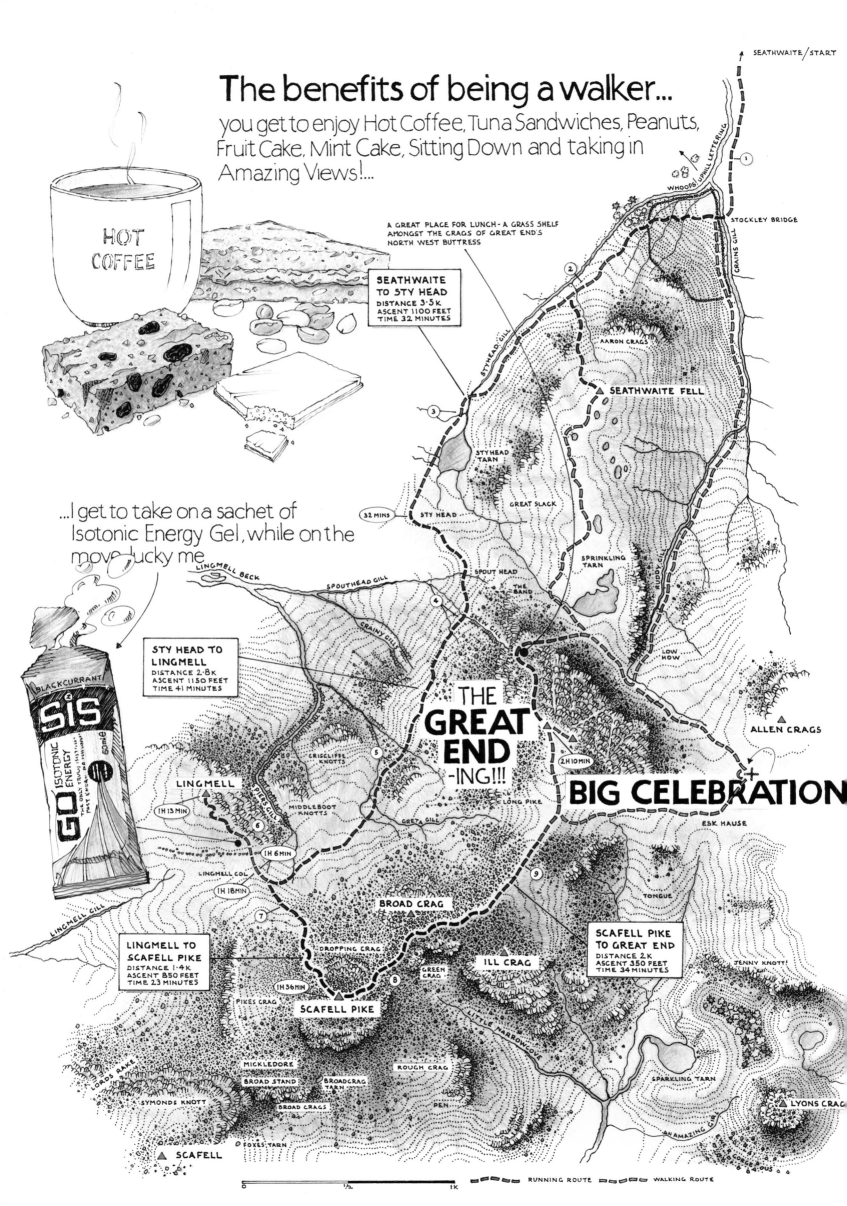

The benefits of being a walker...

you get to enjoy Hot Coffee, Tuna Sandwiches, Peanuts, Fruit Cake, Mint Cake, Sitting Down and taking in Amazing Views!...

HOT COFFEE

...I get to take on a sachet of Isotonic Energy Gel, while on the move...lucky me

BLACKCURRANT
SIS
GO ISOTONIC ENERGY

A GREAT PLACE FOR LUNCH - A GRASS SHELF AMONGST THE CRAGS OF GREAT END'S NORTH WEST BUTTRESS

SEATHWAITE TO STY HEAD
DISTANCE 3·5k
ASCENT 1100 FEET
TIME 32 MINUTES

STY HEAD TO LINGMELL
DISTANCE 2·8k
ASCENT 1150 FEET
TIME 41 MINUTES

LINGMELL TO SCAFELL PIKE
DISTANCE 1·4k
ASCENT 850 FEET
TIME 23 MINUTES

SCAFELL PIKE TO GREAT END
DISTANCE 2k
ASCENT 350 FEET
TIME 34 MINUTES

THE GREAT END-ING!!!

BIG CELEBRATION

SEATHWAITE/START

WHOOPS! UPHILL LETTERING

STOCKLEY BRIDGE

CRAINS GILL

AARON CRAGS

SEATHWAITE FELL

STYHEAD GILL

STYHEAD TARN

GREAT SLACK

SPRINKLING TARN

RUDDY

LOW HOW

ALLEN CRAGS

32 MINS

STY HEAD

SPOUT HEAD

THE BAND

LINGMELL BECK

SPOUTHEAD GILL

GRAINY GILL

SKEW GILL

2H 10MIN

ESK HAUSE

LINGMELL

CRISCLIFFE KNOTTS

1H 13MIN

PIERS GILL

MIDDLEBOOT KNOTTS

GRETA GILL

LONG PIKE

9

TONGUE

1H 6MIN

LINGMELL COL

1H 18MIN

7

BROAD CRAG

ILL CRAG

JENNY KNOTT!

LINGMELL GILL

1H 36MIN

DROPPING CRAG

8

GREEN CRAG

LITTLE NARROW COVE

SPARKLING TARN

PIKES CRAG

SCAFELL PIKE

ROUGH CRAG

PEN

LYONS CRAG

LORDS RAKE

MICKLEDORE

BROAD STAND

BROADCRAG TARN

BROAD CRAGS

AN AMAZING CELEBRATION

SYMONDS KNOTT

FOXES TARN

SCAFELL

0   ½   1K

- - - - RUNNING ROUTE   □□□□ WALKING ROUTE

what could possibly go wrong?

THIS CHALLENGE HAS BEEN MORE OR LESS A SOLO EFFORT, BUT TODAY I'VE ARRANGED TO MEET JENNY AND HER WALKING COMPANION, ROBIN, WHO ALONG WITH JANICE WILL WALK TO MY FINAL SUMMIT, GREAT END, AND GREET ME WITH A BOTTLE OF BUBBLY AND A CHOCOLATE OR TWO. WHAT COULD POSSIBLY GO WRONG..?

fingers crossed

...THE WEATHER FOR STARTERS, AS WE MEET UP AT SEATHWAITE IN DRY CONDITIONS, BUT WITH THICK HILL FOG ON THE HIGH FELLS. I CROSS MY FINGERS THAT IT BREAKS UP AND DISPERSES SOONER RATHER THAN LATER AS WE SET AND CHECK OUR WATCHES, WISH EACH OTHER LUCK AND HEAD DOWN TO STOCKLEY BRIDGE, ME RUNNING AND THE 'SUPPORT GROUP' WALKING. THEIR ROUTE INVOLVES AN ASCENT OF GREAT END VIA THE BAND, WHILE MINE INVOLVES THE ASCENT OF LINGMELL VIA THE CORRIDOR ROUTE, THEN SCAFELL PIKE.

IT'S JUST GONE TEN A.M. AND LOTS OF WALKERS ARE EN ROUTE TO STY HEAD AS I CROSS GRAINS GILL AND PUSH UP THE STONE STEPS, HANDS ON KNEES, THEN RUN ALL THE WAY TO THE BUSY JUNCTION OF STY HEAD.

no sign of improvement

I GLANCE UP TO THE BAND ON GREAT END – WHAT I CAN SEE OF IT IS IMPRESSIVE. GOOD LUCK SUPPORT TEAM! I HEAD DOWN TO THE CORRIDOR ROUTE. APART FROM SMALL SECTIONS OF ROCK IT'S GOOD RUNNING MOST OF THE WAY TO LINGMELL COL, WITH LOTS OF FOLK HEADING TO THE PIKE.

LINGMELL KEEPS PLAYING HIDE-AND-SEEK WITH THE CLOUDS AS I MAKE MY WAY TO THE COL. FROM HERE A GRASS PATH, HEADS FOR THE SUMMIT, TURNING TO SLIPPERY SHALE AS IT ZIGZAGS UP TO THE CAIRN. IT'S NOT QUITE AS TALL AS THE ILLUSTRATION IN MY OLD GUIDEBOOK, BUT IT'S STILL A GOOD LOOKING EDIFICE – BETTER THAN THE VIEWS, THAT'S FOR SURE, WITH NO SIGHT OF GREAT GABLE, AND ONLY A FAINT MISTY VIEW DOWN INTO WASDALE.

time to rejoin the masses

IT'S TIME FOR A TIME CHECK. ONE HOUR THIRTEEN MINUTES FROM THE START AT SEATHWAITE. I'M HAPPY WITH THAT, SO I GRAB A QUICK SUCK ON AN ENERGY GEL AND TAKE A DRINK, THEN I DROP DOWN TO THE COL AND REJOIN THE MAIN PATH AND THE STREAM OF WALKERS TRUDGING UP FROM WASDALE. IT'S HANDS-ON-KNEES TIME AGAIN AS I FOLLOW THE CAIRNS AND PASS WALKERS BOTH ASCENDING AND DESCENDING WHO APPEAR LIKE GHOSTLY FIGURES THROUGH THE MIST.

IT'S ONWARDS AND UPWARDS NOW TO ENGLAND'S HIGHEST CAIRN, AS THE THICK MIST IS JOINED BY THE ARRIVAL OF LIGHT RAIN TO ADD TO THE GLOOM. THERE ARE NOT MANY PEOPLE HANGING AROUND TODAY – CAN'T SAY I BLAME THEM. BEFORE LONG IT'S TIME TO GO MYSELF. FIRST I CHECK THE COMPASS – FOR ONLY THE SECOND OR THIRD TIME DURING THE WHOLE CHALLENGE. THEN I DESCEND OVER WET ROCKS AND BOULDERS, CHECKING WITH APPROACHING WALKERS THAT THEY'VE ARRIVED VIA ESK HAUSE – BETTER TO BE SAFE THAN SORRY. I'M RELIEVED TO HEAR A RESOUNDING YES, SO I PUSH ON WITH RENEWED CONFIDENCE, FOLLOWING ONE CAIRN TO ANOTHER, STILL OVER ROCKS AND BOULDERS, ALL THE WAY TO BROAD CRAG COL.

into the void

I CAN'T SEE A THING OTHER THAN GHOSTLY FIGURES APPEARING OUT OF THE GLOOM ASKING ME IF THEY ARE ON THE SUMMIT, OR NEARLY AT THE SUMMIT, OR HOW FAR TO THE SUMMIT. UP AND DOWN TO ILL CRAG COL I HEAD, ON A SLIGHTLY BETTER SURFACE, THEN PICK UP THE PACE TO CALF COVE ON GRASS. HERE I SPOT THE THIN TRACK OFF TO GREAT END, SO PUSH ON. THANK GOODNESS FOR CAIRNS AS I STILL CAN'T SEE A THING, THOUGH MY FAITH PAYS OFF AS I ARRIVE SAFE AND SOUND AT THE SUMMIT.

IT'S OVER! FINISHED THE END

CHALLENGE COMPLETED!!!

...I JUST NEED TO MEET UP WITH JANICE JENNY AND ROBIN, CELEBRATE, THEN HEAD BACK TO THE CAR...

GREAT END-ING FROM STY HEAD

DISTANCE **10**k

TIME **2**hrs**10**mins

ASCENT **3,630**ft

WHAT HAPPENS NEXT? QUICK, TURN OVER ⟶

nowhere in sight

I'M STANDING IN THE MIST AND DRIZZLE WITH MIXED EMOTIONS WHEN I REALISE I AM ALONE! WHERE ARE THEY? THEY ARE NOWHERE IN SIGHT. MIND YOU, NEITHER IS ANYTHING ELSE. AS I STAND I START TO COOL, SO I DON A COUPLE OF DOWN JACKETS PACKED SPECIFICALLY FOR THIS RUN JUST IN CASE.

I SHOUT INTO THE GLOOM BUT THERE'S NO REPLY. I THOUGHT THEY'D BE HERE BY NOW, SO I GET OUT THE PHONE: NO SIGNAL, OF COURSE. A SMALL WINDOW IN THE MIST ALLOWS ME A GLIMPSE OF THE OTHER SUMMIT JUST TO THE EAST. COULD THEY BE THERE?

I ARRIVE AT THE CAIRN BUT THERE'S NOT A SOUL IN SIGHT. SO BACK I GO TO THE FIRST CAIRN - STILL NO SIGN OF LIFE.

BACK AND FORTH I GO UNTIL FORTY MINUTES HAVE PASSED SINCE I ARRIVED AND EVEN WITH TWO JACKETS ON I'M BEGINNING TO FEEL THE COLD.

WHO'S BROUGHT THE GLASSES?

doubts set in

HAVE THEY TURNED BACK DUE TO THE BAD WEATHER AND DECIDED TO WALK UP VIA ESK HAUSE?, I ASK MYSELF. I DON'T KNOW. SO I MAKE A PLAN.

IT INVOLVES PLACING THE FOIL BIRTHDAY BANNER, WHICH I'VE CARRIED READY FOR MY PHOTOSHOOT AT THE FINISH, ON THE SUMMIT CAIRN SO THEY WILL AT LEAST KNOW THAT I'VE BEEN AND GONE AND THEY WON'T HAVE TO HANG ABOUT WAITING FOR ME TO ARRIVE UNNECESSARILY. IN THE MEANTIME I'LL RUN DOWN TO ESK HAUSE, FIRSTLY TO WARM UP, AND SECONDLY TO SEE IF I CAN SPOT THEM WALKING UP TO THE HAUSE. SO OFF I GO, OUT OF THE WIND, MIST AND RAIN TO ESK HAUSE, BUT THERE'S NO SIGN OF THE 'SUPPORT GROUP' - AND STILL NO PHONE SIGNAL. WHAT NEXT?

oh yes it can

MY HEAD'S DOWN, WHEN OUT OF THE GLOOM I SPOT FOUR WALKERS HEADING DOWN TOWARDS ME. IT CAN'T BE THEM, THOUGH, AS THERE'S FOUR OF THEM, NOT THREE - JANICE, JENNY AND ROBIN.

I'M TO BE PROVED WRONG.
IT IS THEM!

EVERYONE'S ELATED, AND THERE ARE LOTS OF HUGS AND CONGRATULATIONS. WE THEN DECIDE TO HEAD DOWN TO THE SHELTER JUST BELOW ESK HAUSE TO POP THE CORK AND OPEN THE CHOCS. YUMMY YUMMY!

THE FOURTH PERSON TURNED OUT TO BE A YOUNG GUY NAMED ARRON ON HIS FIRST VISIT TO THE LAKES. HE WAS ON HIS WAY TO CLIMB SCAFELL PIKE AND SEEMED A LITTLE OUT OF HIS DEPTH WHEN THE SUPPORT GROUP TOOK HIM UNDER THEIR WING. HE ALSO HAD A POCKET FULL OF MINT CAKE, WHICH MIGHT HAVE HAD SOMETHING TO DO WITH IT, TOO.

say our farewells

A COUPLE OF DRINKS AND CHOCS LATER IT'S TIME TO GO. WE POP OVER SEATHWAITE FELL TO TICK OFF ONE OF ROBIN'S 'TO DO' WAINWRIGHTS. THEN - SOD'S LAW - AS WE DESCEND THE SKY BRIGHTENS TO REVEAL GREAT GABLE AND DISTANT VIEWS OF DERWENT WATER AND SKIDDAW. SOUTHWARDS GREAT END IS STILL SHROUDED IN MIST.

OVER THE NORTH SUMMIT OF SEATHWAITE FELL WE GO, AND THEN DOWN TO STOCKLEY BRIDGE AND THE FINAL MILE OR SO TO SEATHWAITE VILLAGE.

THERE ARE MORE HUGS, HANDSHAKES AND BEST WISHES AS WE SAY OUR FAREWELLS AND HEAD OUR SEPERATE WAYS.

BUT WE'LL MEET AGAIN.
I'M SURE OF IT!

HALF EMPTY OR HALF FULL?

THE BUBBLY, CHOCS AND MINT CAKE TASTED SO MUCH BETTER THAN THEY LOOK HERE, BELIEVE ME!

and the # GRAND TOTAL is

852·4 k in distance

50,330 metres of ascent

142 hours **47** minutes

OR

529·3 miles in distance

165,125 feet of ascent

5 days **22** hours **47** mins

AVERAGE PER RUN (APPROX)

11·2 k – **6·9** mls DISTANCE

662 mtrs – **2,173** ft ASCENT

1 hr **54** mins TIME

2·8 SUMMITS

TEMBER 30th 2015
ONISTER QUARRY 10·15am
10·35
Y KNOTTS 10·4..
RANDRETH ..04
BASE BROWN 11·23
GREEN GABLE 11·36
GREAT GABLE 11·58
STY HEAD 12·17
SEATHWAITE FELL 12·51
FINISH SEATHWAITE

SHORTEST in DISTANCE

- (34) RAVEN CRAG - **2**k
- (62) HARD KNOTT - **2·1**k
- (52) BINSEY - **2·5**k
- (71) HOLME FELL - **3·5**k
- (28) WHINLATTER - **3·5**k

a few
facts &

SHORTEST in TIME

- (52) BINSEY - **15**mins
- (62) HARD KNOTT - **20**mins
- (49) CASTLE CRAG - **27**mins
- (34) RAVEN CRAG - **29**mins
- (58) BLACK CRAG - **30**mins

LEAST ASCENT

- (58) BLACK CRAG - **450**ft
- (19) LITTLE MELL FELL - **450**ft
- (62) HARD KNOTT - **550**ft
- (18) HIGH RIGG - **610**ft
- (52) BINSEY - **620**ft

LONGEST IN DISTANCE

57 HARTER FELL, KENTMERE PIKE, SHIPMAN KNOTTS, YOKE, ILL BELL, FROSWICK & MARDALE ILL BELL **24·7**k

11 MUNGRISDALE COMMON, LONSCALE FELL, SKIDDAW, LITTLE MAN & LATRIGG **21·0**k

31 HOPEGILL HEAD, WHITESIDE, GRASMOOR, WANDOPE, EEL CRAG, SAIL & SCAR CRAGS **20·75**k

36 TARN CRAG, SERGEANT MAN, HIGH RAISE, THUNACAR KNOTT, PIKE O' STICKLE, LOFT CRAG, HARRISON STICKLE, PAVEY ARK & BLEA RIGG **19·75**k

25 BAKESTALL **18·0**k

47 PIKE O' BLISCO, COLD PIKE, CRINKLE CRAGS, BOWFELL & ROSSETT PIKE **18·0**k

figures...

LONGEST IN TIME

57 HARTER FELL, KENTMERE PIKE, SHIPMAN KNOTTS, YOKE, ILL BELL, FROSWICK & MARDALE ILL BELL **4**hrs **26**mins

36 TARN CRAG, SERGEANT MAN, HIGH RAISE, THUNACAR KNOTT, PIKE O' STICKLE, LOFT CRAG, HARRISON STICKLE, PAVEY ARK & BLEA RIGG **3**hrs **59**mins

47 PIKE O' BLISCO, COLD PIKE, CRINKLE CRAGS, BOWFELL & ROSSETT PIKE **3**hrs **55**mins

73 KIRK FELL, PILLAR, SCOAT FELL, STEEPLE, RED PIKE & YEWBARROW **3**hrs **54**mins

31 HOPEGILL HEAD, WHITESIDE, GRASMOOR, WANDOPE, EEL CRAG, SAIL & SCAR CRAGS **3**hrs **47**mins

MOST ASCENT

73 KIRK FELL, PILLAR, SCOAT FELL, STEEPLE, RED PIKE & YEWBARROW **4,870**ft

57 HARTER FELL, KENTMERE PIKE, SHIPMAN KNOTTS, YOKE, ILL BELL, FROSWICK & MARDALE ILL BELL **4,775**ft

47 PIKE O' BLISCO, COLD PIKE, CRINKLE CRAGS, BOWFELL & ROSSETT PIKE **4,600**ft

13 SEAT SANDAL, DOLLYWAGGON PIKE, NETHERMOST PIKE, HELVELLYN, WHITESIDE & RAISE **4,260**ft

11 MUNGRISDALE COMMON, LONSCALE FELL, SKIDDAW, LITTLE MAN & LATRIGG **4,033**ft

that's that then

PHEW! THAT'S THAT THEN. I FINALLY COMPLETED MY CHALLENGE ON MY 66th BIRTHDAY, THE 15th OCTOBER 2016, SOME 6 YEARS AFTER THE INITIAL FELL RUN THAT TRIGGERED THE IDEA TO RUN ALL THE WAINWRIGHT SUMMITS OF LAKELAND.

IT'S BASICALLY BEEN A PURELY SELFISH CHALLENGE. I HAD NO LIFE-THREATENING DISEASE OR NEAR-DEATH EXPERIENCE TO SPUR ME ON, NO WORTHWHILE CHARITIES OR GOOD CAUSES TO RAISE MONEY FOR. IT WAS JUST TO SEE IF I COULD DO IT ALL BY MYSELF. AND I DID!

JANICE, MY BETTER HALF (BY FAR) ACCOMPANIED ME ON 3 SHORT AND EASY RUNS, JUST TO SHOW A BIT OF INTEREST ON HER PART AND TO SEE WHAT I WAS UP TO, I THINK, LEAVING ME WITH WHAT TURNED OUT TO BE A TOTAL OF 73 SOLO EFFORTS. THIS FACT PLAYED A BIG PART, ACTUALLY, ON HOW I APPROACHED MY CHALLENGE, WITH ROUTE CHOICE AND EFFORT BEING THE MOST AFFECTED. RUNNING SOLO MEANT I DIDN'T HAVE TO WAIT FOR ANYONE TO CATCH UP OR VICE VERSA, SO I WAS ABLE TO DICTATE MY OWN PACE AT ALL TIMES - A BIG BONUS. I DECIDED EARLY ON THAT FOR SAFETY REASONS ALL MY DESCENTS WOULD BE MADE AT A CONTROLLED PACE WITH NO RISKS TAKEN, AS THAT'S THE MOST LIKELY TIME TO TAKE A NASTY TUMBLE AND SUSTAIN A SERIOUS INJURY - UNLESS YOU'RE ON NICE GREEN GRASS, OF COURSE, WHEN IT'S JUST A FORWARD ROLL, BACK ONTO YOUR FEET AND OFF YOU GO. SO NONE OF MY RUNS ARE AT FULL PELT - ALTHOUGH THE ASCENTS ARE PROBABLY AS FAST AS I COULD MANAGE ON THE DAY. IT WAS STEADY AS YOU GO ON THE DESCENTS.

I FOUND A BIT OF REVERSAL WITH WALKING WHEN IT CAME TO THE ROUTES I TOOK. MOST OF MY FAVOURITE WALKS ARE THOSE OVER ROUGH AND ROCKY GROUND WITH STEEP ASCENTS AND DESCENTS. BUT THOSE SORT OF CONDITIONS AREN'T CONDUSIVE FOR ENJOYABLE FELL RUNNING, WITH EVERY FOOTSTEP AND EVERY STRIDE REQUIRING EXTREME CAUTION AND CONCENTRATION. EG:- CRINKLE CRAGS TO BOWFELL IS A BEAUTIFUL WALK, BUT A HORRENDOUS RUN, WHILE THE 'BORING' GREEN GRASSY SUMMITS OF THE EASTERN, FAR EASTERN AND NORTHERN FELLS PROVIDED BY FAR THE BEST CONDITIONS FOR CARE-FREE, ENJOYABLE AND SUSTAINED RUNNING.

I ONLY HAD 2 BAD TUMBLES IN TOTAL, THE WORST ONE ON TOP OF PILLAR AND THE OTHER NEAR RED TARN BETWEEN CATSTYCAM AND BIRKHOUSE MOOR, BOTH ON RELATIVELY SMOOTH TERRAIN ODDLY ENOUGH. I'VE MANAGED TO HAVE PLENTY OF LITTLE SLIPS, MAINLY IN DESCENT ON WET GRASS AND PROBABLY CAUSED BY POOR CHOICE OF SHOE. BUT ON THE WHOLE I THINK I GOT OFF QUITE LIGHTLY SEEING AS JUST ONE BAD TUMBLE OR INJURY COULD HAVE PUT ME BACK MONTHS, OR WORSE, IN HOSPITAL.

I'LL BE REVISITING A FEW OF MY RUNS IN THE FUTURE WITH A CHAPERONE - STEVEN - NOW THAT I'M GETTING ON A BIT!

I CAN HIGHLY RECOMMEND ANYBODY THAT CAN RUN A BIT (I'M ONLY A 22 MINUTE PARK RUN SORT OF GUY) AND NAVIGATE THE HILLS TO TAKE UP THE CHALLENGE AND GIVE IT A GO, BUT PLEASE, DON'T WRITE A BOOK ABOUT IT!

THANK YOU.